Urban Diversities – Environmental and Social Issues

Mirilia, Marino, and Giuseppe remember Anna Maria – who suddenly left us after editing this volume – with her gentle presence, her brilliant culture, and her passionate love for life, people, and environments.

Advances in People-Environment Studies

Gabriel Moser; PhD, Prof., Paris, France, Past-President of the International Association for People-Environment Studies (IAPS).

David Uzzell; PhD, FBPsS, FRSA, Prof., Surrey, UK, Past-President of the International Association for People-Environment Studies (IAPS).
(Series Editors)

The new book series *Advances in People-Environment Studies*, published in collaboration with the International Association for People-Environment Studies (IAPS; www.iaps-association.org), is a timely initiative to provide researchers with up-to-date reviews and commentaries on the diverse areas of people-environment studies that are of current concern. The series focuses on significant and currently debated themes. The books are interdisciplinary, drawing on expert authors from the social, environmental, and design disciplines, especially those who are working at the interface between the design (e.g., architects, landscape planners, urban designers, urban planners) and the social sciences (e.g., environmental psychologists, sociologists, geographers). Each volume reports on the latest research and applications of research in the field. The series is meant to provide a bridge, not only between disciplines but also between cultures. The authors and contributors come from many different countries and are undertaking research and practicing in culturally diverse environments. Books in the series are therefore a precious source for those who want to know what is going on in a specific field elsewhere and to find ideas and inspiration for their own work.

Advances in People-Environment Studies Vol. 2

Urban Diversities – Environmental and Social Issues

Marino Bonaiuto
Mirilia Bonnes
Anna Maria Nenci
Giuseppe Carrus
(Editors)

Library of Congress Cataloging in Publication

is available via the Library of Congress Marc Database under the
LC Control Number 2010941815

Library and Archives Canada Cataloguing in Publication

Urban diversities: environmental and social issues / Marino Bonaiuto ... [et al.], editors.

(Advances in people-environment studies ; v. 2)
Includes bibliographical references and index.
ISBN 978-0-88937-385-3

1. Urban ecology (Sociology). I. Bonaiuto, Marino II. Series: Advances in people-environment studies ; v. 2

HT241.U73 2010   307.76   C2010-906858-0

Cover illustration: Wilfrid Moser (1914–1997). L'Alchimiste gai (Paysage de Métro). 1963/64, oil, collage on canvas, 114 × 146 cm. © Wilfrid Moser Foundation

© 2011 by Hogrefe Publishing

PUBLISHING OFFICES
USA: Hogrefe Publishing, 875 Massachusetts Avenue, 7th Floor, Cambridge, MA 02139
            Phone (866) 823-4726, Fax (617) 354-6875; E-mail customerservice@hogrefe-publishing.com
EUROPE: Hogrefe Publishing, Rohnsweg 25, 37085 Göttingen, Germany
            Phone +49 551 49609-0, Fax +49 551 49609-88, E-mail publishing@hogrefe.com

SALES & DISTRIBUTION
USA: Hogrefe Publishing, Customer Services Department,
            30 Amberwood Parkway, Ashland, OH 44805
            Phone (800) 228-3749, Fax (419) 281-6883, E-mail customerservice@hogrefe.com
EUROPE: Hogrefe Publishing, Rohnsweg 25, 37085 Göttingen, Germany
            Phone +49 551 49609-0, Fax +49 551 49609-88, E-mail publishing@hogrefe.com

OTHER OFFICES
CANADA: Hogrefe Publishing, 660 Eglington Ave. East, Suite 119-514, Toronto, Ontario M4G 2K2
SWITZERLAND: Hogrefe Publishing, Länggass-Strasse 76, CH-3000 Bern 9

Hogrefe Publishing
Incorporated and registered in the Commonwealth of Massachusetts, USA

Hogrefe Publishing
Incorporated and registered in Göttingen, Lower Saxony, Germany

Printed and bound in Germany
ISBN: 978-0-88937-385-3

Table of Contents

Introduction

Environmental and Social Diversities in the City

An Introduction

Mirilia Bonnes,[1] Marino Bonaiuto,[1] Anna Maria Nenci,[2] and Giuseppe Carrus[3]

[1]Sapienza University of Rome, Italy
[2]LUMSA University, Rome, Italy
[3]University of Roma Tre, Italy

The title of the 20th biennial Conference of IAPS (International Association for People-Environment Studies), held in Rome in 2008, focused attention on the multiple diversities that characterize urban environments, and their impact on human well-being. The intention was to explore the need for a strategic and shared approach to designing and managing our urban environments in a sustainable way. This special focus on urban themes was partly a consequence of the location of the conference, since Rome, the so-called "*eternal city*", or the *Urbs* in Latin, represents the city *par excellence*.

Coherent with the mission of IAPS, the Rome conference tried to provide a forum at which the different scientific disciplines interested in environmental issues could gather to engage in a dialogue between themselves and with professionals and decision makers responsible for designing and managing our environments.

The theme of *urban diversity* is addressed in this volume by explicitly focusing on the various diversities that characterize urban settings across different geographical and cultural contexts. For this reason, the reader will frequently find the term "diversities" in the plural form throughout this introductory chapter. The importance of diversity for the future of human affairs is also foremost in many United Nations' programmes for sustainable development, such as the UNESCO-MAB Programme, and the related Convention for the Conservation of Biological Diversity. These initiatives have drawn attention to the relation between biological diversity, or biodiversity and other forms of diversity, in particular human-cultural diversity. This relation is crucial to understanding and addressing the interactions between the biosphere's human and natural processes – from global to local – which affect the quality of the environment and the quality of human life (e.g., Moser, 2009; Uzzell, 2000). Not by chance, the United Nations declared the year 2010 as the International Year of Biodiversity.

A major objective of the conference was to draw attention to the challenges presented by different kinds of diversities within our cities: biological, technological, historical, cultural, ethnic, architectural, and finally social-psychological. Understanding the reciprocal links and interdependencies between these aspects provides the basis for promoting and preserving the well-being of all the components of each urban system (biological and socio-cultural) within the context of sustainability. In other words, managing diversities represents the key objective for more sustainable urban development and for promoting the well-being of people. Such a complex task needs collaboration among the natural and technological sciences (e.g., biology, natural science, engineering, and design) and the human and social sciences (e.g., psychology), and between these and the public and private sectors. Studying and understanding these processes is the necessary foundation of knowledge systems that are capable of fostering synergistic efforts to identify and promote innovation choices, not just in the short term, but also from a medium- and long-term perspective.

Diversities and Ecological Processes

A recent paper by Bonnes, Carrus, Corral-Verdugo, and Passafaro (2010) discussed the implications of the concept of diversity for the study of people-natural environment relations. Bio-ecological sciences assign a key role to biodiversity from genetic, functional and evolutionary points of view (e.g., Barbault, 1995; di Castri, 1995; Wilson, 1999). According to a recent definition put forward by the IUCN – *International Union for Conservation of Nature*, biodiversity is "the variability among living organisms from all sources including terrestrial, marine and other aquatic ecosystems, and the ecological complexes of which they are part; this includes diversity within species, between species, and of ecosystems." (International Union for Conservation of Nature – IUCN, 2010).

Following an evolutionary paradigm of bio-ecological sciences, biodiversity is conceived as a mechanism of pre-adaptation of any living system for facing ecological changes, and thus a fundamental resource for the long-term continuity of life (di Castri & Balayi, 2002; Wilson, 1999). Diversity should then be considered as "the foremost adaptive and evolutionary strategy to face unpredictable changes and to ensure options for the future in all biological, cultural and economic systems" (di Castri & Balayi, 2002, p. 15).

Diversity, in fact, is not only of a biological nature. Several leading scientists have proposed to broaden the concept of biodiversity to include cultural diversity (i.e., *biodiversity* and *socio-diversity*), so to consider both as parts of a broader *diversity* concept (e.g., Alfsen-Norodom & Lane, 2002; Dansereau, 1997; di Castri & Balayi, 2002; Guillitte, 2005). According to this perspective, the human dimension, in its social, economic, and cultural aspects, can act as a major driving force within any ecosystem (e.g., Bonnes & Bonaiuto, 2002). In sum, socio-ecological systems need variety in their constituting elements, in order to survive and develop through the time. This principle applies to both biological and human ecology (Capra & Pauli, 1995).

Despite this widely acknowledged importance, human affairs are having an increasingly negative impact upon biological and cultural diversity over the last decades (Starke, 2008). This impact can seriously affect the quality of life of human and non-human beings. Ecosystems are composed of a large number of species, mutually interdependent in obtaining nutrients and other components of the life cycle: If the biological diversity within an ecosystem is seriously threatened, the entire system might collapse because of the negative consequences on the nutrients cycle (Tonn, 2007). The loss of biodiversity is indeed identified as one of the most serious global environmental changes threatening the biosphere in present time (Wilson, 1999). Not by chance, the specific UN Convention on Biological Diversity (CBD) was available to be signed by all the member countries since the first world summit devoted to launch the UN programme for Sustainable Development held in Rio de Janeiro[1] in 1992. As a consequence, the issue of sustainable use and recovery of biodiversity has been increasingly in the focus of scientific research and political action at the international and intergovernmental level across the last two decades (see the proceedings of a Conference on "Biodiversity, Science and Governance" organized in Paris by UNESCO and the French Government; Le Duc, 2005; see also UNESCO, 2006). Biodiversity is thus recognized at the intergovernmental level as an inalienable good, despite being an increasingly threatened resource.

The loss of plants and animal species is a more tangible manifestation of biodiversity loss. The rate of species extinction caused by human beings in the last decades is 1,000 times more rapid compared to the "normal" rate throughout the history of the planet (Millennium Ecosystem Assessment, 2005). This phenomenon could be even more extreme: The natural extinction rate has ranged between 10 and 100 species per year. In the second half of the 20th century, it was calculated the extinction of about 27,000 species per year only in the tropical forests (Elewa, 2008). In terms of plant biodiversity, the IUCN (2008) reports that 70% of plant species are at risk of extinction, including important species that are used for pharmaceutical production (Hawkins, 2008). A similar situation characterizes animal and marine biodiversity, which are increasingly threatened by global environmental changes, such as global warming (Boyle & Grow, 2008; Elewa, 2008), and by direct human activities such as industrial fishing (Food and Agricultural Organization of the United Nations – FAO, 2007).

In parallel to the loss of biological diversity in the biosphere, a further trend can be found with respect to socio-diversity within human societies (Jimeno, Sotomayor, & Valderrama, 1995). Socio-diversity is related to the variety in languages, religions, customs, and traditions, as well as to diversity in political, economic, generational, and

---

[1] These issues were also outlined within the report produced by the *World Commission on Environment and Development,* preparatory to the Rio summit, titled *"Our common future",* and known as the "Brundtland Report" (World Commission on Environment and Development – WCED, 1987).

sexual orientations within and across human societies (O'Hara, 1995). The extinction of spoken languages around the world seems to parallel the extinction of non-human species in ecosystems. According to recent estimates, the 90% of languages will be extinguished by the next 100 years (Nettle & Romaine, 2000).

Economic globalization and cultural homogenization are also impacting other forms of socio-diversity, such as food and eating practices (Lacy, 1994). The estimates of the UN suggest that this situation could worsen in the future. Based on predictions about population growth, it is estimated that human societies will require the 50% more food production compared to current requirements. This increase could be achieved only by substituting current wild lands with land that can be brought into production for agriculture and animal farming purposes. Likewise, cereal production will require an 80% increase by the year 2030 in order to satisfy increasing human demands.

Interestingly, the causes of this phenomenon have been attributed to the same factors that might underlie environmental degradation in human societies. For example, economic globalization and increasing urbanization are pushing human societies towards the homogenization of cultural systems. This leads to a loss of socio-cultural diversity, which in turn, is a fundamental condition for human evolution (Tonn, 2007). The loss of socio-diversity could then also bring serious consequences to human health and well-being, just as for biological diversity, because the evolutionary basis driving human development requires a sufficient amount of socio-diversity. The same logic applied to biodiversity as a basis for ecosystem sustainability can be applied to socio-diversity: the higher the variety of cultural forms, the higher the potential sustainability of human development. Understanding and investigating the common factors which are the basis of the simultaneous loss of biological and cultural diversity is a crucial step to define strategies aimed at guaranteeing biodiversity within ecosystems and maintaining socio-diversity among human cultures.

A significant growth in population is a key issue in this sense and represents an apparent paradox: To sustain an increasing number of people in the planet, we need to exploit natural resources at an increasingly higher rate, and this might contribute to the loss of both biological and cultural diversity at the same time. All these considerations demonstrate the importance of paying specific attention to the individual and psychological factors that are involved in the simultaneous loss of biological and cultural diversity. A better understanding of these factors might also help in preserving and restoring the existing diversities.

Structure and Contents of the Volume

The present volume is organized around major research issues that are the focus of current investigations on urban diversities in the field of people-environment studies. These research themes are representative of the diversities which are relevant for understanding current and future developments in people-environment relationships and for designing and managing future changes to our common living environments (see also Uzzell & Moser, 2009).

The contributions in this volume are also representative of a plurality of disciplinary backgrounds, which are deemed as necessary to understand human psychological processes and behaviour in relation to the environment. The volume is organized around different research themes, relevant for understanding current trends and future developments in the study of people-urban environment relations with an emphasis on the key concept of diversity in relation to:

- theoretical and methodological approaches;
- urban landscapes and perceptual approaches;
- urban green spaces and well-being;
- lifestyles and urban sustainability;
- social groups and inclusive urban environments.

Section 1: Diversity in Theoretical and Methodological Approaches

The need for interdisciplinary and transdisciplinary collaboration is commonly accepted as a key requirement for the advancement of people-environment studies (e.g., Lawrence & Després, 2004). However, bridging together different disciplinary backgrounds is not always straightforward, especially when it concerns the question of how empirical evidence can be reconciled across neighbouring disciplines and then translated into actual environmental design and management practices. These aspects are also related to the more general implications of people-environment studies for policy-making: In relation to this issue, the identification of communication strategies and inclusive governance practices appears particularly crucial for the pursuit of more sustainable urban management. This section groups together four chapters that address the main theoretical assumptions at the basis of people-environment studies and some of the related methodological implications.

The chapter by Lawrence addresses the issues of how interdisciplinary and transdisciplinary approaches can contribute to urban development in a broad environmental, economic, social, and political context, through the cross-fertilization of ideas and knowledge from different fields. In doing so, Lawrence illustrates how human ecology can achieve this aim by providing an integrated framework for interdisciplinary contributions and common applications that can be extended to implement transdisciplinary contributions.

The chapter by Diaz Moore and Geboy reviews current worldviews in environmental design research and practice, focusing in particular on the development of the concept of evidence-based design. The authors provide critical insights into the strengths and weaknesses of this concept, illustrating its increasing popularity in a number of urban domains ranging from healthcare environments, to long-term care settings, housing, workplaces, and facilities management.

In their chapter, Romice and her co-authors discuss the issue of sustainable communities as a key component of urban design and regeneration, with specific reference to the possible strategies to achieve it. The debate between centralized and state-based planning strategies on the one hand and deregulated and laissez-faire planning procedures on the other hand is critically presented, together with insight and reflections about the relations between markets, time constraints and sustainable urban regeneration.

Finally, Drucker and Gumpert discuss the issue of regulation on public spaces in current societies, with a particular emphasis on the impact of mediated communication upon the experiences, functions and design of public space. The authors stress how both media spaces and physical infrastructures have different regulatory implications affecting social interaction (e.g., manifest *vs.* latent, indirect *vs.* accidental, intentional *vs.* unintended). The basic aspects relating to this regulation of communication are illustrated through an examination of the laws governing public spaces of New York City.

Section 2: Diversity in Urban Landscapes and Perceptual Approaches

The investigation of the visual aspects of the relationship between the city and its inhabitants can be traced back to the beginnings of people-environment studies, with the seminal works of authors such as Lee (1969), Lynch (1960), and Milgram (1970). Following this specific research tradition, the chapters in this section focus in particular on the perceptual processes at the basis of visual experience in urban settings. The research presented in these chapters puts the emphasis, in turn, on a variety of behavioural and psychological outcomes (e.g., wayfinding, environmental preference, social interaction), and cover a range of cultural and geographical contexts.

The chapter of Conroy Dalton and co-authors shows how spatial decisions made by pedestrians when executing a task, exploring novel environments or re-enacting daily habits in familiar environments involve complex thinking processes. The chapter focuses in particular on the dynamic and experiential aspects of this thinking, as well as on the overall methodological approaches within this line of empirical research.

In the paper by Portella, the influence of commercial signs, shopfronts and window displays in the appearance of commercial and historical streetscapes for users from different countries is analysed, combining qualitative and quantitative approaches. The aim is to identify the physical characteristics for developing commercial signage in different urban contexts. Findings show how visual preferences in commercial and historical streetscapes can be based on perception (perceptual constancy) more than on cognition processes.

Silva Gambim and Dias Lay address the effects of particular urban spatial attributes, such as visual appearance, on social interaction between different socio-economic groups in Brazil. The authors discuss the implications of increasing spatial fragmentation and population heterogeneity in large urban contexts in relation to the issues of urban violence and segregation.

Finally, in their chapter on incongruous architecture, Bonaiuto and colleagues analyse how, using an experimental approach, various kinds of architectural incongruities (e.g., position, shape, composition, size, colour) can be found in a variety of different real-life urban contexts and settings, which in turn can affect individual perceptions and evaluations.

Section 3: Diversity in Urban Green Spaces and Well-Being

The study of people-nature relations in the city, and its implications for urban sustainability, is receiving more attention within environmental psychological research (e.g., Van den Berg, Hartig, & Staats, 2007; see also Giuliani & Scopelliti, 2009, for an analysis of the more general trends). Urban diversity might frequently become a source of cognitive overload and psychological distress (Milgram, 1970; Moser, 1988, 1992). However, the presence of green spaces in the city might serve as a buffer to citizen's stress. Research on restorative environments has typically highlighted the beneficial outcomes of contact with nature for "stressed" or mentally fatigued urban dwellers (Hartig, 2004). This aspect relates to the specific and different functions that contribute to define the diversity of green spaces from the rest of the urban landscape. Furthermore, providing more possibilities of contact with nature for urban inhabitants is likely to positively affect the quality of urban environment itself. In fact, frequent and positive experience with nature might, in the long run, promote the adoption of more "sustainable lifestyles" among urban dwellers. The contributions included in this section deal with these issues, adopting different approaches and methods.

The chapter by Landázuri and co-authors addresses the relations between the presence of green areas in residential contexts and housing habitability in Mexico. Starting from previous research in environmental psychology about the positive effects of contact with nearby residential nature, the authors provide results that support the view that the presence of greenery within and surrounding the dwelling has pleasant and relaxing effects over inhabitants' perception of their house.

In a similar vein, the chapter by da Luz Reis and Barcelos refers to the relations between green spaces, vegetation, and well-being in the housing environment, with particular reference to low-income residents in southern Brazil. Their study, based on a combination of individual interviews and Geographical Information System (GIS) techniques, assesses variables such as inhabitants' perceived importance and adequacy of, and satisfaction with, residential vegetation. Reported findings confirm the importance of vegetation in planning for health promotion and people well-being in urban areas.

The paper by Payne analyses the restorative value of soundscapes within urban parks. Starting from classical theories on psychological resoration in the environment, such as Attention Restoration Theory (Kaplan, 1995), this work demonstrates how people's experiences of urban natural environments are not just visually based, but are multi-sensorial. The study explores the relationship between sounds perceived, described, and categorized by users of urban parks, and measures of restorative qualities of the soundscape. As expected, findings show how the sonic environment could be an important component of the restorative experiences within urban parks.

Finally, the chapter by Fornara analyses the perceived restorative properties of attractive built places compared to natural places in the urban environment. The study presented in this chapter, different from most research on restorative environments where participants are asked to rate places represented in images, focuses on the restorative properties and affective qualities of actual places as experienced by people in the place itself. Results show that built places including historic-panoramic properties can be perceived as restorative as urban natural places, as well as being more restorative than other urban attractions, such as shopping malls. However, urban natural places are perceived as more pleasant and relaxing compared to the other two urban contexts considered, thus confirming the generalized preference for nature spots, particularly for relaxation experiences.

Section 4: Diversity in Lifestyles and Urban Sustainability

Changes in the natural environment occurring at a global level have received increasing scientific, political, economic, and social attention over the last two decades. As a consequence, social and behavioural sciences have increasingly focused on the impact of human action and lifestyles upon the quality of our living environments and of the natural resources therein. Facing global environmental issues for the pursuit of sustainable development implies the study of the individual and social determinants of localized environmentally friendly human actions, and their impact on the well-being of human beings and non-human species (e.g., Uzzell, 2000). As a consequence, the performance of pro-ecological behaviours is currently the focus of environmental and social-psychological investigation, in various behavioural domains, such as bioclimatic architecture and "green" housing, energy production and consumption, household recycling, green consumerism, and biodiversity conservation (e.g., Steg & Vlek, 2009; see also Bamberg & Möser, 2007): lifestyle diversity therefore matters for urban sustainability. The contribution of people-environment studies for the prediction of environmentally friendly behaviour in these domains is illustrated and discussed in this section through a variety of theoretical reflections and empirical approaches.

The chapter by Blossom and Blossom explores the collective symbols, patterns, ideals, and ideas of social living represented in the interior of Tibetan homes. The authors critically consider contemporary views of "green" architecture and sustainability, as well as the relation of historic vernacular building approaches to the natural environment. In their analysis, Blossom and Blossom show how vernacular Tibetan tradition strategies are employed to both exploit and mitigate sunlight, and argue that these strategies might influence tangible as well as intangible aspects of the interior. The chapter also discusses the implications for setting up sustainable solar design interventions strategies, both interior and exterior, in relation to features such as layered volumes and light qualities.

The theme of domestic energy consumption is addressed more directly in the chapter by García-Landa and Montero, who examine the relationship between domestic electric consumption and socio-demographic factors. The authors apply the concept of austere consumer lifestyle, characterized by moderation in the acquisition and use of economic goods and services, to energy consumption. A scale of "Rational Electric Power Consumption" was developed covering aspects such as survival, comfort, luxury, and squander, and administered to housewives living in Mexico City. Results showing a negative association between electricity consumption and family income are discussed in relation to the issue of consumers' life satisfaction.

Tabernero and Hernandez analyse the role of collective motivation in environmentally responsible behaviour, with the purpose of exploring the internal motivation leading communities to adopt pro-environmental lifestyle and behaviours. In their study conducted in the city of Cordoba in Southern Spain, the authors set up a measure of observed collective recycling behaviour. The findings show how this variable is linked to motivational factors, such as intrinsic satisfaction and collective efficacy, and how communities sharing reasons for recycling tend to carry out more environmentally responsible actions.

In his chapter, Caddeo investigates the role of ecological concern in consumer's choices of organic and genetically modified (GM) food products. The author argues that personal health and preservation of natural environment are both related to beliefs about responsible food consumption behaviours, including considerations about the difference between organic and GM products. The study assessed consumer evaluations of organic and GM food products in Italy, to ascertain whether ecological motives, such as the natural and healthy food's content and the ecological concern, play a role in consumers' evaluations of these food products. Results confirmed how the health hazard related to GM food products affects consumers' choice, especially consumers with high ecological motivations, while consumers with low ecological motives are more confident towards both organic and GM food.

Section 5: Diversity in Social Groups and Inclusive Urban Environments

A commonly accepted assumption in the field of people-environment studies is the need for inclusive and participatory approaches in the design and management of current urban environments. Promoting social inclusion in the urban environment is indeed a major political aim for global and intergovernmental institutions, such as the United Nations Human Settlements Programme (UN-Habitat). This idea has also been followed by planners and architects at different spatial scales, ranging from building interiors to neighbourhoods and residential contexts, to larger urban and peri-urban spaces (e.g., Goltsman & Iacofano, 2007). Social and environmental psychological research has also often highlighted how the physical space can be used for regulating interpersonal relations between individuals and within small groups (e.g., Festinger, Schacther, & Back, 1950). At a collective level, it has been used as a strategic means for maintaining and reproducing existing societal conditions and intergroup relations (e.g., Dixon, Reicher, & Foster, 1997; see also Uzzell & Räthzel, 2009).

The final section of the book groups together three contributions, which, in different ways and with different approaches, investigate how diversities among individuals, within and between groups of age, residential experience (such as place attachment), and ethnicity, are reflected in the different perceptions, evaluations, and use of the urban physical space. All these three chapters share a common background in their reliance on specific theories, constructs, and processes that have traditionally been employed in social, environmental, and community psychology: the ecological approaches of Bronfenbrenner (1979) and Lewin (1936) for the chapter by Migliorini and Cardinali, the processes of place attachment for the chapter by Devine-Wright and the processes of social identity for the chapter by Dixon, Durrheim, and Tredoux.

The chapter by Migliorini and Cardinali explores children's sense of safety and well-being towards the neighbourhood in the city of Genoa, Italy. They argue that children's experience of the environment is connected with the perception of safety and with the feelings of fear, and that safety is an essential resource for everyday life, needed by individuals and communities to fulfil their aspirations. The chapter presents the results of a research project carried out in neighbourhoods differing in structural and social features. The chapter concludes with further research questions on the links between children's sense of safety and self-esteem, and children's sense of safety and parents' socio-demographic factors. These issues have important implications for the promotion of more inclusive urban environments, such as children-friendly neighbourhoods.

The chapter by Devine-Wright addresses local opposition to development projects of energy supply from renewable sources, such as wind farms. The work critically examines the 'NIMBY' (Not In My Back Yard) concept, commonly used to explain public opposition to land use changes. The author applies a conceptual approach that investigates the social representations of the place in relation to place experience. Empirical data from a case study in the UK show how strong place attachment might predict resident's opposition, enhancing feelings of threat to their place-related identities. The policy implications are also discussed, as these results seem to challenge the commonly held assumption that offshore wind farms might be less controversial than onshore ones.

Finally, the chapter by Dixon, Durrheim, and Tredoux analyses the potential contribution of environmental psychology to understanding and overcoming the persistence and the negative effects of racial segregation. In their study of the consequence of South African racial segregation during the second half of the 20th century, Dixon and colleagues suggest that if the ideal city promotes diversity, interaction, and social justice, then the apartheid city stands as the antithesis of this ideal. The amplification of intergroup divisions, prejudices, and social injustice deriving from environmental racial segregation is illustrated through the example of the use of sea beaches in the city of Cape Town, adopting a discursive analytical approach.

Concluding Remarks

Following the cross-cutting theme of diversity, it is important to underline the plurality of the scientific backgrounds and methods that form the basis for the present book, a key issue for people-environment studies. This volume covers a range of disciplinary and theoretical perspectives, approaches, and research methods. The theoretical background of the papers refers to various domains of psychological research (e.g., environmental psychology, but also cognitive, developmental, social, and community psychology), as well as other disciplinary domains (e.g., architecture, landscape architecture, urban planning, geography, human ecology, communication science, interior design). This disciplinary diversity is also reflected in the research methods used, which range from laboratory experiments, to field surveys, observations, simulations, and discourse analysis. Taken together the content of this volume illustrates how theoretical and methodological diversity is a key in understanding people-urban environment relations, in order to advance the quality of the environment and the lives of its inhabitants.

Acknowledgments

The editors and authors are grateful to Prof. William D. Crano and Dr. Suellen Crano for their kind help in revising the English language for the texts in this volume.

References

Alfsen-Norodom, C., & Lane, B. (2002). Global knowledge networking for site specific strategies: The international conference on biodiversity and society. *Environmental Science & Policy, 5*, 3–8.

Bamberg, S., & Möser, G. (2007). Twenty years after Hines, Hungerford, and Tomera: A new meta-analysis of psycho-social determinants of pro-environmental behaviour. *Journal of Environmental Psychology, 27*, 14–25.

Barbault, R. (1995). Biodiversity: Stakes and opportunities. *Nature & Resources, 31*, 18–26.

Bonnes, M., & Bonaiuto, M. (2002). Environmental psychology: from spatial-physical environment to sustainable development. In R. Bechtel & A. Churchman (Eds.), *Handbook of Environmental Psychology* (pp. 28–54). New York, NY: Wiley.

Bonnes, M., Carrus, G., Corral-Verdugo, G., & Passafaro, P. (2010). The socio-psychological affinity towards diversity: from biodiversity to socio-ecological sustainability. In V. Corral-Verdugo, C. II. García-Cadena, & M. Frías-Armenta (Eds.), *Psychological approaches to sustainability: Current trends in theory, research and practice.* Hauppauge, NY: Nova Science Publishers.

Boyle, P., & Grow, S. (2008). The global amphibian crisis. *Endangered Species Bulletin, 33*, 4–6.

Bronfenbrenner, U. (1979). *The ecology of human development.* Cambridge, MA: The Harvard University Press.

Capra, F., & Pauli, G. (1995). *Steering business toward sustainability.* New York, NY: United Nations University Press.

Dansereau, P. (1997). Biodiversity, ecodiversity, sociodiversity – three aspects of diversity: Part 1. *Global Biodiversity, 6*, 2–9.

di Castri, F. (1995). The chair of sustainable development. *Nature & Resources, 31*, 2–7.

di Castri, F. & Balayi, W. (Eds.). (2002). *Tourism, biodiversity and information.* Leiden: Backhuys Publishers.

Dixon, J. A., Reicher, S., & Foster, D. (1997). Ideology, geography and racial exclusion: The squatter camp as "blot on the landscape". *Text, 17*, 317–348.

Elewa, A. (2008). *Mass extinction.* Berlin: Springer.

FAO – Food, Agriculture Organization of the United Nations. (2007). The state of World fisheries and aquaculture 2006. Rome: FAO. Retrieved August 2008, from ftp://ftp.fao.org/docrep/fao/009/a0699e/a0699e.pdf.

Festinger, L., Shachter, S., & Back, K. (1950). *Social pressure in informal groups*. Stanford, CA: Stanford University Press.

Giuliani, M. V., & Scopelliti, M. (2009). Empirical research in environmental psychology: Past, present and future. *Journal of Environmental Psychology, 29*, 375–386.

Goltsman, S., & Iacofano, D. (2007). *The inclusive city. Design solutions for buildings, neighbourhoods, and urban spaces*. Berkeley, CA: MIG Communications.

Guillitte, O. (2005). Biodiversity and sociodiversity for a sustainable development. *Liaison Energie Francophonie, 68*, 95–98.

Hartig, T. (2004). Restorative environments. In C. Spielberger (Ed.), *Encyclopedia of applied psychology* (Vol. 3, pp. 273–279). New York, NY: Academic Press/Elsevier.

Hawkins, B. (2008). *Plants for life: Medicinal plant conservation and botanic gardens*. Richmond, UK: Botanic Gardens Conservation International.

IUCN – International Union for Conservation of Nature. (2008). 2007 IUCN red list of threatened species. Retrieved August 2008, from www.iucnredlist.org/.

IUCN – International Union for Conservation of Nature. (2010). About biodiversity. Retrieved May 2010, from http://www.iucn.org/iyb/about/.

Jimeno, M., Sotomayor, M., & Valderrama, L. (1995). *Chocó: Diversidad cultural y medio ambiente* [Chocó: Cultural diversity and environment]. Bogotá, Colombia: Fondo FEN.

Kaplan, S. (1995). The restorative benefits of nature – toward an integrative framework. *Journal of Environmental Psychology, 15*, 169–182.

Lacy, W. (1994). Biodiversity, cultural diversity and food equity. *Agriculture and Human Values, 11*, 3–9.

Lawrence, R., & Després, C. (2004). Futures of transdisciplinarity. *Futures, 36*, 397–405.

Le Duc J. P. (Ed.), *Proceedings of the UNESCO International Conference on Biodiversity, Science and Governance*, 24–28. January, Paris. Paris: IFB – Institut Français de la Biodiversité.

Lee, T. (1969). Urban neighbourhood as a socio-spatial scheme. *Human Relations, 21*, 241–267.

Lewin, K. (1936). *Principles of topological psychology*. New York, NY: McGraw-Hill.

Lynch, K. (1960). *The image of the city*. Cambridge, MA: MIT Press.

Millennium Ecosystem Assessment. (2005). *Ecosystems and human well-being: Synthesis*. Washington, DC: Island Press.

Milgram, S. (1970). The experience of living in cities. *Science, 167*, 1461–1468.

Moser, G. (1988). Urban stress and helping behavior: Effects of environmental overload and noise on behavior. *Journal of Environmental Psychology, 8*, 287–298.

Moser, G. (1992). *Les stress urbains*. Paris: Armand Colin.

Moser, G. (2009). *Psychologie environnementale. Les relations homme-environnement*. Bruxelles: De Boeck.

Nettle, D., & Romaine, S. (2000). *Vanishing voices: The extinction of the world's languages*. New York, NY: Oxford University Press.

O'Hara, S. (1995). Valuing sociodiversity. *International Journal of Social Economics, 22*, 31–49.

Starke, L. (2008). *State of the World*. New York, NY: W. W. Norton & Company.

Steg, L., & Vlek, C. (2009). Encouraging pro-environmental behavior: An integrative review and research agenda. *Journal of Environmental Psychology, 29*, 309–317.

Tonn, B. (2007). Futures sustainability. *Futures, 39*, 1097–1116.

UNESCO. (2006). UNESCO: A key factor in the fulfillment of the global biodiversity agenda, 15. Retrieved June 15, from http://www.unesco.org/mab/biodiv.shtml.

Uzzell, D. (2000). The psycho-spatial dimension of global environmental problems. *Journal of Environmental Psychology, 20*, 307–318.

Uzzell, D., & Moser, G. (2009). Introduction: Environmental psychology on the move. *Journal of Environmental Psychology, 29*, 307–308.

Uzzell, D., & Räthzel, N. (2009). Transforming environmental psychology. *Journal of Environmental Psychology, 29*, 340–350.

Van den Berg, A. E., Hartig, T., & Staats, H. (2007). Preference for nature in urbanized societies: Stress, restoration, and the pursuit of sustainability. *Journal of Social Issues, 63*, 79–96.

WCED – World Commission on Environment and Development. (1987). *Our common future*. Oxford: Oxford University Press.

Wilson, E. O. (1999). *The diversity of life*. New York, NY: W.W. Norton.

Diversity in Theoretical and Methodological Approaches

Analysing Urban Diversity

The Pertinence of Interdisciplinary and Transdisciplinary Contributions

Roderick J. Lawrence

Human Ecology and Environmental Sciences, University of Geneva, Switzerland

Abstract

Cities are human-made ecosystems that are meant to meet the requirements of daily life and sustain their population over several generations. Although there are diverse interpretations of cities, it is possible to analyse them according to a set of generic characteristics including centralization, concentration, diversity, information and communication, mechanization, verticality, and political authority. These characteristics will be presented as the conceptual framework for an integrated interdisciplinary analysis based on the core principles of human ecology. Although this kind of analysis has been applied successfully since the 1920s by human ecologists, it has not become mainstream in the field of urban studies. This field is still dominated by disciplinary contributions that fail to deal with the complexity and the diversity of urban ecosystems. This chapter argues that both inter- and transdisciplinary contributions are more effective ways of improving current knowledge about urban ecosystems.

Key words: complexity, diversity, ecosystems, human ecology, interdisciplinarity, transdisciplinarity

Cities and all their buildings, infrastructure, and services must be conceptualized before they are constructed. The foundation and the construction of cities and towns imply that geographical space and environmental resources are appropriated, cultivated, and transformed by people to serve their daily basic requirements and sustain human societies over time. Human sustenance is dependent on the availability of natural resources and the quality of living conditions both within and beyond the geographical boundaries of urban ecosystems (Boyden, 1987). These ecosystems can be interpreted in relation to those collective decisions, lifestyles, and adaptive responses that individuals and groups make in relation to the local environmental conditions of their habitat, the available resources, and their knowledge and know-how. Traditionally, shared lifestyles, conventions, and meanings about the ordering of society have also been used implicitly and explicitly in the construction of urban ecosystems (Lawrence, 2001). This chapter argues that it is necessary to reconsider cities and urban development in a broad environmental, economic, social, and political context. Human ecology can achieve this objective because it has provided an integrated framework for interdisciplinary contributions since the 1920s, and common applications can be extended to implement transdisciplinary contributions.

The term ecosystem is used in the natural sciences to designate a unit of analysis in a delimited geographical area (biotope) that includes all plants, animals, and micro-organisms (biotic components) functioning together with all non-living (a-biotic) components as well as flows of materials, energy, and information between these components. A human ecosystem implies that *Homo sapiens sapiens* are also included in the area (Lawrence, 2001). An urban ecosystem is not easily defined because the definition of a city varies from country to country. The United Nations uses national definitions that are commonly based on population size. Other definitions are based on the administrative or political authority of municipalities, especially the degree of autonomy in relation to the national or regional administration. Some definitions include the socioeconomic status of the resident population, especially their livelihood (such as the proportion of all employed people with non-agricultural occupations). A combination of these characteristics will be used to interpret urban ecosystems using an integrated interdisciplinary analysis based on the core principles of human ecology.

Disciplinary, Interdisciplinary, and Transdisciplinary Contributions

In this chapter, disciplinarity refers to the specialization of academic disciplines that became strong during the 19th century. Each discipline has defined concepts, methods, and criteria for evaluation which are endorsed by specialized peer reviewed publications. Multidisciplinarity refers to research in which each specialist remains within her/his discipline and contributes using disciplinary concepts and methods. For example, civil engineers, geologists, geographers, and representatives of other disciplines and professions each have their own approach to analyse urban areas which they can do independently of each other. In contrast, interdisciplinary contributions can be interpreted as the explicit bringing together of disciplines that retain their own concepts and methods that are applied to a mutually agreed subject such as an urban ecosystem. This kind of contribution can be considered as the exchange of knowledge between academic disciplines in order to better understand the complexity of an urban ecosystem. Finally, transdisciplinary contributions involve the integration of disciplinary scientific knowledge with the know-how of professions and the tacit knowledge of laypeople (Lawrence & Despres, 2004). The combination of these three kinds of knowledge creates a new hybrid that is different from any specific constituent part. This interpretation means that transdisciplinary contributions are not auto-mated processes that stem from the bringing together of people from different disciplines or professions. In addition, they require an ingredient that some have called "transcen-dence". It also implies the giving up of sovereignty over knowledge, the generation of new insights and knowledge by collaboration, and the capacity to consider the viewpoints of professionals and laypeople.

Collectively, interdisciplinary and transdisciplinary contributions enable the cross-fertilization of ideas and knowledge from different contributors. They can lead to an enlarged vision of a subject, especially the complexity of urban ecosystems. Both interdis-ciplinary and transdisciplinary contributions are ways of improving knowledge (Lawrence & Despres, 2004). The relationship between researchers in different disciplines, especially in the human/social and the basic/natural sciences, is often considered to be a source of conflict. Nonetheless, this need not be the case as shown already nearly 30 years ago by the contribution of Boyden and his colleagues in their applied human ecology research about Hong Kong (Boyden, Millar, Newcombe, & O'Neill, 1981). Transdisciplinary con-tributions of this kind can lead to the development of new terminology, innovative con-cepts, and new knowledge. This is an important challenge for those who wish to apply human ecology in research on urban ecosystems.

What Is Human Ecology?

Human ecology usually refers to the study of the dynamic, systemic relationships between human populations and all the physical, biotic, cultural, and social characteristics of their environment and the biosphere. Human ecology transgresses traditional disciplinary boundaries by explicitly applying a broad conceptual and methodological framework that is represented in Figure 1. It is an interdisciplinary interpretation because it includes con-cepts and principles from both the natural and the social sciences. It also underlines the systemic interrelations between sets of biotic, a-biotic, and anthropological factors. Hence, it does not concentrate only on specific components because it considers the whole eco-system as the unit of study for people-environment relations. This interpretation can be applied at different geographical scales including urban ecosystems. It is meant to be reap-plied at different times to explicitly address a short- and long-term perspective during the life cycle. This temporal perspective can identify change to any of the specific components as well as the interrelations between them.

One basic principle of biological life is that all living organisms (irrespective of their species) impact on their surroundings (Boyden, 1987). The livelihood of organisms is dependent on the interrelations between them and their surroundings, the volume and quality of the available local resources, the discharge of waste products, and the creation of new resources. By their existence, all living organisms change the conditions upon which they depend for their subsistence. In addition, all organisms are components of

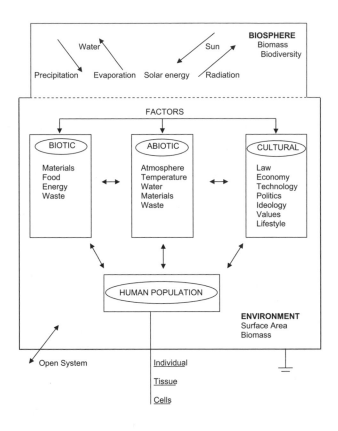

Figure 1. The holistic framework of a human ecology perspective showing the interrelations between genetic biospace, ecospace, cultural space, and artefacts (*copyright, R. Lawrence*).

ecological systems and, therefore, they explicitly influence the living conditions of other species (Marten, 2001). For example, human beings can change their habitat as well as the habitats of animals, insects, and plants to such an extent that they may jeopardize their existence over the long term.

There are certain conditions and limits overriding the sustenance of human groups and societies that are defined by some fundamental principles of human ecology. First, the biosphere and the Earth are finite (Boyden, 1992). Both natural and human ecosystems at all scales of the planet and its atmosphere are circumscribed by certain immutable limits, such as the surface of land, its bio-mass and bio-diversity, the water cycle, biochemical cycles, and thermodynamic principles about the production and transformation of energy, including the accumulation and radiation of heat from the Earth. Although these principles are fundamental, their relative importance has been interpreted in various, sometimes contradictory ways (even by scientists in the same discipline). These divergences highlight the diversity and limitations of current knowledge in many scientific disciplines which have not been well coordinated.

Second, human ecosystems are not closed, finite systems because they are open to external influences of an ecological kind (such as solar energy and earthquakes), as well as to influences of a biological kind and an anthropological kind, such as disease and warfare. This means that research programmes on sustainability that deal with internal conditions and processes should also consider those external factors that impact on them. Unfortunately, recent contributions on this subject include misconceptions about the autonomy of urban ecosystems and the ability of modern technology to overcome ecological constraints.

Third, human beings must create and transform energy using materials, energy, and acquired knowledge to ensure their livelihood (Boyden, 1987). The increasing disparity between ecological and biological processes and products on the one hand, and the products and processes of human societies, on the other hand, is largely attributed to the rapid growth of urban populations, the creation of many synthetic products that cannot be recycled into natural processes, plus increases in energy consumption based on the use of nonrenewable and renewable resources at a greater rate than their replacement. At the global level, the negative consequences of these trends include the depletion of the ozone layer, a reduction in bio-diversity, the accumulation of wastes, the enhancement of the "greenhouse effect," and the incidence of environmental catastrophes including floods, landslides, and famine.

Fourth, human beings can be distinguished from other biological organisms by the kinds of regulators they commonly use to define, modify, and control their living conditions. Human beings have several mechanisms that enable them to adjust to specific environmental conditions. These mechanisms include thermoregulation and circadian rhythms, which are used to ensure and maintain vital needs, such as nutrition. This fundamental need is not only guaranteed by biological and physiological mechanisms, because cultural rules and practices (that vary between ethnic groups, across cultures, and within societies) are also used (Boyden, 1992).

Adaptation is a set of interrelated processes that sustain human ecosystems in the context of a continual change. Evolutionary adaptation refers to processes of natural selection. It is only applicable to populations and it is transgenerational. Innate adaptation refers to physiological and behavioural changes that occur in individuals that are genetically determined and do not depend on learning. Cultural adaptation refers to adaptation by cultural processes that are not innate, such as legal measures, or changes in lifestyle and therefore it includes institutional adaptations. The outcome of adaptation depends on a complex set of biological, ecological, cultural, societal, and individual human mechanisms.

The organizing principles of human ecosystems are derived from people-environment-biosphere relations (Lawrence, 2001). Hence, the substantive characteristics of the environment should be addressed in the same way as the cultural and social characteristics of human populations. This means that a human ecology perspective should not borrow concepts that only refer to animals and plants. For example, successful adaptations to ecological constraints include different means and measures used by human beings and other organisms to deal with flows of materials. There may be a few genetic sets of adaptive processes that are similar among human beings, animals, and plants. However, the crucial role of human culture underlying human adaptability should not be underestimated. The preceding principles will now be applied to interpret urban ecosystems.

Analysing Urban Ecosystems: Applied Human Ecology

Cities and towns can be interpreted as human constructs that result from the interrelations between ecological, economic, material, political, and social factors at the local, national, and international levels. Cities such as Bangkok, Cape Town, or London are interesting examples of the intersection between these sets of factors, and how some of these factors have remained, while others have been modified over thousands of years. Given the changing nature of these factors, it is appropriate to discuss ways and means of sustaining urban ecosystems. This approach underlines the fundamental principle that all human societies regulate their relation to the biosphere and the local environment by using a range of codes, practices, and principles based on scientific knowledge and community know-how. Societies can use legislation, surveillance, monetary incentives, and taxes, as well as behavioural rules and socially agreed conventions in order to ensure their sustenance (Lawrence, 1996).

All living organisms, individuals, and species aspire for survival. The mechanisms used to sustain human beings depend on their capacity to adapt to changing local conditions such as climate and the availability of resources (Laughlin & Brady, 1978). Adaptation for sustaining human settlement processes and outcomes is based on both ecological principles and cultural practices. These principles and practices stem from the fact that specific localities or sites provide intrinsic opportunities and constraints for all living organisms, including human individuals and groups, to sustain themselves. This is well illustrated by the unique site chosen for many cities including Cape Town, Istanbul, and Rome. The site of any human settlement is also a small part of a much larger region that has intrinsic interrelated sets of ecological, biological, geological, and cultural characteristics. Therefore, no site should be interpreted in isolation from these interrelated sets of characteristics.

Human ecology stresses that sustaining urban ecosystems involves a wide range of human practices that ought to adapt to the dynamic circumstances of a constantly changing world at both local and global levels. Human ecology can help bridge the social distance between scientific knowledge, professional practices, and the tacit know-how of citizens.

Urban Ecosystems: Product and Process

In order to redirect the debate between scientists, practitioners, and policy decision makers about sustaining urban ecosystems, some conceptual clarification is required. First, it is important to distinguish between urban ecosystems as a *product* (i.e., the analysis of the urban environment as the physical outcome of decisions about how to accommodate human life in cities) and urban ecosystems as *process* (by referring to the multiple sets of processes that occur in cities and between cities and their hinterlands). It is common to adopt only one of these interpretations as Lawrence (1995) has shown. This chapter suggests that both should be applied simultaneously in order to deal with the complexity of urban ecosystems.

Constructing an urban ecosystem involves choosing between a range of options in order to achieve objectives that may or may not give a high priority to health and quality of life (Galea & Vlahov, 2005). The complexity of building cities and towns raises some critical questions including: What parameters are pertinent for a specific building task, such as the construction of a new residential neighbourhood? Whose values, goals, and intentions will be taken into consideration? How and when will these goals and intentions be achieved? What will be the monetary and non-monetary costs and benefits of specific options? In order to answer these kinds of questions, it is necessary to recall those inherent characteristics of urban ecosystems. In order to distinguish urban ecosystems from other kinds of human settlements, notably rural villages and towns, it is important to identify the distinguishing characteristics of cities.

The first characteristic of cities is *centralization*. The choice of a specific site and the definition of the administrative and political boundaries of a city distinguish it from the hinterlands. Studies in urban history and geography confirm that many factors have been involved in the location of cities (Bairoch, 1988). For example, coastal sites for ports such as New York, Cape Town, or Sydney can be contrasted with sites on inland trade routes such as Geneva or Vienna. It is important to note that modern economic rationality has an interpretation of the World and human societies, which has rarely accounted for the climatic, geological, and biological characteristics of specific localities. This has meant that urban populations have been confronted with unforeseen natural and human-made disasters including earthquakes, floods, and landslides (Mitchell, 1999).

Verticality is the second characteristic of cities. During the long history of cities, urban communities have constructed buildings of several storeys. Bairoch (1988) noted that Jericho included buildings of seven storeys. This characteristic underlies the compact or dense built environment of cities in contrast to the dispersed character of rural villages and towns. The height of residential buildings in cities increased dramatically from the late 19th century with the construction of skyscrapers, first in Chicago, then in other cities around the World. The relations between high-rise housing conditions and quality of life are not easy to decipher owing to the vast number of confounding factors (Lawrence, 2004). However, there is empirical evidence that those residents who do not choose where they live, especially households with young children who are allocated housing units in high-rise buildings, may suffer from stressors that impact negatively on their health (Halpern, 1995).

Concentration is the third characteristic of cities that is directly related to the two preceding ones. Urbanization is dependent on the availability of natural resources and the exportation of waste products in order to sustain their populations (UNCHS, 2001).

Urban ecosystems import energy, fuels, materials, and water that are transformed into goods and services. The high concentrations of activities, objects, and people in cities, and the flows between rural and urban areas, mean that city authorities must manage the supply of food and water as well as the disposal of solid and liquid wastes in a sustainable way. Urban history confirms that cities are localities that favour the rapid spread of infectious diseases, fires, social unrest, and warfare (Bairoch, 1988). In terms of public health, concentration can be quantified in terms of activities, building density, and population density. Empirical studies show that the number of persons per metre of habitable floor area is related to the propagation of infectious diseases such as tuberculosis and cholera (Galea & Vlahov, 2005).

Diversity is a refining characteristic of cities that can be used effectively to promote ecological, economic, and social well-being (Finche & Iveson, 2008). Diversity is known to be an important characteristic of natural ecosystems because it enables adaptation to unforeseen (external) conditions and processes that may impact negatively and even threaten survival (Laughlin & Brady, 1978). In the same way, we have learnt from history that those cities with a diverse local economy have been able to cope much better with economic recessions and globalization (Jacobs, 1969). This was not the case for Detroit, Glasgow, or cities of the mid-West in North America.

Social, cultural, economic, and material diversity are inherent characteristics of cities (Jacobs, 1961). The heterogeneity of urban populations can be considered in terms of age, ethnicity, revenue, and socio-professional status. These kinds of differences are often reflected and reinforced by education, housing conditions, employment status, property ownership, and material wealth. When these dimensions of human differentiation become acute, they are often reflected and reinforced by spatial segregation and social exclusion in urban agglomerations. Several empirical studies show how these characteristics of urban neighbourhoods, especially acute socioeconomic inequalities and lack of social cohesion, are linked to morbidity and mortality (Marmot & Wilkinson, 1999).

Information and communication is the fifth characteristic because cities have always been centres for the development and exchange of ideas, information, and inventions (Castells, 1991). The systematic collection of data and information is a responsibility of civic authorities. No single focus information system can equal the potential of Coordinated Information Systems to support cross-sector policies and programmes. A strategic approach to improving public awareness based on efficient communication and information transfer can reduce the social distance between scientists, professionals, and laypeople. There is much to be learnt from successful marketing strategies by private enterprises (Duffy, 1995).

Mechanization is the sixth characteristic. Cities have depended on machines to import supplies, to treat waste products, and to efficiently use their built environment. Contemporary cities are heavily dependent on machinery for a wide range of functions and services that guarantee sanitary living conditions. Mechanical and technological characteristics of cities that impact directly or indirectly on quality of life include industrial production, transportation, and the processing of mass-produced foods (UNCHS, 2001). In particular, the incidence of accidents in urban areas is a major challenge for public health. For example, in 1998, injuries caused by motor vehicle accidents were ranked 10th among leading causes of mortality worldwide and 9th among the leading causes of disability. Children and young adults in all regions of the World bear a significant burden of these accidents, and the burden is higher in urban areas compared with rural areas, as well as in developing countries compared with developed countries (World Bank, 2001).

Political authority is the seventh characteristic. The city was the polis in ancient Greece, meaning that it had a specific political status, which is still the case today in the form of municipal government. During the 1990s, much attention had been given to urban governance rather than municipal government. Governance can be defined as the process through which individuals and institutions (public and private) plan and manage their common affairs. It is based on the effective coordination of three main components: market-based strategies for the private sector, hierarchical strategies articulated by the public sector, and networking in civil society (Hambleton & Gross, 2008). The goal of governance should be to develop synergies between these partners so that there is a better capacity to deal with the diversity of cities (Finche & Iveson, 2008).

Synthesis

This chapter has argued that our capacity to understand and manage urban ecosystems is insufficient for several reasons including their diversity and complexity; the difficulty in identifying and measuring the interrelations between them and all their components; and the need to understand the relative importance of these components in precise localities at different geographical scales and over time. Therefore, it is necessary to shift from disciplinary to interdisciplinary and transdisciplinary concepts and methods.

Policy makers in most countries still have great difficulty in measuring, describing, and explaining constancy, change, and differences of the human and non-human characteristics of cities (Hambleton & Gross, 2008). Part of the difficulty has been the lack of systematic data collection. A dynamic set covering several characteristics is required across a range of administrative levels and geographical scales. Alone, official statistics based on national census returns do not provide comprehensive accounts of the quantity and quality of the housing stock, urban infrastructure, and services in rapidly developing urban areas and they ignore illegal buildings in informal settlements. There are several kinds of innovative techniques and tools that can be used to monitor and analyse the spatial distribution, dynamics, and interrelated nature of environmental, housing, demographic, and health profiles in urban areas. There have been significant developments in the collection and interpretation of data, indicators, and information during the 1990s, which warrant further systematic applications. For example, geographical information systems represent data from diverse sources (including remote sensing) in order to identify relationships between the components of urban areas.

Conclusion

Urban ecosystems are multidimensional and complex. No single discipline or perspective can understand and explain them in a comprehensive way. Collaboration and coordination of contributions are necessary. However, the study of people-environment relations, in general, still remains divided between the social and natural sciences as well as between the theoretical and applied approaches in specific disciplines including anthropology, biology, epidemiology, human geography, geosciences, psychology, and sociology. The main obstacle that hinders an integrated framework is the compartmentalized disciplinary approach of scientists and professionals who adopt exclusive interpretations rather than developing shared definitions and concepts. There is an urgent need to complement several disciplinary contributions by coordinated interdisciplinary and transdisciplinary contributions in order to improve our understanding of the diversity and complexity of urban ecosystems.

References

Bairoch, P. (1988). *Cities and economic development: From the dawn of history to the present*. London: Mansell.

Boyden, S. (1987). *Western civilisation in biological perspective: Patterns in biohistory*. Oxford: Oxford University Press.

Boyden, S. (1992). *Biohistory: The interplay between human society and the biosphere, past and present*. Paris: UNESCO.

Boyden, S., Millar, S., Newcombe, K., & O'Neill, B. (1981). *The ecology of a city and its people: The case of Hong Kong*. Canberra: Australian National University Press.

Castells, M. (1991). *Informational city: Economic restructuring and urban development*. Oxford: Blackwell.

Duffy, H. (1995). *Competitive cities: Succeeding in a global economy*. London: E & FN Spon.

Finche, R., & Iveson, K. (2008). *Planning for diversity: Redistribution, recognition and encounter*. Basingstoke: Palgrave Macmillan.

Galea, S., & Vlahov, D. (Eds.). (2005). *Handbook of urban health: Populations, methods, and practice*. New York: Springer.

Halpern, D. (1995). *Mental health and the built environment*. London: Taylor and Francis.

Hambleton, R. & Gross, J. (Eds.). (2008). *Governing cities in a global era: Urban innovation, competition and democratic reform*. Basingstoke: Palgrave Macmillan.

Jacobs, J. (1961). *The death and life of great American cities*. New York: Vintage Books.

Jacobs, J. (1969). *The economy of cities*. New York: Vintage Books.

Laughlin, C., & Brady, I. (1978). *Extinction and survival in human populations*. New York: Columbia University Press.

Lawrence, R. (1995). Meeting the challenge: Barriers to integrated cross-sectoral urban policies. In M. Rolén (Ed.), *Urban policies for an environmentally sustainable world* (pp. 9–37). Stockholm: Swedish Council for Planning and Co-ordination of Research.

Lawrence, R. (1996). Urban environment, health and the economy: Cues for conceptual clarification and more effective policy implementation. In C. Price & A. Tsouros (Eds.), *Our cities, our future:*

Policies and action plans for health and sustainable development (pp. 38–64). Copenhagen: World Health Organization European Office for Europe.

Lawrence, R. (2001). Human ecology. In M. K. Tolba (Ed.), *Our fragile world: Challenges and opportunities for sustainable development* (Vol. 1, pp. 675–693). Oxford: EOLSS.

Lawrence, R. (2004). Housing and health: From interdisciplinary principles to transdisciplinary research and practice. *Futures, 36*(4), 487–502.

Lawrence, R. & Despres C. (Eds.). (2004). Futures of transdisciplinarity [Special issue]. *Futures, 36*(4).

Marmot, M., & Wilkinson, R. (Eds.). (1999). *Social determinants of health.* Oxford: Oxford University Press.

Marten, G. (2001). *Human ecology: Basic concepts for sustainable development.* London: Earthscan.

Mitchell, J. (Ed.). (1999). *Crucibles of hazards: Mega-cities and disasters in transition.* Tokyo: United Nations University Press.

United Nations Commission on Human Settlements (UNCHS). (2001). *The state of the world's cities.* Nairobi: United Nations Commission on Human Settlements (UNCHS Habitat), document HS/619/01E.

World Bank. (2001). *Attacking poverty: World development report 2000/2001.* New York: Oxford University Press.

Regarding the Question of Evidence

Current Worldviews in Environmental Design Research and Practice

Keith Diaz Moore[1] and Lyn Geboy[2]

[1]University of Kansas, KS, USA
[2]Milwaukee, WI, USA

Abstract

The popularity of the concept of evidence-based design (EBD), an emergent mode of linking environmental design research and environmental design, has exploded in recent years. Its emphasis on the term "evidence" raises the epistemological question, "What constitutes evidence in the design discipline?" To answer this question, this paper begins with an historical overview of the EBD concept, highlighting the epistemological assumptions that undergird the current approach to EBD. The discussion then broadens to address the five general approaches to knowledge generation in environmental design research and design practice. Our point is that in current discussions of EBD, a certain mode of knowledge generation is privileged yet the applicability of that sort of knowledge to design practice is problematic as it violates certain presumptions of practice. A more inclusive definition of evidence-based design is called for, one which values evidence produced through various modes of environmental design research.

Key words: environmental design research, environmental design practice, epistemology, worldviews

The popularity of the concept of evidence-based design (EBD) has exploded over the past five years, picking up speed as a topic of attention in environmental design conferences (e.g., Berlage Institute, 2008; Center for Health Design, 2006; ICADI, 2008; WCDH, 2007), papers and articles (e.g., Geboy & Keller, 2006; Hamilton, 2004; Shepley, 2004; Ulrich, Zimring, Joseph, Quan, & Choudhary, 2004), and books (e.g., Malkin, 2008;

Verderber, 2005; Zeisel, 2006). Rooted in the healthcare environment arena, the EBD concept has now bridged out to the design of long-term care settings (e.g., Calkins & Cassella, 2007), housing (e.g., Ahrentzen, 2006), and workplaces (e.g., Sailer, Budgen, Lonsdale, Turner, & Penn, 2008) as well as facilities management (e.g., Martin & Guerin, 2006). While "evidence-based design" is indeed a seductive term for those of us interested in advancing research-informed design, portending linkages between research-derived evidence and environmental design, in its current conceptualization, its clout is stronger than its clarity. At this point, the concept of EBD is emergent, warranting careful, critical examination regarding its meaning and underlying assumptions.

The idea of EBD raises the question, "What constitutes evidence in the design discipline?" This is an epistemological question requiring epistemological inquiry, and, as interested parties, that is the challenge we have taken up here. For the purposes of this chapter, the range of epistemological perspectives we have examined is limited to five: traditional science and its applied partner, technical rationality; interpretivism; intuitionism; and pragmatism. We have confined ourselves to these perspectives – what Altman and Rogoff (1987) termed "worldviews" – because we believe these five to be illustrative of the range of "natures of knowledge" that are present within design discourse. Note we are not suggesting that these worldview perspectives are isolated "silos"; in fact, our premise is that designers and researchers move very fluidly between these positions and are rarely dogmatic. And, we argue that dogmatism is the precise problem with the current approach to defining "evidence" for EBD.

This chapter begins with an historical overview of the concept of EBD, highlighting the epistemological assumptions that undergird the current approach to EBD. The discussion then broadens to address the five general approaches to knowledge generation. Our point is that in current discussions of EBD, a certain mode of knowledge generation is privileged, yet the applicability of that sort of knowledge to practice is questionable as it violates certain presumptions of practice. A more inclusive definition of EBD, one which values evidence produced via various modes of environmental design research, is proposed.

Evidence-Based Design

Best appreciated as a coalescent movement aimed at linking environmental design and research with the intent of improving outcomes, EBD is "the natural parallel and analog to evidence-based medicine" (Hamilton, 2004a, para 3). For its part, evidence-based medicine (EBM) emphasizes the use of research evidence generated through the scientific method as the basis for patient care (Guyatt et al., 1992). According to early EBM advocates Sackett, Rosenberg, Gray, and Richardson (1996), EBM is "the conscientious, explicit and judicious use of current best evidence in making decisions about the care of the individual patient. The practice of EBM means integrating individual clinical expertise with the best available external clinical evidence from systematic research" (para 2). Following this lead, EBD came to be defined as design "based on the best available information from credible research and evaluations of projects" (Hamilton, 2004b, para 2). Complications with parallelism arise promptly, however, with respect to the issue of "best available" evidence. In the case of EBM, the presumption is that "best evidence" is "research evidence and more specifically, research evidence from the quantitative tradition" (Rycroft-Malone et al., 2004, p. 83). EBM advocates' teleological confidence prompted the development and widespread influence of a hierarchy of evidence, typically depicted as a pyramid with systematic reviews, meta-analysis, and randomized control trials positioned at the top (e.g., Guyatt et al., 1995).

Meanwhile, the evidentiary situation is not so clear-cut for EBD. As it happens, most environmental design research does not take the form of randomized control trials and rarely if ever qualifies as a true experiment. However, the characteristics of "best evidence" found in EBM have clearly influenced the definition of "best evidence" for EBD, regardless that these characteristics are extraordinarily difficult to achieve in environmental design research (Groat & Wang, 2002; Zeisel, 2006). For example, Ulrich and colleagues conducted a landmark literature review covering more than 600 studies linking design of healthcare environments with clinical outcomes in an attempt to ascertain the existing evidence base. This literature review provides useful insight into the foundational assumptions held by pioneers in the EBD movement. As the authors' articulated criteria for inclusion state: "research studies were assessed on their rigor, quality of research design, sample sizes, and degree of control" and further that studies be "high impact, in that the outcomes they explore are of importance to healthcare decision-makers, patients, clinicians, and society" (Ulrich et al., 2004, p. 3). In effect, the initial set of criteria implies certain assumptions regarding the kind of research that generates evidence. The "high impact" criterion refers to both the saliency of the research topic and the potential influence of the findings. Together, these criteria suggest that studies with large sample sizes, significant degrees of control, and the greatest potential utility constitute the "best evidence," a presumption worth scrutiny of the greater environmental design research community on behalf of the design discipline.

Five Worldviews of Design-Oriented Knowledge

To effectively answer, "What constitutes good evidence in design?" several questions pertaining to the epistemology of each of the five worldviews necessarily precede and inform our response. Clarification of these epistemological points illuminates similarities and differences between worldviews, which in turn, increases awareness, understanding, and hopefully, appreciation. Table 1 is a summary comparison of the five worldviews (in columns) in terms of the epistemological questions (in rows).

Traditional Science

In traditional science, the nature of knowledge is to be objective, meaning to be related to a phenomenon in the realm of the senses independent of individual thought. For instance, the

Table 1. Five worldviews in environmental design research

	Traditional science	Technical rationality	Pragmatism	Interpretivism	Intuitionism
What is the nature of knowledge?	Objective	Applied, objective	Constructed	Subjective (at times constructed)	Received
What is the nature of the problem?	Discrete, reducible, existent	Discrete, reducible, projectional	Systemic, existent, or projectional	Holistic, existent, perspectival	Holistic, singular perspective, projectional
What is the purpose of knowledge?	Explanation (ideally, causal)	Instrumentality	Utility	Perspective	Insight
What is the exemplary habit of mind?	Analytic	Procedural	Practical	Synthesis	Creative
What is the typical form of knowledge?	Statistics	Protocols	Patterns, case studies	Narrative, stories	Patterns
What is truth?	Causal laws are the ideal, data produced through approved methodologies	Causal adjustment	Operational	Persuasive rhetoric	Correspondence
What is good evidence?	Internally and externally valid, reliable, objective data	Valid, reliable, objective data that when applied, achieves its ends	That which is efficacious	A persuasive, trustworthy, (perhaps inspiring) narrative	That which is inspiring

Celsius scale is considered an objective measure of temperature, reflective of a tactile sensation. Thus, sensation is the primary source of knowledge in traditional science. The problems that are addressed are existent, meaning they exist in the world. The nature of those problems is conceptualized as discrete and reducible. Often the word "control" is utilized due to this assumption and the need to reduce the nature of the phenomenon by "controlling" certain variables. The purpose of knowledge is to provide explanation of observed phenomena, particularly causal explanations. Truth is those causal laws that are based on findings resulting from the data generated using agreed-to methodologies of research and analysis. As the hegemonic view within inquiry, traditional science has finely honed criteria for good evidence: internally and externally valid, reliable, objective data.

Technical Rationality

Technical rationality is a term that reflects the perspective that professional practice is the instrumental application of scientifically developed knowledge and theory to confronted problems. Accordingly, the primary source of knowledge remains sensation. Knowledge is first and foremost to be objective; within technical rationality it is to be applied to well-defined problems with clear outcomes. Also as with traditional science, the nature of the problem remains discrete and reducible, but in this case, knowledge is applied to a world of projection. The purpose of knowledge is to achieve an instrumental outcome. If that outcome is not achieved, the knowledge base is to be questioned and researched. Thus, good evidence not only has the characteristics of evidence of traditional science – internally and externally valid, reliable, objective data – but additionally, when applied, achieves its ends.

Interpretivism

This is a broad-ranging worldview, incorporating (for the purposes of this paper) phenomenological methods, such as hermeneutics, grounded theory, and critical theory (Neuman, 1997). Within interpretivism, the focus is on meaning (which is therefore the primary source of knowledge) and developing an ideographic understanding of the phenomenon in question. The nature of knowledge is viewed as subjective, as being possessed within each individual's perception, although in some modes, multiple perspectives are triangulated and therefore knowledge becomes constructed. The goal is to maintain an understanding of the phenomenon as whole and complete as possible, thus synthesis is the exemplary habit of mind. Interpretivists value thick description and thus research reports often read like novels. In this mode, truth is rhetoric, that which is persuasive – persuasive to those being studied and those for whom it provides deeper understanding. In this case, evidence should also be persuasive, rooted in trustworthy methods of knowledge accumulation and offered in a holistic narrative. Those narratives that inspire often compel action.

Intuitionism

Intuitionism is often argued as the primary epistemological position within architectural design practice (Johnson, 1994; Zumthor, 2006). Knowledge may be intuited, which is to say, complete, integrated knowledge gained in a flash of insight (although the patterns assembled into the intuition may have been percolating for some time [Duggan, 2007]). As knowledge is complete and holistic, so, too, is the nature of the problem. This linkage is effectively described by Rowe (1982), whereby he characterizes architectural problems as "ill-defined," demanding heuristic reasoning that is embedded with a priori knowledge. Intuitionism, like technical rationality (and pragmatism, description follows), addresses knowledge largely within the framework of projection, rather than existence. The purpose of intuition-based inquiry is to provide creative insight that guides the solution that is generated in order to resolve the ill-defined problem. Truth is that wherein an action guided by intuition corresponds to a desired intent: Note that the actual outcome is not as important as the correspondence with intentionality, in fact, the exemplary habit of mind is to maximize intentionality through action. Goodness of evidence is an effect of the action-intention correspondence and the degree to which the truth resolution is inspiring.

Pragmatism

In many ways, the pragmatism of Pierce, James, and Dewey may be viewed as a response to technical rationality. Dewey (1916/1966) suggested that the primary source of knowledge could not be limited to what he called "sensationalistic empiricism." Pragmatism contrasts with traditional science and technical rationality in three important ways: truth is mutable not absolute; experiential knowledge gained through professional practice is valued rather than disregarded; and the significance of an idea is gauged on the basis of its practical utility. Knowledge is constructed within pragmatism and therefore subject to re-view and re-construction. Problems are systemic in nature, demanding focus on the relationships between the discrete and the holistic. Utility is the ultimate purpose of inquiry. The best evidence – that knowledge which compels acceptance of a truth – is that which proves efficacious.

Situating EBD Within the Five Worldviews

One of the core differences between the five worldviews lies in regard to the fundamental natures of the problems they address. Two particularly salient continua on which these problem natures differ are (1) discrete to holistic and (2) existent to projectional. Figure 1 maps the five worldviews onto a graph where the abscissa ranges from discrete to holistic and the ordinate from existent to projectional. As described above, the fundamental way of environmental designers knowing is through intuition, wherein problems are viewed as holistic and projectional. Thus, intuitionism is mapped in quadrant 1. Contrast that with the underlying assumptions of the current approach to EBD. Recall that Ulrich et al. (2004) articulated sample size and degree of control as crucial criteria for research conducted to inform EBD. Issues such as these are concerns within the traditional science paradigm, wherein problems are existent and discrete, therefore situating traditional science in quadrant 3. Hence, these two positions are fundamentally juxtaposed with respect to this

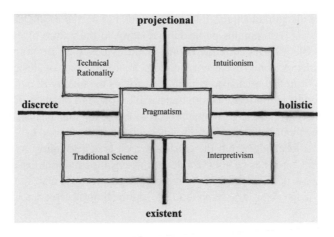

Figure 1. Mapping the five worldviews in relation to the nature of the problem.

fundamental epistemological issue. Hamilton's (2004b, para 2) description of practice as being where decisions are made "based on the best available information from credible research" clearly reflects the spirit of technical rationality, which takes discrete knowledge and applies it to projectional problems (quadrant 2). As an architect, Hamilton acknowledges that EBD is "additional," not an alternative to what architects already do – which is intuition-informed decision making. But he makes clear that in this view, "conscientious architects will experience fewer doubts as they increase the percentage of decisions based on research" (Hamilton, 2004b, para 10). This reflects an instrumental use of research in which there is direct application of a specific, discrete research finding.

Seidel (1985) provides a useful distinction between instrumental and conceptual research use. In contrast to the instrumental use as advocated within the current approach to EBD, conceptual use is indirect application of a general understanding of research, theory, or models to assist decision making. Heuristics, particularly as discussed by Rowe (1982), serve a conceptual purpose within the design decision-making process, highlighting certain aspects while obscuring others. In fact, in describing "environmental relations" as a type of heuristic, Rowe suggests that, yes, specific information about the relationship between a person and the environment is incorporated, but so too are broader principles that may not be empirically derived. The current approach to EBD appears to leave out the potential of the conceptual and/or provocative use of research and yet these are the questions of concern early and throughout the design process.

As we have described here, the nature of knowledge differs among worldviews, and since evidence can be complementarily defined as "information or signs indicating whether a belief or proposition is true or valid" (Compact Oxford English Dictionary, 2009) and "that knowledge which compels acceptance by the mind of a truth" (Webster's, 1990), how one defines evidence for EBD may well depend upon one's worldview. Herein lies the danger of the current approach to EBD, which has been constructed on implicit but powerful underlying assumptions particularly relating to the nature of evidence and the nature of the problem. EBD currently defines good evidence as stemming from a mode of inquiry that shares none of the epistemological foundations of design practice, and which, inferring from the articulated criteria, downplays the quality of evidence stemming from research conducted in modes more translatable to design practice. Thus, an inherent contradiction exists within the current approach to EBD, for this analysis suggests that if research is pursued within the traditional science model, its likelihood of "high impact" in design is rife with challenges, not the least of which is accessibility. As it stands, then, EBD in its current form has been assembled on an ideal of research based on epistemological assumptions that are contrary to that of design practice, with the latent effect of producing knowledge with little likelihood of "compelling acceptance by the mind" of designers.

This conclusion is not at all to suggest that traditional science research should not be conducted in environmental design. However, we should not delude ourselves that findings within traditional research will become evidence without a process of translation into a form that communicates with designers. Rather, the large implication of this conclusion for EBD is to reconsider the genesis of this concept. Rather than beginning with the definition of evidence stemming from EBM, we posit that EBD would be better off by recognizing the diversity of inquiry that occurs within the environmental design enterprise. From there one can proceed to ask what would be evidence within that broader spectrum and then consider what constitutes good evidence.

Toward an Enhanced Approach to EBD

Let us return to the core question of "What constitutes evidence in the design discipline?" This clearly depends upon the question at hand. There are three basic types of questions that research may address and three types of questions typically asked in any learning activity. Research addresses questions that are either causal, relational, or descriptive (Trochim, 2006). Learning asks questions that are factual, conceptual, or provocative in nature. Figure 2 maps the knowledge generation worldviews found in environmental design onto a table with research question types in rows and learning questions in columns. Not surprisingly, traditional science is viewed as engaging primarily in causal types of research which most likely result in findings of a factual nature. Interpretivism, which produces narratives of thick description, addresses descriptive research questions and largely provides understandings that may prove provocative in nature. Again, note how pragmatism bridges the middle, largely relational, and systemic, producing patterns and case studies that may be convergent or divergent, or that may offer evaluative insight (e.g., POEs).

We advocate for a more inclusive definition of evidence in design, wherein evidence is that research-based knowledge which is the most appropriate to the question at hand and of the highest rigor as defined by the worldview within which the research was conducted.

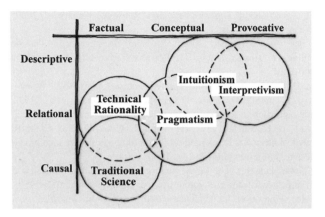

Figure 2. Mapping the five worldviews in relation to research and learning questions.

Sample size and control are very important to causal research, but problematic in interpretive research where ecological and descriptive validity are of paramount concern. With this understanding, we propose that EBD should be defined as environmental design that is informed by the best available evidence provided from the most up-to-date, credible research conducted according to the highest standards of rigor appropriate for that research approach, which is then applied in a critical and appropriate manner in order to achieve collective intentions.

References

Ahrentzen, S. (2006). *Actionable knowledge: A research synthesis project for affordable housing design practice*. Washington, DC: American Institute of Architects.

Altman, I., & Rogoff, B. (1987). World views in psychology: Trait, interactional, organismic, and transactional perspectives. In D. Stokols & I. Altman (Eds.), *Handbook of environmental psychology* (Vol. 1, pp. 7–40). New York: Academic Press.

Berlage Institute. (2008). *Hospital architecture: Master class evidence-based design for critical care*. The Netherlands: Rotterdam, 7–11 January.

Calkins, M., & Cassella, C. (2007). Exploring the cost and value of private versus shared bedrooms in nursing homes. *The Gerontologist, 47*, 169–183.

Center for Health Design. (2006). *HealthCare Design 06*. Chicago, IL, 4–7 November.

Dewey, J. (1916/1966). *Democracy and education: An introduction to philosophy of education*. New York: Free Press.

Duggan, W. (2007). *Strategic intuition: The creative spark in human achievement*. New York: Columbia University Press.

Evidence. (1990). *Webster's ninth new collegiate dictionary*. Springfield, MA: Merriam Webster.

Evidence. (2009). *Compact Oxford English Dictionary.* Retrieved January 12, 2009, from http://www. askoxford.com/concise_oed/evidence.

Geboy, L., & Keller, A. (November, 2006). Research in practice – The design researcher's perspective (online). *InformeDesign*(4), 11. Retrieved from http://www.informedesign.umn.edu/ _news/nov_v04r-p.pdf

Groat, L., & Wang, D. (2002). *Architectural research methods.* New York: Wiley.

Guyatt, G., Cairns, J., Churchill, D., Cook, D., Haynes, B., Hirsh, J., et al. (1992). Evidence-based medicine: A new approach to teaching the practice of medicine. *JAMA, 268*, 2420–2425.

Guyatt, G. H., Sackett, D. L., Sinclair, J. C., Hayward, R., Cook, D. J., & Cook, R. J. (1995). Users' guides to the medical literature. IX. A method for grading health care recommendations: Evidence-based medicine working group. *JAMA, 274*, 1800–1804.

Hamilton, D. K. (2004a, January). The new evidence-based designers. *Interiors & Sources,* 58–59. Retrieved from http://www.isdesignet.com/articles/detail.aspx?contentID=3960

Hamilton, K. (2004b). Four levels of evidence-based practice. In *American Institute of Architects Newsletter.* Retrieved from http://www.aia.org/nwsltr_print.cfm?pagename=aiaj_a_20041201_ fourlevels

International Conference on Aging, Disability and Independence (ICADI). (2008). Advancing technology and services to promote quality of life, St. Petersburg, FL, 20–23 February.

Johnson, P. A. (1994). *The theory of architecture.* New York: Van Nostrand Reinhold.

Malkin, J. (2008). *A visual reference for evidence-based design.* Concord, CA: Center for Health Design.

Martin, C. S., & Guerin, D. A. (2006). Using research to inform design solutions. *Journal of Facilities Management, 4*(3), 167–180.

Neuman, L. (1997). *Social research methods: Qualitative and quantitative approaches.* Boston, MA: Allyn and Bacon.

Rowe, P. (1982). A priori knowledge and heuristic reasoning in architectural design. *Journal of Architectural Education, 36*(1), 18–23.

Rycroft-Malone, J., Seers, K., Titchen, A., Kitson, A., Harvey, G., & McCormack, B. (2004). What counts as evidence in evidence-based practice? *Journal of Advanced Nursing, 47*(1), 81–90.

Sackett, D., Rosenberg, W. M., Gray, J. A., & Richardson, W. S. (1996). Evidence-based medicine: What is it and what it isn't (online). *British Medical Journal, 312*, 71–72. Retrieved from http:// www.pubmedcentral.nih.gov/picrender.fcgi?artid=2349778&blobtype=pdf

Sailer, K., Budgen, A., Lonsdale, N., Turner, A., & Penn, A. (2008) *Evidence-based design: Theoretical and practical reflections of an emerging approach in office architecture* (online). 4th Design Research Society Conference, Sheffield, UK, 16–19 July.

Seidel, A. (1985). What is success in E&B research utilization? *Environment and Behavior, 17*(1), 47–70.

Shepley, M. M. (2004). Evidence-based design for infants and staff in the neonatal intensive care unit. *Clinics in Perinatology, 31*(2), 299–311.

Trochim, W. (2006). *The research methods knowledge base.* Ithaca, NY: Atomic Dog.

Ulrich, R., Zimring, C., Joseph, A., Quan, X., & Choudhary, R. (2004). *The role of the physical environment in the hospital of the 21st century: A once-in-a lifetime opportunity.* Concord, CA: Center for Health Design.

Verderber, S. (2005). *Compassion in architecture: Evidence-based design for health in Louisiana.* Lafayette, LA: Center for Louisiana Studies.

World Congress & Exhibition – Design & Health (WCDH). (2007). Glasgow, UK, 27 June–1 July.

Zeisel, J. (2006). *Inquiry by design: Environment/behavior/neuroscience in. architecture, interiors, landscape and planning* (Rev. ed.). New York: W. W. Norton.

Zumthor, P. (2006). *Thinking architecture.* Basel: Birkhauser Basel.

Time, Market Pressures, and Urban Regeneration

A Feasible Mix?

Ombretta Romice,[1] Robert Rogerson,[2] Kevin Thwaites,[3]
Mark Greaves,[4] Rolf Roscher,[5] and David Hasson[6]

[1]Department of Architecture, University of Strathclyde, Glasgow, UK
[2]Department of Geography, University of Strathclyde, Glasgow, UK
[3]Department of Landscape Architecture, University of Sheffield, UK
[4]The Princes Foundation for the Built Environment, London, UK
[5]ERZ Design Limited, Glasgow, UK
[6]Ryder Architects, Glasgow, UK

Abstract

While acknowledging that urban regeneration is currently achieving significant positive results – innovative design, economic prosperity, and increase in numbers of urban inhabitants – this paper questions the capacity of prevailing approaches to develop socially sustainable solutions, in their search for compress development timescales to satisfy political and economic pressures. Looking at the process of regulation and management of development, the paper argues the potential role of design codes in shaping urban form based upon the experience of place as a way to structure an environment that can be inhabited, modified, and transformed to better suit changing demands. Urban design is proposed as a discipline that can design and manage change, although its theoretical base and education are in need of advancement and reform, to include the essential understanding of the human and social dimensions of space.

Key words: place experience, planning, urban regeneration

Across Europe and further afield, there is a growing awareness in academic, policy, and practitioner debates that creating and maintaining sustainable communities is a key component of urban design and regeneration. There is however less agreement about how such communities can be developed, or indeed about what constitutes a "sustainable community". Within these debates there are those who argue for greater central control over the planning, design, and construction of communities, including an enhanced role for the state. Others take a different perspective, arguing for less state-led regulation and more control embedded within those directly involved in the construction process, what has loosely been termed the "free market". With demographic pressures for increasing numbers of new homes and smaller households, there are suggestions that regeneration and renewal of communities and the development of new communities need to be "freed" to move forward apace, meeting the high targets for new buildings set by governments and meeting the demands for new houses. Others caution against this, often arguing that wider concerns linked to environmental and social spheres should not be compromised in the development process.

Resolving these contestations is difficult and this chapter does not aim to do so directly. Rather it explores the extent to which different technologies, or tools, might assist to offer a more sustainable future, one that enables sustainable communities to be developed.

Our thesis is: the desired development of mixed communities that are more sustainable socially will be the outcome of a "natural" cycle of "creative destruction" within local areas. We refer not only to physical regeneration and renewal – its visible expression – but also to renewal of the regulatory and institutional arrangements which shape development. This process of creative destruction arises from a sense of "crisis" and dissatisfaction with the existing regulation and control over regeneration (Brenner & Theodore, 2002).

There are two strands to the case we wish to make. First, our view is that the regeneration of many towns and cities across Europe is yielding certain benefits: The transformation of neglected city quarters is, in many cases, bringing innovative design, economic prosperity, and significant increase in numbers of urban inhabitants, albeit across a limited socio-economic spectrum. There is, however, growing evidence that prevailing approaches to urban regeneration may compromise the capability to achieve socially sustainable solutions because political and economic pressures compress development timescales to an extent that overprivileges commercial interests over social interests. In so doing, there is a conflation of the "natural" process of regeneration of urban areas; the three occupation phases have been identified by sociologists: undertaken by the risk-oblivious, the risk-aware, and the risk-adverse.

Second, the current process of regulation and management of the development process – the key elements of the planning system and urban design guidance – is proving inadequate to ensure that socially sustainable communities are being created. In this respect, the system is moving towards a crisis where key policy goals are not being met. In making a case for the adoption of more creative instruments, we are interested in developing design codes beyond their current use in identifying the physicality of the urban environment. Critically, we argue that to date the use of design codes has all too often neglected the social experience of place.

O. Romice et al.
Time, Market Pressures, and Urban Regeneration

43

The British Planning System

There are worrying symptoms that in the UK the current planning practices which purport to support the regeneration of communities, towns, and cities are underperforming. The creative renewal process is not achieving its targets and we believe that some interventions are required. The planning system is meant to provide the means to encourage appropriate urban design; however in its current format in the UK, it has weaknesses affecting how appropriate design and management of places can be delivered, not only reactively through the development management of proposals but proactively through such mechanisms as design codes. However, those mechanisms designed to be proactive are often instead a pre-emptive reaction.

The planning profession is suffering from a skills gap that impairs its ability to deliver appropriate design and management of places. The concession that the current UK planning system is stifling appropriate design and development has seen the establishment of performance standards and the recent adoption of design codes to help rebalance guidance and control with quality design.

Urban design, thanks to its overlap with other disciplines such as architecture, planning, landscape architecture, geography, and sociology, is a key profession in the design management of change. However, there are challenges for urban design in undertaking this key role, mainly due to its theoretical underpinning (especially the close alignment with traditional master-planning and building design) and the "skills gap" of those with strategic visioning and design responsibilities.

Urban design could add definition and therefore clear goals and directions by expanding the currently mainly formal character of design codes to incorporate aspects of environment-behaviour research. At the moment, market pressures often make it difficult or not commercially expedient for the planning and design profession to adequately respond to, interpret, and follow current guidance, leaving socially responsive regeneration too often to fate and talent. By amending design codes to include current environment-behaviour research thus ensuring the codes address the social dimensions of place-making, it is possible to reinforce the effectiveness and applicability of planning guidance.

Conclusions from recent ESRC funded series of seminars (Cardiff, Birmingham, Nottingham, Bristol – Manchester, Newcastle upon Tyne, Leeds, and Sheffield – Edinburgh, Glasgow, Liverpool, Belfast) have revealed that to achieve some of the 2021 Urban Task Force goals, British cities must equip themselves with strategic conception, delivery, and management tools for urban regeneration (i.e., citywide masterplans). Design-led regeneration needs to be redefined to include performance standards at its core to prevent the push for high-quality urbanism more often than not becoming the "pull of bling" or the "Bilbao effect" (Hebbert, 2008). The specific importance is that design codes are often better able to accommodate an assessment of the large gesture or gestures when a series of smaller, more time-consuming measures may be more effective and appropriate. The issue of performance standards then relates to the establishment of such standards, the roles of those involved in their establishment, management, and implementation.

Some Background to Urban Regeneration in the UK

Natural, "bottom-up" socially responsive urban transformation can be characterised as a synthesis of occupation over time by three population groups, according to their perception of risk level (Duany, 2001). The spontaneous revitalisation of disused and neglected urban areas begins with colonisation by those who are risk-oblivious, attracted by perceptions of character, social interaction, freedom of expression rather than the prospect of capital gain. This tends to be an organic, community-led form of occupation that generates social rather than physical or economic benefit. Once this social benefit is established and recognised, a second wave of population becomes attracted to the area; those who appreciate the lifestyle opportunities and physical potential that the risk-oblivious have created. This second wave is risk-aware and includes those from secure socio-economic groups attracted by lifestyle and the investment potential of their activities. This tier of occupation over time retains the setting's fundamental character while introducing physical upgrades that eventually become reflected in increasing property prices and rental values. Growing economic value and the retention and enhancement of intrinsic physical and social character then attract a third tier of occupant. These are the risk-adverse: Investors interested primarily by the prospect of commercial gain and who may not have further interest in the urban area after that commercial gain has been achieved. The net result of this can often be a mixed community of wide-ranging occupants with diverse socio-economic profiles that can collectively sustain the setting's economic and social heart and its environmental quality.

Urban renaissance policies adopted across the EU have viewed the formation of such a blend of mixed communities and enhanced economic value as essential for the formation of sustainable development and sustainable communities. In so doing, however, they have often focused attention on the goal, the third and therefore risk-adverse phase, rather more than the process that leads to it, inadvertently enhancing the value of this third phase and devaluing the urban spaces created in the earlier phases. Overlooked here is that the formation of such characteristics is associated with a process which takes time. The problem today is that often those responsible for urban regeneration and renewal cannot afford (both financially and temporally) such rhythms to take their own course. Because of market pressures, the need for rapid economic return, and low perceived value attached to the nature of renewal and community arising from first and second phase, they seek interventions which guide and implement urban renewal to phase 3 as rapidly as possible. A corollary of this is that socially responsive aspects of well meaning (but perhaps not strong enough) current guidance in development are undervalued or ignored where socially beneficial messages are perceived of little relevance to the commercially oriented third phase. This is a question, in practice, of what is considered essential, and what is incidental, and from what point of view. Design codes often

O. Romice et al.
Time, Market Pressures, and Urban Regeneration

45

understandably attempt to engage the risk adverse on their own ground, and hence fall into the trap of mistaking the essential (social sustainability) for the incidental (minimising risk and speeding up development).

There are clear references to Jane Jacobs, G. Cullen, C. Alexander, et al. currently included in urban design guidance and several places possess/represent fine design and civic pride but too often "regeneration" produces places that succeed in attracting people to the city centres, but fail in keeping them there, putting down roots, raising their families, and developing a sustainable neighbourhood. Their success depends on a continuous supply of well-paid, transient professional people, attracted by "boutique" environments marketed for lifestyle opportunities that are often sterile and experientially vacuous, and could be gradually abandoned to become the slums of tomorrow. Max Hutchinson warned of this possibility 5 years ago in a BBC TV local news report about the, then, ongoing construction of Leeds' Clarence Dock development. Recent economic downturn has graphically demonstrated how vulnerable such development practice is, as now Hutchinson's warning is starting to look very much like a prophecy (Hutchinson, 2006).

Perhaps urban design guidance so far has overlooked some of the messages implicit in the writings of Jacobs et al., that an urban order defined in terms of the dynamic actions of human subjects must be allowed space and time to unfold gradually, to grow and evolve, mature and settle. Because of the complexity, the interrelation, reciprocal influence, and implications of the aspects which entail change, the key to pursue well-being and quality of life lies in the design management of change, which begs the questions: Which are the professionals that should be in charge of this very strategic task? Is there sufficient provision of such figures, and do they have the tools to do so?

Discussion and Conclusion

The Urban Designer

Cuthbert (2007) suggests that urban design, because of its in-betweenness between architecture and planning, has so-far been characterised by a fairly chaotic, anarchic, unfounded sequence of creative ideas bearing little or no coherence with each other and has consequently failed in establishing a relationship between design and societal processes. He argues the need for legitimisation of urban design through the establishment of theoretical grounds, connected to the economic, political, social, and cultural processes which shape social life (ibid.: 1). Ultimately, this would allow the fruitful establishment of "performance standards", as suggested by Hebbert, and consequently the significant assessment of projects before they are ordained, and after, to understand necessary modifications and determine needed change (ibid.: 179).

Assuming that this will happen in the future, and offering ideas for the establishment of some of such theoretical grounding from within the field of environment-behaviour studies, this discussion suggests that urban design would be a well-placed discipline to take up the challenge, thanks to its complex range of expertise, its versatile approach to problem solving and method of working, and its understanding of issues at different scales. Obviously, this description of urban design depends upon (1) the education, (2) the practice, and (3) the role and status of urban design within policy and planning, and depends once again on the definition of a theoretic framework which disentangles itself from the various professions and new corporations which hold interests in shaping the built environment (ibid.).

There is some degree of concern to the news of studies that indicate a dramatic skills shortage in strategic visioning and design among, primarily, the municipality staff. Among this, a recent report by Arup called "Mind the Skills Gap" has revealed that *in most built environment professions more and more people are retiring and recruitment levels cannot keep up with demand* and this is a major problem in that it is not only a question of adding capacity, but of replacing it. Urban designers are the worst hit, with 91% of positions expected to be vacant by 2012 (Morris, 2007). Equally worrying is that it is the public sector which struggles most to recruit and retain young talented professionals who possess the skills to deliver sustainable communities and places, much less so the private sector, revealing a structural weakness of British civic life, the limited fiscal and decisional autonomy that municipalities hold (Hebbert, 2008).

A number of initiatives are on the way to address this skills shortage but there is still a catch: Urban designers work within the planning context, following its guidance and laws. The structure and thrust of this context plays therefore a crucial role in how effective urban design can be.

Urban Design in Context: Strength and Weaknesses of the British (Planning) System

Most Western capitalist societies allow the marketplace to be the major arbitrator of competing goals and means for establishing the nature of the society. In some countries, the public sector has intervened more strongly than in others in establishing priorities for the quality of the city form. In these, the professional designer as policy maker (or, more likely, as the advisor of the policy maker) tends to play a larger role than, say, in the United States, where power is spread more diffusely among individuals, albeit within certain limits. Thus professional designers have had greater impact on the design of the cities in Western Europe than on those in the United States (Lang, 1994).

Within the British system designers have had an impact but there is the potential for the designer to have an even more profound effect, especially if the system can address its shortcomings and if the design professions step forward in creating places based on sound UD principles; that is where codes and more stringent standards, especially if they are underpinned by environment behaviour studies, come into the picture (and where addressing the skills gap becomes paramount if planners are to work in such mediums).

The nature of the British planning system requires that nearly all development receives permission from the local planning authority (as opposed to, for example, the American zoning system in which whole classes of development are permitted as of right).

This has the attraction of being able to restrict certain development as a matter of principle. However over the years, the system has developed a set of instruments that offer guidance primarily to prevent the worst abuses rather than promote and deliver quality urban design and development. The result has been a form of institutional inertia to new design and practices. In this constraining context, the question is from where can the aspiration for quality come? What space is there for quality and innovation? Is this likely to come from local authorities or developers?

Planning advice and guidance have in the UK a great challenge, which needs to be resolved: They must be guarantor of design quality, maintain a protective dimension, and guarantee economic development. It is often the case that the argument for economic development prevails, no matter how ill founded (i.e., in Scotland until the mid-1990s, often any development was good, quality was a secondary issue). To be able to remedy all this, design guidance must be comprehensive, clear, and prescriptive.

The Difference Between Guidance and Statement: The Nut to Crack

Substantial planning guidance is produced every year in the UK. Beautifully illustrated, superficially persuasive documents are published regularly. There is, nevertheless, a substantial quality gap between such guidance and what gets built. Guidance suggests without requesting, leaving the final decision open to human arbitration (Duany, 2008). Development control and planning consent are often given on the basis of compliance of uses and economic targets and, in the case of substantial regeneration schemes, do not go to design, delivery, and management detail, leaving this to developers.

Precision and adoption of assessment criteria and targets are the most powerful tools to achieve and control outcomes. They are also best able to gain a well-deserved place with those that today are among the stronger determinants of development, such as transport engineers and environmentalists. This requires theoretical frameworks from which to clarify problems, criteria of analysis assessment, and creative action which urban design does not yet possess.

The reason behind this is twofold: (1) urban design is still very much self-referential and (2) urban design, as most of all other disciplines related to the design of the built environment, is not yet substantially engaged with theory and does not yet possess a breadth of knowledge which could enable urban designers to study and understand, and consequently act upon many urban problems (Cuthbert, 2007). All attempts to date to define urban design have missed the key step of defining its theoretical object (civic society) and its real object (the public realm).

If these main issues were addressed, then it could be possible to give precise and clear guidance and guarantee more appropriate production of places which more correctly respond to shared systems of values and needs (Castells' (1997) "urban meaning", "urban functions", "urban form", "urban social change", and finally "urban design" as a related set of interdependent levels, context, relativity, and processes). At this point, the use of standards rather than guidance, or at least the availability of both, could become a fruitful tool towards clarity.

Cuthbert's reference for urban design is spatial political economy. Our suggestion is that environment-behaviour studies, in their focus on the relationships between people and space at every level, could be an equally substantiating ground.

Design Codes Can Raise Quality

Design codes attempt to identify the physical components of place-making, a nebulous figment within practically all planning guidance documents that is rarely, if ever, substantiated except by perhaps some pictures of a café strewn street. Design codes are usually written in the hope that they can provide the physical framework that will allow a place to succeed over the long term. Recent experience in England has highlighted advantages of design codes to speed up the planning process, provide certainty for developers, and help achieve environmental standards. In addition the study also suggested that design codes generated a consensus, by which the design aspirations could be agreed with local authority planners (and often with the local community), and then made mandatory for developers.

While design codes may quantify the physical elements of successful places, for example, street and pavement width, scale and massing of buildings, building material, environmental resources, etc. what is missing are the psychological and ultimately the social elements. In other words urban designers are usually just guessing when it comes to how people will respond to them. Infusing design codes with research and evidence, both quantifiable and qualifiable, based on how people experience places would certainly mitigate some of the risk in this regard. Certainly in this age when sustainability is at the heart of all guidance related to the built environment, the element of sustainability that gets overlooked the most in favour of green standards is the socially responsive element, that giving a place the best chance to succeed in the long term requires more than just acceptance or tolerance of place by the inhabitants but rather conceptions such as affinity, affection, and even intimacy with places. To be "sustainable" buildings and communities must last over time and if environmental psychology can provide critical knowledge in the way people relate to their environments then it is only logical they be used within prescriptive planning and design methods such as codes in order to achieve maximum effect.

The planning system should address the use of codes and their potential benefit at all tiers – national, regional, and local. Codes generally work best at a more local scale; hence they are most effective when used within supplementary planning guidance, masterplans, local development strategies, etc. However, given the negative perceptions of them within the design community (based usually on unfounded criticisms that they inhibit the creative freedom of the architect or favour one type of architecture over another) the more explicit references to their use at levels the better. Advocation should cascade down the planning system extending from national (through policy, guidance documents, advice notes, circulars, etc.) to the regional tier and then embedded within local plan policies.

Our suggestion is that supplementary planning guidance could raise the quality bar avoiding the risk and limitations of having to rely upon individuals with ambitions to deliver effectively, and in particular that design codes be formulated to keep creativity and allow for guidance and framework.

The challenge is dual: On the one side, develop ambitious, considered, informed guidance; on the other, create a delivery and management system which can ensure the pursuit of multidimensional quality (i.e., sustainable places for a sustainable life).

The authors of this chapter are currently engaged on both fronts.

References

Brenner, N., & Theodore, N. (2002). Cities and the geographies of "Actually Existing Neoliberalism". *Antipode: A Radical Journal of Geography, 34*, 349–379.

Castells, M. (1997). *The urban question: A Marxist approach.* Cambridge, MA: MIT Press.

Cuthbert, A. (2007). Urban design: Requiem for an era – Review and critique of the last 50 years. *URBAN DESIGN International, 12*, 177–223.

Duany, A. (2001, April/May). Three cheers for gentrification. *The American Enterprise, 12*(3), 36–39.

Duany, A. (2008). *Speech at Scottish Council for Development and Industry Influencers Dinner.* UK: Edinburgh.

Hebbert, M. (2008). Urban design and the British renaissance, part 2: Manchester, Newcastle, Sheffield and Leeds. *Urban Design, 107*(Summer), 10–13.

Hutchinson, M. (2006). *Is Leeds missing out? One's inside out.* Retrieved September 18, 2006 from E-mail: http://www.bbc.co.uk/leeds/content/articles/2006/09/13/skyline_inside_out_feature.shtml.

Lang, J. (1994). *Urban design: The American experience.* New York: Van Nostrand.

Morris, H. (2007). Staffing shortage hits home. *Planning, 1378*, 25.

Regulating Augmented Public Spaces

Susan Drucker[1] and Gary Gumpert[2]

[1]Department of Journalism, Media Studies and Public Relations, Hofstra University, NY, USA
[2]Urban Communication Foundation, NY, USA

Abstract

The physical environment is characterized by the fixed feature of topography, dwellings and structures, streets, public space, and by those who inhabit places. Both media spaces and physical infrastructures carry regulatory implications. That environment, in the name of safety, security, and economics, requires regulation and government control of some type. The growing media environment has a long tradition of regulation as well and this environment has generally been regulated in the name of public interest, convenience, and necessity. This chapter proposes a regulatory taxonomy in which some regulations directly control communication through the regulation of communication behavior or through control over communication content or control of media access. Other regulations function indirectly controlling communication by regulating communicative behavior in public space through surveillance technology. The authors conclude that challenges abound for those concerned with publish spaces in which diverse media transforms regulation and design.

Key words: augmented spaces, media, public space, regulation, technology

Rome provides a reminder that communication and public space have a long history. To be sure, conversation, advocacy, and people watching are particularly Italian sports of the public space.

In 1501 Cardinal Oliviero Carafa put in a small square near *Piazza Navona* the torso of a statue representing Menelaus with the body of Patroclus. Each year on April 25 the Cardinal chaired a sort of Latin literary competition and poems were posted on the statue and occasionally this happened outside the competition period. In this way Pasquino (the name given to the statue) became the first talking statue of Rome and it is still used from time to time for posting messages and claims. The little square is named after him *Piazza di Pasquino* and *pasquinata* (pasquinade) is the word used for a short satire exhibited in a public place. Pope Adrianus VI (1522–23) considered throwing Pasquino into the Tiber and other popes had similar thoughts, but they feared to fall into ridicule by punishing a statue. Severe laws however were issued to stop the practice and Pasquino was put under surveillance. This led to the undesired result of multiplying the talking statues of Rome. The colossal statue of a river-god at the foot of the Capitol Hill became soon a second Pasquino. It was named Marforio and it added zest to the lampooning of the popes as Pasquino and Marforio started talking to each other (Talking Statues of Rome).

These are known as the Talking Statues of Rome.

Surveillance and fear of expression are not new forms of regulation. What is changing is the medium being suppressed or doing the suppressing. In the 21st century, the social uses of public spaces are being altered by the introduction of media technology that provides individuals with the ability to control connection. Media technology in public space, urban media, and digital technologies is proliferating and having a profound effect on traditional public space.

Not only have we entered into digital online public spaces such as online gaming environments and social networking sites, but we have also entered into immersive virtual environments such as *Second Life*. These virtual places are all accessible from physical public spaces. While experientially distinct from the physical equivalent, the media experience alters the perception and evaluation of the built environment.

William Gibson (1998) wrote in "Cyborg Civics:"

For millennia, architects have been concerned with skin bounded body and its immediate sensory environment – with providing shelter, warmth and safety, with casting light on the surfaces that surround it, with creating conditions for conversation and music, with orchestrating the touch of hard and soft and rough and smooth materials, and with breezes and scents … [N]ow [architects] must contemplate electronically augmented, reconfigurable, virtual bodies that can sense and act at a distance, but that also remain partially anchored in their immediate surroundings (p. 173).

Gibson's theorization of the "digital native" points to an increasingly complex relationship between the individual and the built environment (Wiley, 2008). Digitally based infrastructures, such as wireless local area networks, remote surveillance, and coordinated digital signage systems, demonstrate the development of a highly mediated urban space providing interaction between electronic information and communication environments.

It is this complex interface that Manual Castells refers to when he states "cities … are transformed by the interface between electronic communication and physical interaction, by the combination of networks and places …" (Castells, 2004, p. 85). Thus, "augmented pubic space" is physical space in which technologies have been incorporated adding to the contextual dimensions of that space.

From mobile phones to Wi-Fi to the pull of media-filled private spaces, communication technologies are redefining this human-environment relationship. Portable public privacy meets the needs of a public alienated, disconnected, and distrusting of public spaces. Engagement with Wi-Fi computing or mobile telephony in public space affects not only attitudes and behavior in public space but also psychological presence in those spaces. Public interaction is being transformed into "disembodied private space" by mobile technologies. Individuals are provided with the ability to insulate themselves by controlling connection and exposure. Unpredictability or serendipity is reduced in an environment in which content and connection "on demand" are available. While much literature spotlights the connection of individuals in an electronic public space transcending physicality of the environment, the symbiotic relationship between public space and mediated communication ought not be neglected. "As mobile connection beckons, people can become immersed or absorbed in media connection, altering their awareness and interaction with the physical environment .... At heart is the essential value of human as communicator gliding between physical and media environments" (Gumpert & Drucker, 2007).

The impact of mediated communication upon the experiences, functions, and design of physical public space is vital to the maintenance of community. Both media spaces and physical infrastructures carry regulatory implications.

Regulatory Taxonomy

Several years ago, we began developing a taxonomy of the manifest and latent, indirect or accidental, intentional, or unintended regulations that influence social interaction in public spaces. We argued that a vast complex of legal regulations govern public space and the built environment thereby shaping the opportunity for and nature of social behavior (Drucker & Gumpert, 1996). Some regulations *directly control communication* through licensing and control of content. Other regulations indirectly control communication ostensibly targeting *non-communication-related activities*, but purposefully or accidentally determine the nature of communicative interaction. These include land use regulation, primarily, zoning laws. Zoning laws in their countless variations include the determination of signage, facade, parking, display windows, take-out, and delivery service, and vending machines, plus the segregation of functions or design districts which all influence communication patterns. Other indirect regulations address loitering, gambling, and public nuisance, and the licensing of alcoholic beverages, minimum drinking age and driving age, the regulation of smoking in a public place, and even the requirements imposed upon a place of public accommodation found, for example, within the Americans With Disabilities Act – all form the regulatory web.

For purposes of the following discussion, regulation of communication will be explored through an examination of the laws governing public spaces of New York City. It is essential to remember that law always lags behind technological developments. Simply put, the law plays catch-up with technologies.

Direct Control of Communication

Regulation of Communication Behavior

Public nuisance laws have long been used to regulate *communicative behavior* in public space. Public nuisance involves activity that endangers health, safety, property, comfort, and convenience or offends public morals (*Black's Law Dictionary*, 1979). Nuisance laws have been directly linked with communicative activities (e.g., adult movie houses and profanity), and influence social interaction in public places by governing excessive noise (which may result from association or assembly in public places) and the use of sound systems and even boom boxes. One example of a New York City regulation in this area requires performers to use a city-supplied sound system and sound technician (*Ward v. Rock Against Racism*, 1989).[1] While much sound in public space has become increasingly personal and privatized with the ubiquitous iPod, regulation of the mediated acoustical environment remains an issue.

The linking of territory and sound is central to understanding attitudes toward media use. The concept of acoustical space and its relation to territoriality are not new. R. Murray Schafer noted this in *The Tuning of the World*, arguing that acoustical space can be imperialistic (1981). Acoustical aggression resulting from or aided by media technologies may be unacceptable forms of behavior subject to regulation. "Responses to the problems of acoustical space violations have taken many forms including regulatory responses such as creating mobile phone-free environments in restaurants, hospitals and theatres or providing designated areas for use in aptly named commuter train 'babble cars' " (Gumpert & Drucker, 2007). Noise pollution or noise control codes are common forms of regulation with most communities prohibiting excessive and unreasonable noise. In New York, noise has been cited as one of the most annoying features of urban life: "Noise is the number one complaint to the City's 311 citizen service hotline" (Department of Environmental Protection, 2008). Noise-related calls reached 38,660 in 2005 and 41,856 in 2006 (Long, 2007). New York became the first city in the United States to adopt a noise code in 1972. The code forbids things such as commercial music. The code also prohibits businesses from using loudspeakers that can be heard on the sidewalk, enforcement is primarily through the Department of Environmental Protection. The acoustical environment has been a priority under Mayor Michael Bloomberg's administration. In 2002, *Operation Silent Night* was introduced as a program targeting 24 high-noise neighborhoods throughout the City with intensive enforcement measures including the seizure of audio equipment, summonses, fines, and arrests.

In 2007, new regulations took effect representing the first revisions in the city's noise code in more than three decades. Under the new code, reasonableness rather than decibel measurement is the key. So, for example, a bar or a club can be ticketed if

---

[1]   The regulation was challenged on First Amendment grounds by Rock Against Racism but the US Supreme Court upheld the city regulations (*Ward v. Rock Against Racism*, 491 US 781, 1989).

music is "plainly audible" to a police officer or an enforcement agent 15 feet outside the establishment (Long, 2007). Personal audio devices are addressed in the revised law: The law §2. Section 24-203 *(43)* defines these devices as: "a portable sound reproduction device as normally and customarily used for personal purposes including but not limited to a personal radio, phonograph, television receiver, tape recorder or compact disc player. For the purposes of this definition such term shall include a sound reproduction device installed in or operated from a motor vehicle whether or not portable." Section 24-233 stipulates that

> §24-233 Personal audio devices. (a) No person shall operate or use or cause to be operated or used any personal audio device in such a manner as to create an unreasonable noise. (b) For the purposes of this section unreasonable noise shall include but shall not be limited to: (1) the operation or use of a personal audio device on or in any public right-of-way so that sound emanating from such device is plainly audible to another individual at distance of 25 feet or more from the source. Noise Code (Local Law 113 of 2005).

Directly Regulating Communicative Content and Structures in Public Space

The US Constitution only permits the regulation of the time, place, and manner of communication. While reasonable content-neutral regulation is generally found to be constitutional, content-based regulations are not.

Billboards illustrate the overlap of regulation of communication medium and communication content in public spaces. Billboards became part of New York landscape in the 1830s, when P. T. Barnum put up advertisements for the circus that were slightly bigger than your average poster in 1835. In 1850, exterior advertising was first used on street railways. In the 1890s, reformers condemned billboards, not just as eyesores, but as hiding places for "immoral acts" (History of Outdoor Advertising, 2008). Federal and local regulations developed addressing public policy concerns associated with outdoor advertising (e.g., Highway Beautification Act of 1965 limited billboards). As long ago as 1954, the US Supreme Court ruled that esthetic justification alone could permit government regulation over land issues (*Berman v. Parker*, 1954). The totality of US Supreme Court decision on the regulation of billboards in public places suggests different criteria for commercial and noncommercial content. Since commercial speech receives less constitutional protection than noncommercial content, regulation of content is permitted if the regulation must directly advance a substantial government interest in the narrowest way possible. For noncommercial content, billboards need to be prohibited in a manner that is content neutral (*Metromedia Inc. v. City of San Diego*, 1981).

Outdoor advertising has changed greatly since the first 50 square foot circus poster appeared in New York. Within the last few years, size restrictions changed as technologies have developed to enlarge the size of billboards. The former restrictions limited billboards to about 1,200 square feet (about the size of a three-story town house), but advances in advertising technology have made it possible to make one 3,000 square feet (or about the size of a six-story office building). Add to the expansion in size the new intensity in illumination and you have an area of regulation undergoing revision. Since most municipalities already have ordinances dealing with roadside billboards, most officials elect to amend current legislation to incorporate the newer technology.

Urban screens refer to various kinds of dynamic digital displays and interfaces in urban space such as LED signs, plasma screens, projection boards, JumboTrons, information terminals as well as skins or intelligent architectural surfaces. Some regulation comes from changes in zoning laws, some emerge from highway safety rules growing from fear that moving signage or JumboTrons will be dangerous, since driving safety researchers, including the Traffic Injury Research Foundation, believe that digital billboards not only keep drivers' attention focused longer, but are also more "cognitively demanding" (Story, 2007).

Anthony Townsend, an urban design critic, argues that New York's Times Square illustrates a new standard of digitally enhanced surfaces in public spaces (Wiley, p. 20):

> Located at 3 Times Square, the Reuters sign presents live news and photos from the news agency feed, selected without intervention by a sophisticated content and 7th Avenue, the architecture firm Kohn Pederson Fox wove a digital skin of LED panels around the building's first 3 floors. This digitally enhanced façade displays a series of landscape and nature scenes embossed with subtle Lehman Brothers branding ... The Reuters and Lehman Brothers signs point towards a possible future for Times Square in which reprogrammable building facades provide an endless variation of content, subtle marketing, and environmental enhancement (Townsend, 2004, p. 103).

The former Lehman Brothers signage, Lehman Brothers a victim of our current economic catastrophe, suggests that adaptable surfaces and variable imagery are defining new public spaces. All temporary signage must comply with zoning regulations on signage and must have a permit from the Department of Buildings. The zoning laws and building codes include provisions addressing the billboards. In 2001, the City enacted a law with an enforcement mechanism giving the city official greater power over signage in public spaces. In 2006, the Buildings Department of New York City issued new rules for the city for billboards.

> In 2007, the city was also sued by another advertiser: Metro Fuel LLC which ... has erected 360 illuminated "panel signs" throughout the city. By the company's own estimate, 90% of its signs are technically illegal – their brightness is considered a safety hazard, and their locations violate zoning ordinances. (Panel signs look like rectangular flaps or flags and are attached to the signs of buildings.) Jacksonville-based attorney Bill Brinton, who has fought more than 30 cases against advertising companies in the past two decades, says Metro Fuel is following a pattern around the country: putting up illegal signs and, when a city objects, challenging the constitutionality of sign laws (Dwoskin, 2008).

Lawyers for advertisers respond that the city has not effectively enforced its own codes nor has it been consistent in enforcement. They argue that New York City seeks to regulate privately owned outdoor advertising, while not regulating those sites where the city receives revenue for advertisements placed on publicly owned sites such as the 13,000 public phone kiosks that bring in an estimated $13 million annually (Dwoskin, 2008). The policy by which these publicly owned spaces are rented for advertising has been the subject of criticism by those against the privatization of public space including the Municipal Art Society.

Direct Control of Communication: Media Access

Another manifestation of direct regulation of communication comes in the form of media access. Older forms of media available in public space have resulted in a body of law regarding newsstands/kiosks and newsracks. Perhaps, the newsrack is the modern equivalent of the corner newspaper boy. The issue of newsracks relates to two primary concerns: esthetics and safety. Cities seek to regulate on the basis of visual clutter or pedestrian safety creating obstacles particularly for the disabled. These cases have often ended up in federal court in the US;[2] the newsracks and kiosks may seem to be relics of a bygone media age, but they remain a significant method of distributing news and information to millions. In the US, they raise specific issues associated with constitutionally protected free press.

Mobile media access has been the most significant new feature of public space including mobile telephony and Wi-Fi. Zoning laws shape the communication infrastructure as municipalities determine where mobile towers may be located, when public property may be used to supply Wi-Fi hot spots, and whether there is a right to broadband access or wireless connection as suggested by the Mayor of San Francisco (Orlowski, 2005).

Municipalities are increasingly aware that widespread broadband availability is essential for their social and economic health. In order to foster such services, municipalities are turning to Wi-Fi. City authorities are extending old notions of utility regulation, highway metaphors, and the government's appropriate role as a player in protecting and promoting economic and social welfare to support city subsidized municipal wireless.

Diverse models are emerging for the equitable deployment of broadband and Wi-Fi. The world's biggest municipal wireless rollout is Taipei, Taiwan. Japan and Korea have been at the forefront of public policy supporting public broadband rollout. The European

---

[2] The Supreme Court has twice decided cases involving newsracks. In its 1988 decision, *City of Lakewood v. Plain Dealer Publishing Co.*, the High Court invalidated a city ordinance that gave the Mayor unbridled discretion to determine whether publishers could place newsracks in various locations.

Union's stated policy encourages member states to make a public investment in broadband and Wi-Fi, despite its historic approach of encouraging market competition. Sweden and the Netherlands have emerged as leaders in the muni movement. Some credit Sweden with developing the most successful business model that is a "wholesale" model where the municipality owns the network, but private sector companies provide the actual broadband services running over the network. While municipal Wi-Fi is one approach, other cities have relied upon a public/private partnership or contract for services with private providers (e.g., Philadelphia and San Francisco). Each model has proven problematic. Some cities such as Orlando and Florida have pulled the plug on municipal Wi-Fi. More than 175 US cities have attempted to build citywide or partial systems with little success in providing the coverage promised. Most recently, the concept of a Wi-Fi cloud hovering over a city has been proposed in which a "city could make do by piggybacking on the many residential and business hotspots already dotting most cities. Among the many difficulties in making such a scheme work, one of the main ones is determining just how large and dense the existing Wi-Fi clouds are" (Hsu, 2008).[3] In the US, there is a question as to whether the regulatory environment even permits municipalities to offer Wi-Fi. The policy and regulatory issues are currently before the United States Congress.[4]

The Mayor of New York City announced a comprehensive Telecommunication Action Plan that called for a partnership between the private and the public sector. The partnership will include a "CBS Mobile Zone" that will provide Wi-Fi access points on its billboards and signage above the subway entrances in central areas. The plan is to place antennae and telecommunication equipment on city-owned street poles throughout the five boroughs of New York City.

What everyone seemed to forget is that while public space is generally regulated on a local/municipal basis, media technologies are generally regulated at a national level. Spectrum allocation for Wi-Fi in the US is determined by the Federal Communications Commission. The same wireless technologies that promise increased user flexibility, that entice people back into public spaces, potentially expose users to considerable risks stemming from privacy concerns, data security, and the unauthorized access of ISPS to data. Diverse regulations exist addressing minimum levels of security for such Internet access with the

---

[3] The concept of the cloud has also been associated with specific computer services. The *cloud* is a metaphor for the Internet in which users access technology enabled services from the cloud. Companies such as Amazon.com, Google, and Salesforce.com offer "platforms as a service" providing server computing power and storage (Hoover, 2008).

[4] In June 2005, Sen. John McCain introduced legislation promoting local governments' rights to launch wireless networks in direct competition with incumbent carriers. The Community Broadband Act of 2005 (S. 1294) adds provisions to the Telecommunications Act of 1996 to allow a municipality to offer high-Internet access to its citizens. *As of March, 2005,* "at least 15 states have laws regulating or prohibiting municipalities from deploying, owning, and/or operating broadband and/or telecommunications networks." Bills have been introduced in at least 14 state legislatures in 2005 aimed at prohibiting municipal Wi-Fi, passing in at least Pennsylvania, Colorado, Nebraska, and Florida.

US lacking a standard, the EU providing a clearer directive, and Japan having a specific and somewhat demanding standard.[5]

Perhaps, no technology rivals the mobile phone in terms of presence in public space. To date, mobile phone regulation is yet another medium regulated at the national level. Regulation of mobile phone use as a public nuisance may be possible, but is not yet a widespread policy. New York has a law banning making a call or talking on a mobile phone during public performances at theaters and concerts. It is the first major US city to bring such legislation to fruition and carries with it a $50 fine. The policy does not extend to presence in other public places such as parks and plazas.

The revised noise code of New York City went into effect on July 1, 2007 administered by the New York City Department of Environmental Protection. The department also offers "sound advice" recommending "Keep cell phone conversations to a minimum in public places: Cell phone conversations can be disruptive especially in confined areas like public transit, where they should be avoided whenever possible" (Have you heard, 2007).

A bill was introduced in 2007 that would ban the use of MP3 players, cell phones, and any other electronic device used by pedestrians crossing the street in New York City or other "big cities" in the state (Mayors Archive, 2008). This proposal follows two pedestrian deaths attributable, in part, to a person "listening to his iPod"(Ricker, 2007). State Senator Carl Kruger equates this with a public safety measure noting that he is: "talking about people walking sort of tuned in and in the process of being tuned in, tuned out. Tuned out to the world around them. They're walking into speeding cars. They're walking into buses. They're walking into one another and it's creating a number of fatalities that have been documented right here in the city" (Gatlan, 2007).

The issue of freedom from connection and the potential nuisance of mediated connectivity are of particular interest. Should there be a media-free zone in augmented public spaces? If smoke-free zones exist in the name of public health, are media-free zones in the name of community or interactional health feasible?

Any discussion on the regulation of use of technology in public space needs to be understood within the larger context requiring a reassessment of what is meant by public space. Private ownership of public space is growing. Private ownership and management of the public realm is part of the process that has been identified by the government as the "urban renaissance." Jerold Kayden, a Professor of Urban Planning at the Harvard Graduate School of Design, defines privately owned public space as "a physical place

---

[5]   In the US, although there are no specific federal statutes that define a minimum level of security for companies operating on the Internet, the issue is regularly an item of discussion among lawmakers and the information technology (IT) security industry. The European Union has a clearer regulation for information security than the United States. Thus far, Denmark, Sweden, Spain, and Finland have fully adapted regulation, to meet the EU "technology-neutral" standard that was issued in 2002. Japan has the best preparation in their laws for wireless. In 1998, "Guidelines on the Protection of Personal Data in Telecommunications Business" were launched by The Japanese Ministry of Posts and Telecommunication giving the clear guidelines.

located on private property to which the owner has granted legally binding rights of access and use to members of the public, most often in return for something of value from the city to the owner" (Kayden, 2000, n. 2, p. 21). Quasi-public spaces carry with them significant legal implications because a privately owned property may limit access and communicative activities more freely, and in the US, without full consideration of First Amendment rights. (The Supreme Court's 1972 decision in *PruneYard Shopping Center v. Robins* ruled that the US Constitution did not give citizens the right to distribute handbills in privately owned malls.)

Regulation of Communicative Behavior in Public Space Through Technology

Public space is being transformed from the ungoverned place of interaction to the formalized, controlled, less interactive, designed place. Communication technology makes possible the control and privatization of public space by private, corporate interests. Evermore video cameras along with GSM tracking make the public space a place of regulated behavior. November 2008 brought the introduction of a "ring of steel" around downtown New York. The "Lower Manhattan Security Initiative" includes 3,000 cameras (public and private) below Canal Street to monitor people and cars (i.e., license plate readers). The project shifts from cameras capturing images to be reviewed and analyzed after subsequent downloading to a new system in which images are transferred directly to a surveillance center capable of immediate analysis and fast response (Josselson, 2007).

The awareness of cameras is thought to foster a sense of safety and therefore intended to serve as a means of revitalizing public spaces, making them more inviting as sites of public social life and political activity. Privacy rights and communication freedoms are among those areas particularly intertwined with psychological and functional expectations in using a public space, but these rights and freedoms are entangled with conflicting interests in safety and security offered by the surveillance industry. Surveillance portends consequences for freedom of association and the less clearly articulated right of anonymity associated with public places as well as the right to move freely.

Does the presence of the camera create a "chilling effect" on the use of public space for social interaction, conversation, and gatherings? From a legal standpoint, at risk are privacy, associational rights, and the future of the social functions of public places. Surveillance cameras placed in publicly and privately owned places by security forces and police departments and cameras linked for transmission via the Internet represent variation in the increasing complexity of technological connection and public life. Surveillance technology illustrates the difficulties in fixing boundaries of publicness and privateness. The European approach seems to be that those subject to surveillance should be made aware of it. Article 8 of the European Convention on Human Rights along with developing case law addresses privacy and CCT emphasizing the legal concept of "consent."

Consent in the context of public space is not simple and the issue becomes what constitutes "valid full consent."[6]

Networked surveillance also called IP (Internet provider) surveillance is rapidly changing surveillance in public and private institutions. With IP surveillance, individual cameras and camera systems are attached to an IP data network camera and views can be accessed at any machine with an Internet browser and Internet connection including those placed in police cars. IP surveillance has emerged as a new leading security solution that combines networking infrastructure and video equipment providing for the harvesting of digital images (with all the implications inherent with digitalization). It is, however, important to note that the laws governing surveillance by public (i.e., government) entities are different than those for private entities, yet the technologies comingle the systems. While this technology promises faster audits when reviewing images along with efficient sharing of data, it also brings the law of the physical public space directly into the murky realm of Internet regulation.

Discussion and Conclusions

We began our critique of public space 20 years ago with the observation that we were witnessing the demise of public space. We observed fear, distrust, decay, and the abandonment of cities and public spaces as their social functions shifted to controllable private spaces. The automobile, the insulating character of air conditioners, and the ability to transcend local sites through telecommunication offered options siphoning life from public spaces. We lamented the fall of the city and public space. The pendulum has begun to shift back with the newly placed emphasis on safe "media connected," that is to say augmented public spaces. Perhaps, mediated interaction without face-to-face social contacts does not fully satisfy the human need for interaction and association. Perhaps, it is the introduction into public space of the very media technologies that enticed us to leave public spaces in the first place. The physical environment is augmented by cell phones, Wi-Fi, an increase in public screens (e.g., televisions and JumboTrons), iPods, the rise of surveillance

---

[6] So in places such as Britain in which there are rules governing CCTV and data privacy, the introduction of a digital system utilizing the Internet reopens many issues. In Britain, the legal context is permissive. CCTV falls under the Data Protection Act of 1998. By 2003, all CCTV system controllers were required to register with the Information Commissioner and to ensure that they were operating in line with the data protection principles. These were made explicitly applicable to all CCTV systems. With no written constitution and until the incorporation of the Human Rights Act into British law (now a statutory provision for the protection of privacy) there was no legal or constitutional basis to inhibit system developers. These acts have been weak in regulating cameras once in place. Article 8 of the European Convention on Human Rights gives citizens a right to privacy and this has been incorporated in the legislative and judicial activities in this area. There have been a couple of cases to reach the ECHR dealing with surveillance video (including *Herbecq v. Belgium*). France, Sweden, and the Netherlands require attention be drawn to surveillance signs placed outside the surveillance area, so that a person is made aware upon entering the area.

technologies offering comfort, and the illusion of safety, all contributing to the creation of new and improved urban space.

Ironically, what media taketh away, media can return. "Although interaction has been emancipated from place, public places still function as sites of face-to-face interaction" (Drucker & Gumpert, 1991, p. 294). Every electronic communication device allows us to extend our relationship with others, but alters the way we link to and relate to those that inhabit our immediate space. We are emancipated from place and are free to roam the globe – with the possibility of no connection to our next-door neighbor – we might not even know their name. Subsequent technological advances, mobile telephony, in particular, result in a peculiar situation. As technologies emancipate us from place, they simultaneously invite reentry by enhancing the communication possibilities of that place, yet, in the process, introduce a plethora of legal issues.

The social life of public space now competes with media technology that shifts interaction inward. The rise of private space has been dominant, but public space may once again draw people to those spaces that are rejuvenated through media access and mobile communication technologies. An effectively designed new public space should complement physical environment and media alternatives. Ultimately, challenges abound for those concerned with public space since diverse media transform regulation and design.

References

Berman v. Parker. (1954). 348 US 26.

Castells, M. (2004). Space of flows, space of places: Materials for a theory of urbanism in the information age. In S. Graham (Ed.), *The cybercities reader* (pp. 82–93). New York: Routledge.

Drucker, S., & Gumpert, G. (1996). The regulation of public social life: Communication law revisited. *Communication Quarterly, 44*(3, Summer), 280–296.

Dwoskin, E. (2008, August 12). *New York city's struggle to take down illegal billboards.* Site visited September 19, 2008, http://www.villagevoice.com/2008-08-12/news/new-york-city-s-struggle-to-take-down-illegal-billboards/.

Gatlan, S. (2007, February 8). *Cellphone ban in New York.* Site visited October 30, 2008, http://news.softpedia.com/news/Cellphone-Ban-In-New-York-46590.shtml.

Gibson, W. (1998). Cyborg civics. *Harvard Architecture Review, 10*(1), 164–775.

Gumpert, G., & Drucker, S. (2007). The parable of the mobile rock: Displacing place mobile communication in the 21st century or "Everybody, Everywhere, At Any Time". In S. Kleinman (Ed.), *Displacing place: Mobile communication in the 21st century* (pp. 7–20). Peter Lang.

Have you heard. (2007). Site visited October 30, 2008, http://nyc.gov/dep/html/airnoise.html.

History of Outdoor advertising, Outdoor Adverting Association of America Inc. (2008). Site visited October 30, 2008, http://www.oaaa.org/outdoor/sales/history.asp.

Hoover, J. N. (2008, November 3). A stake in the cloud. *Information Week, 26*, 22–24.

Hsu, J. (2008). *Wi-Fi cloud hovers over salt lake city IEEE spectrum online* Site visited October 30, 2008, http://www.spectrum.ieee.org/feb08/6025.

Josselson, S. (2007, September 4). New York's "Ring of Steel". Site visited November 10, 2008, http:// www.gothamgazette.com/article/issueoftheweek/20070904/200/2278.

Kayden, J. S. (2000). *Privately owned public space: The New York city experience.* New Jersey: Wiley.

Local Laws of the City of New York. (2005). Site visited July 5, 2008, http://www.nyc.gov/html/dep/ pdf/law05113.pdf.

Long, C. (2007, June 22). Shhhh: New NYC noise code to take effect. Site visited November 10, 2008, http://www.washingtonpost.com/wp-dyn/content/article/2007/06/22/AR2007062201823_2.html? hpid=sec-nations.

Mayors Archive. Site visited, November 10, 2008, http://www.citymayors.com/environment/ nyc_noise.html.

Metromedia Inc. v. City of San Diego. (1981). 453 US 490.

Orlowski, A. (2005, October 4). *Wi-Fi a basic human right, says SF Mayor.* Site visited July 5, 2008, http://www.theregister.co.uk/2005/10/04/sf_wifi/.

Rickcr, T. (2007, February 7). Bill banning iPods and cellphones on New York City streets coming. Site visited October 30, 2008, http://www.engadget.com/2007/02/07/bill-banning-ipods-and-cellphones-on-new-york-city-streets-comin/.

Story, L. (2007, January 11). *Digital billboard up ahead: New-wave sign or hazard?* Site visited November 10, 2008, http://www.nytimes.com/2007/01/11/business/media/11outdoor.html.

Talking Statues of Rome. Site visited May 11, 2008, http://www.romeartlover.it/Talking.html.

Townsend, A. (2004). Digitally mediated urban space: New lessons for design. *Praxis: Journal of Writing and Building, 6,* 100–105.

Wiley, D. (2008). The public square: Remediating public space. *Stream: Culture/Politics/Technology*(1), 1. http://www.streamjournal.org.

Diversity in Urban Landscapes and Perceptual Approaches

Visual Information in the Built Environment and its Effect on Wayfinding and Explorative Behaviour

Ruth Conroy Dalton,[1] Renato Troffa,[2] John Zacharias,[3] and Christoph Hoelscher[4]

[1]The Bartlett School of Graduate Studies, University College London, UK
[2]DRES – Department of Economic and Social Research, University of Cagliari, Italy
[3]Department of Geography, Planning and Environment, Concordia University, Montréal (Québec), Canada
[4]Center for Cognitive Science, University of Freiburg, Germany

Abstract

The spatial decisions pedestrians make as they execute a task, explore a novel environment, or reenact daily habits in familiar environments engage complex thinking processes. A continuous stream of information is available to the perambulating individual that may combine with the plans and expectations that individual pedestrians have. The dynamic and experiential aspects of this thinking, as well as the overall methodological approach to such research, are the focus of this chapter.

Key words: architectural design, pedestrian movement, spatial cognition, urban planning, wayfinding

This chapter aims to approach the relationship between urban diversities and human movement in the built environment. It also attempts to suggest how the study of the processes implied in urban navigation can contribute to the larger dialog on urban diversities, biosphere, and well-being.

The cognitive and behavioral determinants of human movement in the built environment have been a subject of investigation for several decades. Human movement in the built environment can be highly faceted, depending on environmental factors and the task structure of the human agent. For example, researchers are looking at both wayfinding and free exploration of indoor as well as outdoor environments.

Wayfinding can be defined as the process of traversing a chosen route connecting an origin to a destination. It is a target-directed process and any phase of this process requires the performer to read, understand, interpret, and correctly use environmental cues. To do so, travelers use various spatial, behavioral, and cognitive abilities and use several kinds of environmental cues, depending on the variety of the task and/or on the characteristics of the navigation setting (for instance, to move in a city is different from navigation in a building). Studies in this field have approached differently the question of how people select and read environmental cues: For example, they focus more on social or physical characteristics of the environment, use different kinds of instruments to approach the topic through field studies or laboratory experiments, and target more social or cognitive aspects of performance.

Configurational Features and Wayfinding

As regards the topic of urban mobility, this chapter stresses the influence of configurational structure on people's movement in built environments. Evidence suggests the influence of spatial configuration on people's representations of space. That is, a study carried out by Troffa suggests that in order to adapt to the complex settings in which they live, people need to reduce environmental complexity. When navigating through built environments, one simplification strategy could be the identification of a restricted representation of the different route-choice options. The constituents of the environmental structure can be perceived differently depending on what they suggest, in terms of spatial information (their affordances), to the individuals (Gibson, 1979). Troffa's work focused on the effects of two main features that could be investigated in a controlled experiment, visibility and angularity:

(1) Visibility is defined as the number of elements that can be perceived by participants when selecting their next route leg.
(2) Angular incidence refers to the angle with which any possible route option crosses a choice point (i.e., junction).

This study aimed to investigate the effect of these configurational features on wayfinding and, furthermore, if such an effect is related to the cognitive abilities of the subjects. Troffa introduced the following hypotheses:

H1: The manipulation of visibility influences subjects' choices. (A high incidence option was expected to be chosen more frequently when the level of visibility was raised.)

H2: The manipulation of visibility acts in a different manner depending on the level of familiarity.

H3: Subjects will select paths characterized by the least angular incidence (expected even if it resulted in a longer route).

H4: Spatial abilities influence participants' choices in the navigation task.

The experiment was based on a sample of 120 participants balanced by gender, familiarity with the setting, and age. Participants completed a simulated real-world wayfinding task using the navigational software FINDyourWAY (Nenci & Troffa, 2007). They made a controlled number of route choices (high/low angular incidence and high/low visibility options). A subsample performed the task in survey perspective, indicating the route on a blind map. Cognitive spatial abilities were investigated through the administration of a spatial orientation and wayfinding test.

The results of Troffa's work reinforced previous findings that configurational features of the environment appear to influence spatial behavior. When participants had to choose among different routes, they more frequently selected the routes with the highest visibility. This output is significant only for people with a low level of familiarity ($z(1) = 3.83$, $p < .01$). Non-familiar people have to "read" the environment based on immediate affordances, whereas participants with a high level of familiarity can use preexisting representations of the environment, decreasing the effect of the experimental manipulation.

Furthermore, people chose routes that intersected choice nodes with the lowest angle ($z(1) = 6.16$, $p < .01$) and that the level of familiarity had no influence. Both highly familiar and unfamiliar subjects significantly preferred the "straightest" options. This behavior is mimicked in survey perspective. Because of the structure of the setting, Troffa controlled the influence of distance, so that the route characterized by the sequence of least-angle options was the longest one, whereas the one formed by the set of highest angle options was, conversely, the shortest route. Such results show that the least-angle option is chosen even when it results in an increase of metric distance. Cognitive abilities do not seem to influence the effect of environmental features: Configurational characteristics of the built environment appear to be the primary influence, unmediated by individual abilities. Taken together these results confirm the influence of spatial configuration on wayfinding and should be seen as a crucial issue for the design of human paths in all built environments.

The Presence of Others as an Indeterminate Wayfinding Variable

Another factor influencing route decisions in urban environments was explored by Conroy Dalton, in order to answer a number of questions, "Have you ever got off a train, or emerged at an airport gate and blithely followed the flow of people only to discover that they are leading you somewhere other than your intended destination? Have you ever hesitated to walk down a street because of the presence of a group of people that seems, somehow, unexpectedly 'out of place' and hence potentially threatening?" Conroy Dalton suggests that the presence or absence of other people in the environment has a direct effect on wayfinding behavior. The new hypothesis is that people, in uncrowded, relatively sparse environments (i.e., the "normal" milieu), influence others in one of two ways which she termed "person-place cues" and "person-space cues."

The "person-place cues" hypothesis is that the location of people in an environment is suggestive of the popularity of that place (Conroy Dalton makes a clear distinction between space, as neutral container and place, as experiential, "lived-space"). This might be due to a temporary event that is taking place in the space or more permanent activities located there (e.g., shops). She suggests that we "read" this inferred popularity and make decisions accordingly. This type of inference is more likely to affect exploratory type behaviors such as exploring a new city, wandering through an art gallery, or even spontaneous shopping trips.

With regard to "person-space cues," space syntax research is based upon the fact that all spatial systems (complex buildings, settlements, etc.) form configurations or "sets of spatial relations" and within each complex environment there exists a spatial hierarchy, with some spaces being intrinsically more important or strategic, while others are more segregated and less important (Hillier & Hanson, 1984). Space syntax theories suggest that we are able to "pick up" visual cues leading to inferences about a space's importance. We "read" these visual cues unconsciously having learnt their spatial significance as part of our early development. On the whole there will be an agreement between the numbers of people walking along the street and that street's strategic importance, and this is also something that we are unconsciously aware of. If you walk along Oxford Street in the city of London, you would expect it to be crowded and if you turn into a minor side street, you would experience a sudden and significant drop in the numbers of people encountered. However, if there is a sudden mismatch between the perceived spatial hierarchy of a street and the number of people present, that is, the pattern of occupancy, then this will be read as being a somewhat "strange" or "unexpected" phenomenon (i.e., if you were to walk down Oxford Street and find it almost empty).

This could contribute to the process of wayfinding decision making. For example, if there were fewer people than one would expect, you might begin to wonder if you had stumbled into the middle of an "emergency situation" and therefore, it would be most prudent to attempt to return to a place of personal safety. Conversely, if you were about to turn down a relatively minor side street, where the expectation would be that it would be occupied by few or even no others, and, instead, you were to observe a small group of people gathered. You would, again, register this mismatch and make other inferences (possibly that the reason for their presence may potentially be nefarious) and change your route plan accordingly.

Conroy Dalton confirms that the above-mentioned hypotheses are connected and admits that this is one of the challenges of developing an experimental framework to test the effects of the person-space and person-place cues. Over time, more popular streets will tend to attract shops, which, in turn, will attract more people and so a multiplier effect will take place.

Path Choices in a Public Market

Various aspects of the two presented factors were elegantly encapsulated by a work of Zacharias. He carried out a statistical study on observed walking itineraries to see how they could be related to certain aspects of layout and to explore an observed tendency for such walking itineraries to take a simple, recognizable shape (Zacharias, 1997).

The literature strongly supports a shared response in individuals when faced with similar environments and sets of tasks. Thus, it is important to know the cognitive and physical bounds that individuals have or impose upon themselves in their daily behaviors. Such bounds may be related to a need to avoid getting lost, finding food, and finding specific locations. At the same time, movement through the environment introduces information serially, which can then be stored by the individual for handy retrieval later. The very act of moving and seeing is closely related to the mental construct of the executed path (McNaughton et al., 1991). Zacharias stresses the importance of relating the series of spatial decisions taken by the pedestrian and to code the environments along the way so that specific factors can be drawn out.

The field study involved tracking 250 individuals from four entrances to the relatively large and complex Yuyuan Garden Market, a popular tourist attraction in Shanghai, recording their paths and stops on a scaled map. Each segment of the trip was timed, including time taken within shops and restaurants. Sex and approximate age of the tracked individual were also recorded. Figure 1 shows the distribution of paths, aggregated by the number of individual pedestrians on pathway segments. It will be seen that the distributions are characteristic, with choice proportions at intersections varying from .05 to .95 and distinct path preferences expressed at 15 of the 22 decision points in the market area ($p < .05$). It can be seen that individuals are making choices that generally agree with those made by other visitors, also for the great majority first-time visitors.

If pedestrians generally agreed on the spatial choice made at a decision point, did the direction of movement have an important effect on this decision? It is conceivable that the choices would appear differently if they were approached from a different direction

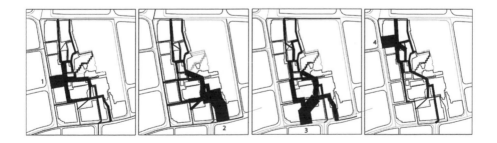

Figure 1. Accumulated trips on pathway segments from tracking records for four entrances to the inner market.

at the choice point. Zacharias noted that the most popular path choice at intersections was also the most popular with those individuals approaching the intersection from the less-traveled pathway segments into the intersection ($r = .596$, $n = 78$, $z = 5.95$, $p < .0001$). It was also seen that trips had a definite forward movement bias. There was also a slight but significant bias toward right-hand choices ($\chi^2 = 210$, $p < .001$), 457 right-hand movements against 378 left-hand ones.

Some proportion of the spatial choices made by these pedestrians is impacted by other local factors in the environment. Some of these might be physical and spatial in nature, and some relating to the dynamic and experiential qualities of the environment. Based on the finding that path choices can be conditioned by human activity and human presence (Zacharias, 2001), occupancy counts were conducted in all of the pathway segments to determine the people density in the spaces or persons per unit area. Generally speaking, spaces that attract people who elect to stand, engage in conversation, or people-watch have a high people density (as related to Conroy Dalton's hypothesis, above), while channels for movement tend to have somewhat lower density. Choice and people density are clearly related ($r = .360$, $p = .001$, one-tailed). The great majority of paths taken by visitors can be described in a small set of configurations. Seven unique path configurations account for 189 of the 250 itineraries, suggesting a high level of agreement among visitors in terms of the degree of complexity and spatial shape of their itineraries.

The high agreement in path choices made by visitors strongly suggests that environmental factors are entering into the decisions, particularly when detailed knowledge of the larger environment is not available. These results point to the importance of both environment-based factors and person-based factors in path choices in such tourist-oriented, commercial walking environments.

Connecting Spatial Cognition Research to Architectural Design

The ongoing project "ArchWay – Architectural Design and Wayfinding Cognition" (Hoelscher and colleagues) aims to help bridge the gap between basic wayfinding research (e.g., Troffa, Conroy Dalton, and Zacharias) and a professional application of the knowledge, by addressing several separating forces in architecture and behavioral science. For example, cognitive psychologists pursue their research from a highly analytic perspective, aiming to separate environmental features from each other in the most controlled fashion, often resulting in studies that test human performance in systematic permutations of abstract mazes rather than real-world settings. Designers, on the other hand, seem to prefer an approach driven by synthesizing factors into a complex design solution, mostly based on precedence, individual case-studies, and intuition. The basic approach of the project, Hoelscher and colleagues, is to investigate both the users of complex building settings and the architectural designers who envision these environments.

On the user side they combined classic measures of spatial behavior and human spatial memory with attempts to model the real-world task structure of a person navigating the complex, public buildings to find their desired goal location. Subjects show distinct behavioral and cognitive preferences when dealing with navigation tasks in such settings. Understanding these route-choice preferences and wayfinding strategies is a key to comprehending wayfinding problems per se, since human beings have to fall back to these mechanisms when they have no adequate prior knowledge about a particular building.

The research goals of the ArchWay project relate to basic research questions in cognitive psychology as well as to practical goals for architectural design by investigating environmental factors as well as internal cognitive processes that determine route-choice preferences and strategies. Environmental factors are investigated on different levels, following a general distinction of local, visually available stimuli at the vista space level (i.e., Troffa's visibility measure) and non-local configurational features at the environmental space level. Real-life experiments and virtual reality studies help us to assess how such features contribute to human wayfinding behavior. Measures from the architectural theory of space syntax (Hillier & Hanson, 1984) are employed to analyze the experimental settings and thus identify systematic relationships between building properties and human wayfinding behavior (Figure 2), primarily via a set of newly developed measures of architectural features along chosen routes (Hölscher, Brösamle, & Vrachliotis, in press).

The practice-oriented aims of the project are centered on identifying concrete wayfinding problems in buildings as well as on understanding the cognitive processes of the architects responsible for such buildings. Despite a body of research in the Design Cognition community on architectural design processes, it is largely unknown how architects reason when they

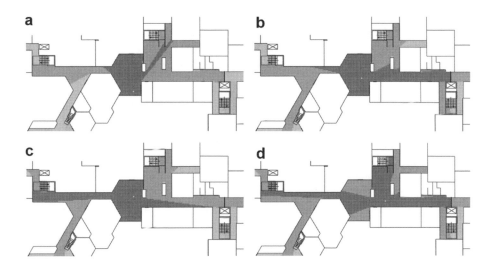

Figure 2. Space syntax analysis of visibility in the entrance area of a complex building, revealing deficits in visual connection to navigation choices, especially staircases. (Images a–d illustrate the visibility around a person moving from the entrance to the main hall.)

try to integrate wayfinding-friendly factors into their designs. We tackle the relevant aspects of wayfinding issues in architectural design processes by interviews and design experiments, capturing design knowledge, guidelines, and a process model of wayfinding design. Initial results indicate that it is difficult for designers to properly anticipate the cognitive abilities and movement behaviors of building visitors, partly due to differences in appreciating layout complexity.

The next major step of this research program will be to translate these results into technical support for architectural designers providing a true Pre-Occupancy Evaluation, curing deficits when changes to the building layout are still feasible, thus overcoming the classic bottleneck of a typical Post-Occupancy Evaluation. On this basis, psychological research can help make buildings more supportive of human well-being and thus be more successful in the long run.

Conclusions

This collection of data, theories, and methods approaches the topic of urban diversities, with the aim to contribute both individually and in combination to the improving of design and management in the direction of sustainable built environments.

First, let us consider the issue of scale, which is highly critical to any discussion of environmental design. The presentations described above represent a wide range of scales from the global-urban, to local-urban and micro-building scale: Troffa and Conroy Dalton at the level of urban route choices, Zacharias at the level of the neighborhood and finally, Hoelscher, at building level. In order to approach and understand the issue of urban diversity and well-being, it is vital to understand the interactions between these differing scales of movement and then to move on to understanding how movement at these different scales combines.

Cultural diversity, considered in the context of this contribution, can be held to be about the cultural differences and similarities that exist between individuals, in particular in the context of their relationship with the built environment. These studies represent a series of experiments in different locations, Italy (Troffa), China (Zacharias), and Germany and London (Hoelscher), representing a breadth of focus that makes the cross-cultural similarities all the more noteworthy.

Conroy Dalton considered the influence that the presence of others in an environment may have over wayfinding choices. The investigation into the effect of this variable has the potential to bring to the foreground how and why certain groups may find the urban environment potentially threatening and by implication find themselves excluded from the city in certain situations and how this knowledge may contribute to the design of a more inclusive environment, hence increasing urban diversity.

Zacharias suggested that by understanding the determinants of route choice in a traditional market (often highly embedded in the local culture), it should be possible to uncover those aspects of route choice that unify people. We believe that the approach taken by all the contributions to the symposium has been to understand common responses to the environment, which has the potential to liberate designers/architects/planners by permitting them to respond to local and cultural differences. All of the studies in this chapter also contribute to the argument of what constitutes a sustainable city, in particular the importance of pedestrian movement for the life and well-being of a city. If designers ignore or simply misunderstand the dynamics at play in pedestrian movement, we risk the creation of moribund or even threatening cities and neighborhoods as well as perplexing, stress-inducing buildings. This is of great importance to the promotion of a psychological feeling of well-being. The more we can understand how and why people find their way around everyday spaces, the more we can design a built environment that encourages and promotes pedestrian behavior, resulting in an increase in walking (and hence our physical well-being) and a reduction in car use (and hence lowering of environmental costs).

So we arrive at the second goal of this field of studies: promoting good design. Hoelscher outlines one approach pioneered through the ArchWay project, a project with practical aims, those of providing tools to designers to design better environments, particularly buildings. This is the potential bridge between research and practice which may permit the medium- and long-term promotion of good environmental design.

References

Gibson, J. J. (1979). *The ecological approach to visual perception*. Boston: Houghton Mifflin.

Hillier, B., & Hanson, J. (1984). *The social logic of space*. Cambridge: Cambridge University Press.

Hölscher, C., Brösamle, M., & Vrachliotis, G. (in press). Challenges in multi-level wayfinding: A case-study with space syntax technique. *Environment and Planning B: Planning and Design*.

McNaughton, B., Chen, L., & Markus, E. (1991). 'Dead reckoning', landmark learning, and the sense of direction: A neurophysiological and computational hypothesis. *Journal of the Cognitive Neuroscience, 3*, 190–202.

Nenci, A. M., & Troffa, R. (2007). Integrating space syntax in wayfinding analysis. In C. Hölscher, R. C. Dalton & A. Turner (Eds.), *Space Syntax and Spatial Cognition*. Proceedings of the Workshop held in Bremen, 24th September 2006. Bremen, Germany: University of Bremen, 181–184.

Zacharias, J. (1997). The impact of layout and visual stimuli on the itineraries and perceptions of pedestrians in a public market. *Environment and Planning B: Planning and Design, 24*, 23–35.

Zacharias, J. (2001). Path choice and visual stimuli: Signs of human activity and architecture. *Journal of Environmental Psychology, 21*, 341–352.

Perceptual Constancy Between Users from Different Countries in Commercial and Historic Streetscapes

Adriana Portella[1,2,3]

[1]School of Architecture and Planning, Federal University of Pelotas, Brazil
[2]Bartlett School of Planning, University College London, England
[3]Joint Centre for Urban Design, Oxford Brookes University, England

Abstract

This chapter discusses the influence of commercial signage on the appearance of historical streetscapes taking into account the perception and evaluation of users from different countries. As part of the historic context of many countries, historic centres have been through a process of physical transformation. This transformation involves updating of historic buildings to accommodate commercial activities and the insertion of contemporary architecture in existing streetscapes. This is a common process and there is nothing wrong with that; problems begin when historic buildings are harmed by this global change. The aim here is to inform those factors that need to be taken into account in the development of commercial signage controls with regard to the preservation of historic heritage and visual quality of urban sites. The empirical investigation adopted the Environment Behavioural approach, that involves theories, concepts and methodologies related to environmental psychology, architecture, planning, and urban design. The findings demonstrated that visual preferences related to historical streetscapes were based on the process of user perception more than on the process of user cognition. The choice of developing the empirical investigation in different countries allowed for a better understanding of the application of techniques to get people involved in surveys.

Key words: evaluation, historic city centres, perception, visual pollution

Studies emanating from disciplines such as architecture, planning, and environmental psychology have explored the negative consequences that disordered commercial signs have on the visual quality of urban areas. At the same time, studies have been done to see how commercial signs affect people's quality of life as these media can influence user perception of the physical environment and user behaviour (Nasar, 1988; Nasar & Hong, 1999; Portella, 2003; Portella & Reeve, 2006).

In relation to the presence of commercial signs in historic cities, the fact that these places are being harmed by the uncontrolled display of shopfronts, franchise signs, window displays, and billboards is evident and has been explored by many researchers, as the literature demonstrates (Ashihara, 1983; Cullen, 2000; Dunn, 2006; Klein, 2000; Nasar, 1988; Passini, 1992; Plummer, 2006). Historic cities have been through a process of physical transformation, which involves the satisfaction of new social and commercial needs. This transformation usually involves updating old buildings to accommodate commercial activities and the insertion of contemporary architecture in existing streetscapes. This is a common process and there is nothing wrong with that; problems begin when historic buildings and places are harmed by this transformation.

This chapter concerns the problem of visual pollution in historic city centres. "Visual pollution" is an established expression commonly used in countries of North, Central, and South America. In this study, this expression relates to the degradation of the visual quality of historic city centres caused by commercial signs displayed on building facades. It is important to highlight that the concept of visual pollution cannot be associated with places such as Times Squares in New York and Piccadilly Circus in London. In these cases, the commercial signage is ordered and displayed to promote the commercial and cosmopolitan character of these areas. Visual pollution is related with the lack of order and character, which are not characteristics of Piccadilly Circus, for example (Figure 1). In London, the City of Westminster gives special consideration to proposals for advertisements in Piccadilly Circus, where existing commercial signs make a positive contribution to the visual character and appearance of this place.

Despite the fact that the problem of visual pollution caused by commercial signage is well described and familiar to many, there is a lack in the literature of any evidence that might relate the physical characteristics of commercial streetscapes to the perception and evaluation of users from different countries; such evidence could allow clear conclusions to be drawn about the universality of this relationship. The literature shows that there are many theoretical concepts that suggest what users from different urban contexts prefer in terms of the aesthetic composition of building facades (Arnheim, 1977; Lang, 1987; Weber, 1995). However, there are no theories that inform universal preferences between users from different countries in terms of the aesthetic composition of commercial signs.

This chapter recognizes that other researchers already have proved that visual preferences with respect to the built environment can differ among people from distinct backgrounds (Bartuska & Young, 1994; Coolican, 2004; Golledge & Stimson, 1996; Lang, 1987; Lynch, 1960; Oliver, 2002). However, what this study explores is that, as argued by Nasar (1988), some visual preferences might be common to the majority of users, independent of their urban context, and these common views might be useful to identify design principles to control commercial signage in historic city centres of different countries. This idea is supported by Reekie (1975 quoted in Uzzell & Jones, 2000, p. 331) who said three decades ago: "What

Figure 1. Piccadilly Circus in London.

is needed is an objective approach based upon design principles that meet with common agreements, and that will lead to an environment visually acceptable to the great majority." Moreover, according to Bentley, Alcock, McGlynn, and Smith (1985), the built environment should be appropriated to a wide range of people and their needs.

In this regard, the investigation presented in this chapter seeks to answer the following question: *Are there common perceptions and evaluations among users from different countries in terms of the appearance of commercial street facades in historic city centres?*

Concepts of Perception, Cognition, and Satisfaction

The process of user evaluation of public spaces involves two principles: perception and cognition (Kaplan & Kaplan, 1982, 1989; Zube & Pitt, 1981; Zube, Sell, & Taylor, 1982). The first one is related to the process by which users get information of places through stimuli that can be related to four human senses: sight, hearing, smell, and touch. In regard to the appearance of city centres, visual stimuli can be commercial signs, shapes, and colours of buildings, and so on. The latter principle (cognition) does not need to be related directly to stimuli linked to physical characteristics of places. The cognition process concerns symbolic meanings associated with places and can be

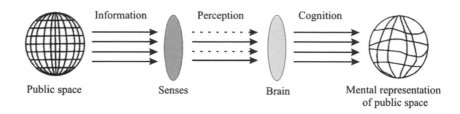

Figure 2. Process of perception and cognition of a public space (*Source*: Golledge & Stimsom, 1996, p. 191).

influenced by users' urban contexts, values, culture, and individual experiences (Bartuska & Young, 1994, p. 69; Biederman & Ju, 1988, pp. 38–64; Carr, Francis, Rivlin, & Stone, 1992, pp. 233–237; Fischer, 1997, p. 27; Golledge & Stimsom, 1996, pp. 19–189; Lang, 1987, pp. 86–92; Passini, 1992, pp. 59–60). This definition agrees with what Meader, Uzzell, and Gatersleben (2006, p. 61) say: "people do not perceive the environment through clear eyes, but through perceptual lenses coloured by their world view" (Figure 2).

The concept of satisfaction also is taken into account to evaluate the appearance of commercial historic city centres. According to Guest and Barrett (1983, p. 234), satisfaction is "the utilitarian value [of a place] to meet certain basic needs," which can range from social activities to physical characteristics (Fried, 1982; Herting & Guess, 1985; Stedman, 2002; St. John, Austin, & Baba, 1986). This is involved in aesthetic judgments, which may correspond to scales of evaluation such as beautiful-ugly and pleasant-unpleasant. This kind of judgement allows comparison: (i) among different users in terms of perception and evaluation of streetscapes, and (ii) among physical characteristics of buildings and commercial signs and user evaluation of city centres (Stamps, 2000, pp. 34–35).

Methods

The methodology in this investigation is designed to bear in mind the practicality of developing a survey in countries with different languages and cultures. Questionnaires and a focus group were applied. A multiple case study approach has been adopted for the empirical study. A frequent criticism of the case study methodology is based on the assumption that its dependence on a single case can render it incapable of providing generalizing conclusions (Cherulnik, 1993, pp. 5–11; Silverman, 2005, pp. 113–115). Therefore, more than one city has been selected as case studies; the results were considered more reliable when the data from two or more case studies led to the same conclusions.

The selection of the countries, where potential case studies could be located, began from the following stratification factors:

- One country where a national approach designed to help local authorities guide and control commercial signage in historic city centres is applied in practice.
- Another country where there is no national approach to guide and control commercial signage, leaving local authorities with the total responsibility for developing commercial signage controls and to decide whether these are necessary in historic city centres.

The choice for the sample of countries was also based on the researcher's previous knowledge of commercial signage approaches applied in countries in South America (Portella, 2003, 2007).

These facts contributed to the selection of England and Brazil. In England, there is a national approach designed to help local authorities to guide and control commercial signage, while in Brazil there is no national approach. In England, this study was focused in Oxfordshire as it represents one of the most historical counties of England. With regard to Brazil, this investigation concentrated the analysis in the southern most Federal State, Rio Grande do Sul. The territorial dimension of this country ($8,514,876.599$ km^2) was taken into account to this selection; the concentration of this study in one Brazilian Federal State avoided data collection becoming exhausting and impractical in terms of financial resources and time spent travelling (Figure 3).

In England there is one common scenario that represents the majority of historic city centres: Commercial signage controls usually are applied to preserve the historic character of these places. In Brazil, two typical cases illustrate the majority of historic city centres: (i) commercial signage controls are designed and applied by the local authority to reinforce a manufactured image of the place and (ii) commercial signage controls are not applied. These last two scenarios were used as criteria in the selection of two case studies in Brazil. The following cities were selected: Oxford in England, and Gramado and Pelotas in Brazil (Figures 3 and 4).

Two commercial streets in each case study were selected for this study. Ideally, to ensure maximum realism, the users from the two countries should observe the same streets *in situ*. However, because of the impracticality of bringing users from England to Brazil and vice versa, part of the experiment was based on colour photomontages, which were shown to residents in Oxford, Gramado, and Pelotas (Figure 5). As already discussed by other researchers, methods using visual stimuli, such as colour photographs and photomontages, are scientifically valid (Light & Pillemer, 1984; Rosenthal & Rubin, 1986; Sanoff, 1991; Sommer & Sommer, 2002; Stamps, 2000).

Questionnaire

Open- and closed-ended questions were designed to investigate perception and evaluation of users when observing the colour photomontages of the streets in the sample (Figure 6). The prerequisites to be part of this sample were (i) to be resident in the case study location surveyed and (ii) to be 18 years old or more. The following techniques were used to

Case Studies in England

England: around 137.940 km² of territorial
extension.

Case Studies in Brazil

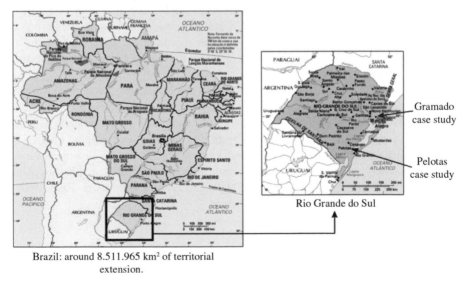

Brazil: around 8.511.965 km² of territorial
extension.

Figure 3. Case studies – Oxfordshire and the Federal State of Rio Grande do Sul.

Oxford city centre   Gramado city centre   Pelotas city centre

Figure 4. Case studies.

Figure 5. Example of photomontage – each building was photographed separately and the photographs pasted together to form an elevation montage.

search for volunteers: Posters were displayed in universities, cafes, public places, and City Council halls, and given to pedestrians in Oxford, Gramado, and Pelotas as pamphlets. Invitation letters were also sent by post to professionals and laypeople selected randomly from phone lists. In addition, a snowball approach was adopted: Volunteers were allowed to invite friends to participate. Articles in local newspapers of the Brazilian case studies were published to encourage people to become involved in the survey. 114 people answered the questionnaires in Oxford, 120 in Gramado, and 127 in Pelotas. Non-parametric statistical tests were applied to the data analysis.

Figure 6. Poster attached to the questionnaire.

Focus Group

A purposive and opportunity sample was selected because the main objective of the focus group discussion was to explore what a specific set of people (City Council officers, professionals, and lay people) think and feel about the impacts of commercial signs in one case study. The focus group was conducted in the case study where the commercial street facades with the lowest user satisfaction in terms of appearance are located. The shop owners located in these commercial streets were also invited; however, they did not show interest in participating. The techniques applied to get volunteers were (i) posters displayed in universities, cafes, public places, and in the City Council hall, and given to pedestrians as pamphlets, and (ii) an article published in a local newspaper inviting people to play a part in the discussion (Figure 7). As suggested by Morgan and Krueger (1998, p. 46), the data analysis was based (i) on notes made by the researcher and by participants during the debate, and (ii) on a document produced at the end of the discussion. Twenty-two people participated in the focus group.

Figure 7. Focus group (*Source*: Author, 2008).

Results

According to responses of users from the entire sample, the highest user satisfaction is related to the appearance of street 1, while the lowest user satisfaction is related to the appearance of street 6 (Figures 8 and 9). Street 1 has the lowest percentage of street facade covered by commercial signs (2.70%) when compared to the other streets in the sample, and only 0.31 m^2 of commercial signs per linear street metre. This street also is characterized by ordered streetscape, high complexity, and preserved historic buildings. On the other hand, street 6 has the second highest percentage of street facade covered by commercial signs (9.11%) when compared to the other streets in the sample and 1.00 m^2 of commercial signs per linear street metre (three times more than street 1). This street is also characterized by disordered commercial signs, high variation of signs, and historic buildings harmed by shopfronts and window displays. The majority of users from Oxford, Gramado, and Pelotas "really like" or "like" the commercial street facades where commercial signage controls are effective and the streetscape is ordered (streets 1, 2, 3, and 4).

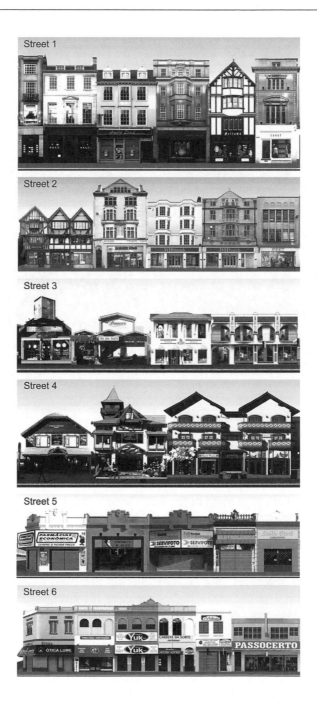

Figure 8. Details of the street facades analysed in this study.

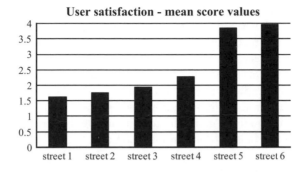

Figure 9. Mean score values related to responses of users from the whole sample. The higher the value, the lower the user satisfaction with the street facade.

At the same time, they "do not like" or "really do not like" the street facades where these controls are ineffective and the streetscape is disordered (streets 5 and 6; Figure 10).

There are statistical differences between users from Oxford, Gramado, and Pelotas in terms of satisfaction with the appearance of street 2 (KW = 20.63, df = 2, p ⁻ .001), street 3 (KW = 39.16, df = 2, p = .001), street 4 (KW = 15.42, df = 2, p = .001), street 5 (KW = 9.23, df = 2, p = .001), and street 6 (KW = 6.63, df = 2, p = .036). The findings show that (i) users from Oxford evaluate streets 5 and 6 more positively than users from Gramado, (ii) users from Gramado evaluate streets 3 and 4 more positively than users from the other case studies, and (iii) users from Pelotas evaluate street 2 more positively than users from Oxford. These results can be related to (i) user familiarity with the streetscape and symbolic meanings attributed to buildings when residents in Gramado evaluated streets 3 and 4 (both located in Gramado), and (ii) user urban context when residents in

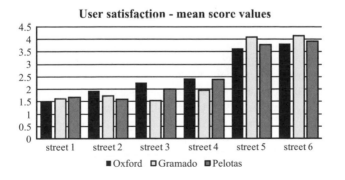

Figure 10. Mean score values related to responses of users from Oxford, Gramado, and Pelotas. The higher the value, the lower the user satisfaction with the street facade.

Pelotas evaluated street 2 and residents in Oxford evaluated streets 5 and 6. In this last case, users from Oxford, where the streetscape is characterized by historic buildings, tend to evaluate streets 5 and 6 characterized by historic buildings more positively than users from Gramado, where very few historic buildings remain preserved in the city centre. Moreover, users from Pelotas, where the majority of streetscapes are comprised of historic and ordinary buildings, tend to evaluate street 2, comprised of historic and ordinary buildings, more positively than users from the other case studies.

The participants of the focus group discussion indicate that the relationship between commercial signage and building form in the historic city centre of Pelotas is negative. They agree with the results obtained from the questionnaire, which show that users from different urban contexts evaluate the commercial street facades located in Pelotas as the worst streets in the sample in terms of appearance. The majority of them suggest that those evaluations are the result of (i) the current commercial signage control adopted in Pelotas, the Code of Postures, that is too permissive (e.g., shop owners can install new commercial signs without the knowledge of the City Council), and (ii) the attitude of the local authority in dealing with shop owners who display commercial signs that harm building facades.

The City Council officers, who participated in the discussion, mentioned that asking shop owners to remove irregular signs can create "a heavy atmosphere in the local community." The other participants in the focus group argue that it is just an excuse to not apply commercial signage controls in practice. On the other hand, the officers said that it is difficult to ask shop owners to remove their signs without the support of effective commercial signage controls, which regulate the physical characteristics of shopfronts and advertisements, such as size, colour, and proportion. According to them, planning officers need the support of an effective legislation to approach shop owners; otherwise the decision of what is an "appropriate" sign becomes a subjective matter.

City Council officers explained that a new commercial signage control that attempts to regulate the physical characteristics of commercial signs has been designed. However, the other participants in the focus group discussion did not know about this initiative because a public meeting to discuss the development of this regulation had not been organized by the Council. According to these participants, the lack of public meetings, which would allow members of the local community to get involved in the development of commercial signage controls, is another negative aspect of the approach adopted by Pelotas City Council to control shopfronts and window displays.

The participants in the focus group also suggest that the lack of interest of shop owners in discussing the negative effects that visual pollution causes to the city centre is another factor that increases the disorder of commercial signs. According to them, this lack of interest is one of the main reasons that make the implementation of commercial signage controls difficult. In general, shop owners do not understand that an ordered city centre may attract more people, and, consequently, increase their profits (Portella, 2003, pp. 46–47). In this regard, the participants of the focus group believe that it is necessary to convince this user group that ordered commercial signs will improve the appearance of the streetscape in the city centre, and consequently this improvement will increase the social and economic vitality of the whole place. City Council officers said that to persuade shop owners to get involved in the development of the new commercial signage control has been one of their aims. However, their initiatives to get these people involved have been always ignored by the majority of shop owners. According to these officers, invitation letters and telephone calls inviting shop owners to come to the City Council to discuss the new commercial signage control were not well received by them.

Results from the discussion related to the support material presented in the focus group (photographs and postcards of Pelotas city centre) show that residents in Pelotas would like the appearance of the city centre to be similar to the images advertised by postcards. They mentioned that the postcards do not reflect the actual appearance of the historic city centre. A participant said "these media just illustrate a few historic buildings still preserved and do not show the chaos created by commercial signs that is the main characteristic of the city centre at present moment" (Figure 11). Participants suggest that the implementation of an effective commercial signage control is one of the main tools to improve the appearance of the city centre and make this place similar to the image promoted by the postcards.

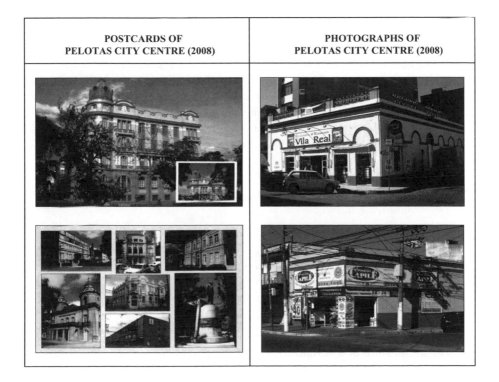

Figure 11. Postcards and photographs of the historic city centre of Pelotas.

From the discussion relating to what can be done to reduce the visual pollution in the historic city centre of Pelotas, eight proposed actions (see section below) were suggested by the participants.

Proposed Actions to Decrease Visual Pollution in Historic City Centre

1. **The persuasion of shop owners to support commercial signage controls**: One of the main conclusions of the focus group discussion is that the shop owners need to get involved in discussions related to (i) the problems caused by the visual pollution in the historic city centre, and (ii) the importance of commercial signage controls as tools to improve the appearance of the place. To get the involvement of these users, two actions were suggested:

   (i) Publication of articles in local newspapers, distribution of pamphlets to shop owners, and promotion of debates broadcast on local TV. The objective here is to promulgate the negative effects caused by the visual pollution, and the positive results that ordered commercial signs can bring to historic city centres in terms of tourist and economic development.

   (ii) Design of a handbook, which introduces to the local community the main issues taken into account in the new commercial signage control that has been designed by the local authority. This handbook should be distributed to shop owners and all members of society interested in this subject. In England, there is a print guide, which explains the guidelines proposed by PPG19 (Great Britain, 1992). Some copies of this guide were shown to the participants of the focus group, and all agreed that it is a good way to help shop owners to understand the issues taken into account in commercial signage controls, and what in terms of design does not affect the historic character of places.

   After the implementation of these actions, the participants of the focus group suggested the application of the following initiative:

   (iii) Organization of workshops to (i) discuss with shop owners the physical characteristics of commercial signs that should be regulated by commercial signage controls, and (ii) show, through examples of other cities, that ordered commercial signs improve the appearance of city centres, attract more visitors, and, consequently, increase the social and economic vitality of these places (Portella, 2003; Scenic America, 1999). The meetings should be open to all members of the local community and be advertised by the local media.

2. **The application of a commercial signage control approach, which takes into account the character of the whole city centre**: A commercial signage control approach, which focuses just on individual buildings and does not take into account their surrounding areas, is a contributory factor to decreasing the visual

quality of historic city centres. This is seen in Pelotas case study where, even when historic building facades are free of signs, commercial signs on their adjacent buildings harm their appearance. The design of commercial signage controls should take into account the character of the whole historic city centre.

3. **The use of computer simulations to illustrate how the appearance of the city centre will be improved with the implementation of commercial signage controls**: Simulations of street facades in the city centre showing how the appearance of this area will improve with the implementation of effective commercial signage controls can be printed out in local guides and distributed to the local community. This kind of visual appeal can persuade shop owners to support commercial signage controls proposed by the local authority.

4. **The delimitation of "street models" to test commercial signage controls**: The implementation of commercial signage controls on one or two street facades in the city centre can allow shop owners and the local community to evaluate the improvement of the appearance of commercial streetscapes *on-site*. This action can also help the local authority to analyse how shopfronts and window displays can be designed with regard to the preservation of the historic heritage *on-site*. The participants of the focus group suggested that these "street models" should be selected by the City Council with the support of the local shop owners. The City Council can give financial support to the shop owners in these streets to adapt their commercial signs to the proposed guidelines. In initiatives already implemented to control visual pollution in some Brazilian cities, such as Rio de Janeiro, the local authority gives exemption of IPUT (equivalent of the Council Tax in England) to owners who agree to restore and preserve the historic character of their properties.

5. **The control of physical characteristics of commercial signs and the definition of a maximum percentage of building facade that can be covered by signs**: Commercial signage controls should be designed in order to (i) regulate physical characteristics of shopfronts and window displays (such as size, colour, shape, and location on facades), and (ii) define a maximum percentage of a building facade that can be covered by these media. Simulations of 3%, 5%, and 10% of a historic building facade covered by commercial signs were shown to the participants of the focus group. Looking at these simulations, the majority of them indicated that a maximum of 3% of the building facade covered by these media is the best alternative to the historic city centre of Pelotas. However, the new commercial signage regulation designed by the City Council of Pelotas defines a maximum limit of 5% of a building facade covered by commercial signs. City Council officers presented in the focus group said that a maximum of 3% is the best option; however, they believe that shop owners will not respect this limit. The City Council does not have a strong enough position to enforce commercial signage controls to be respected by shop

owners. This study recognizes that this attitude is affecting even the design of the new commercial signage control.

6. **The control of the quantity of information displayed on commercial signs**: A limit on the amount of information displayed by commercial signs should be considered in commercial signage controls. The shopfront, for example, should be designed to communicate the name of the shop. Additional information, such as "here you have the best price in the city," "great deals," and "good value," should not be allowed in shopfronts and limited in window displays.

7. **The fragmentation of a building facade by colour and commercial signs should be avoided**: Usually, when more than one shop is located in one historic building, shop owners in Pelotas case study tend to divide the building facade into different parts using colours and commercial signs. They believe that it helps consumers identify each shop; however, according to the focus group, it just contributes to decreasing the visual quality of the building and the historic city centre. The results show that colours and commercial signs of different shops located in the same building should be designed as a group.

8. **The involvement of the local universities in discussions about visual pollution**: Lectures and informal discussions organized among students and meetings to debate the consequences that visual pollution can bring to historic city centres are an initiative that can be promoted by local universities. This kind of discussion can contribute to making students aware of the problem of visual pollution and proactive in terms of avoiding this in their future professional projects. It is interesting to note that the subject of the investigation presented in this chapter is the result of a preliminary academic work developed by the researcher when she was a student of architecture.

Discussion and Conclusion

This chapter provided results for further theoretical discussions in the Environment Behavioural research field. The findings demonstrated that user satisfaction with the appearance of commercial streetscapes was based on the process of user perception (perceptual constancy) more than on the process of user cognition. This is because standard judgments related to the appearance of commercial streetscapes were found between users from different cities and countries. In this regard, this study has begun to fill the gap in the literature of what relates the operation of commercial signage controls and the physical characteristics of commercial streetscapes to the perception and evaluation of users from different urban contexts. Very few studies of user satisfaction in relation to the appearance of commercial streetscapes have been conducted by researchers, with the exception of Nasar (1988) and Nasar and Hong (1999); but these works are based on individual case studies.

The choice of developing the empirical investigation in two countries allowed for a better understanding of the application of techniques to get people involved in surveys. Depending on the urban and cultural context in which potential users live, some techniques will be more successful than others. For example, in the English context, letters, e-mails, and posters displayed in public areas were sufficient to get volunteers to answer the questionnaires. On the other hand, these techniques did not work in Brazil. In the Brazilian context, people are more likely to participate in surveys if these are promoted by the local media (newspapers and/or broadcast TV). Only after articles were published in local newspapers explaining the aim of this study did volunteers contact the researcher to answer the questionnaires. So, it proved to be worthwhile to conduct a pilot study to

Table 1. Factors related to the visual pollution in a historic city centre according to user perception and evaluation

Factor that increase visual pollution	Initiative that decrease visual pollution
1. Legislation is too permissive.	1. Persuasion of shop owners to support commercial signage controls.
2. Attitude of the local authority in dealing with the removal of irregular signs.	2. Application of a commercial signage control approach, which takes into account the character of the whole city centre.
3. Lack of effective commercial signage controls described in objective terms.	3. Use of computer simulations to illustrate how the appearance of the city centre can be improved with the implementation of commercial signage controls.
4. Lack of interest of shop owners in discussing the negative effects that the visual pollution is causing to the historic city centre.	4. Delimitation of "street models" in the city centre in order to test commercial signage controls.
5. Lack of public meetings to allow the local community to get involved in the development of commercial signage controls.	5. Control of physical characteristics of commercial signs and the definition of a maximum percentage of building facade that can be covered by these media.
	6. Control of the quantity of information displayed on commercial signs.
	7. Avoidance of the fragmentation of building facades by colours and commercial signs.
	8. Involvement of local universities in discussions about visual pollution.

search for the most appropriate techniques to get people from different cultures involved in surveys before undertaking the fieldwork. Clearly, this can save money and time.

A possible future stage of research in the topic of "visual pollution caused by shopfronts and window displays in historic city centres" might be the application of the same methodology to other countries to test whether the same universal perceptions and evaluations found here can be verified. If the findings of this chapter can be found consistently among users from other urban contexts, then urban design principles that incorporate user perception and evaluation of the appearance of historic and commercial streetscapes can be addressed as theoretical concepts to combat visual pollution in historic cities around the world. In terms of practical recommendations which can help local authorities design commercial signage controls, this study suggests that questionnaires and focus groups should be undertaken before the design of commercial signage controls begins, and the findings from these should be used as a theoretical background to the development of commercial signage guidelines.

This chapter also identifies and summarizes proposed actions that, according to user perception and evaluation, improve the appearance of historic city centres and convince shop owners and members of local communities to support commercial signage controls (Table 1).

References

Arnheim, R. (1977). *Dynamic of architectural form*. Berkeley: University of California Press.
Ashihara, Y. (1983). *The aesthetic townscape*. Massachusetts: MIT Press.
Bartuska, T. J., & Young, G. L. (1994). *The build environment creative inquiry into design and planning*. California: Crisp Publications.
Bentley, I., Alcock, A., McGlynn, S., & Smith, G. (1985). *Responsive environments: A manual for designers*. Oxford: Butterworth-Heinemann.
Biederman, I., & Ju, G. (1988). Surface versus edged-based determinants of visual recognition. *Cognitive Psychology, 20*, 38–64.
Carr, S. M., Francis, M., Rivlin, L. G., & Stone, A. (1992). *Public spaces: Human qualities of the public environment*. New York: Cambridge University Press.
Cherulnik, P. D. (1993). *Application of environment-behaviour research, case studies and analysis*. Cambridge: Cambridge University Press.
Coolican, H. (2004). *Research methods and statistics in psychology* (4th ed.). London: Hodder & Stoughton Educational.
Cullen, G. (2000). *The concise townscape*. Oxford: Architectural Press.
Dunn, M. (2006). *Educating for a sustainable community. Environmental topic: Visual pollution*. Retrieved March 2006, from http://www.cabq.gov/aes/s5vp.html.
Fischer, G. N. (1997). *Individuals and environment: A psychosocial approach to workspace*. New York: Gruyter.
Fried, M. (1982). Residential attachment: Sources of residential and community satisfaction. *Journal of Social Issues, 38*, 107–120.
Golledge, R. G., & Stimsom, R. J. (1996). *Spatial behavior: A geographic perspective*. New York: Guilford Press.

Guest, A. M., & Barrett, A. L. (1983). Sentiment and evaluation as ecological variables. *Sociological Perspectives, 26*, 159–184.

Herting, J. R., & Guess, A. M. (1985). Components of satisfaction with local areas in the metropolis. *Sociological Quarterly, 26*, 99–115.

Kaplan, R., & Kaplan, S. (1982). *Cognition and environment: Functioning in an uncertain world*. New York: Praeger.

Kaplan, R., & Kaplan, S. (1989). *The experience of nature: A psychological perspective*. New York: Cambridge University Press.

Klein, N. (2000). *No Logo*. London: Flamingo.

Lang, J. (1987). *Creating architectural theory, the role of the behavioral sciences in environmental design*. New York: Van Nostrand Reinhold.

Light, R., & Pillemer, D. B. (1984). *Summing up: The science of reviewing research*. Cambridge: Harvard University Press.

Lynch, K. (1960). *The image of the city*. Cambridge: MIT Press.

Meader, N., Uzzell, D., & Gatersleben, B. (2006). Cultural theory and quality of life. *European Review of Applied Psychology, 56*(1), 61–69.

Morgan, D., & Krueger, R. (1998). *The focus group kit*. Thousand Oaks, CA: Sage.

Nasar, J. L. (1988). *Environmental aesthetics: Theory, research and applications*. Cambridge: University Press.

Nasar, J., & Hong, X. (1999). Visual preferences in urban signscapes. *Environment and Behavior, 31*(5), 671–691.

Oliver, K. (2002). *Psychology in practice: Environment*. London: Hodder & Stoughton.

Passini, R. (1992). *Wayfinding in architecture*. New York: Van Nostrand Reinhold.

Plummer, R. (2006). Brazil's Ad Men Face Billboard Ban. *BBC News*. Retrieved March 2006, from: http://news.bbc.co.uk/go/pr/fr/-/1/hi/business/5355692.stm.

Portella, A. A. (2003). *A Qualidade Visual dos Centros de Comercio e a Legibilidade dos Anuncios comerciais* [The visual quality of commercial city centres and the legibility of commercial signs]. Porto Alegre, Brazil: Federal University of Rio Grande do Sul, Architecture School, Master Dissertation in Town Planning.

Portella, A. A. (2007). *Evaluating commercial signs in historic streetscapes: The effects of the control of advertising and signage on user's sense of environmental quality*. Oxford, UK: Oxford Brookes University. Unpublished doctoral thesis in Urban Design.

Portella, A. A., & Reeve, A. R. (2006, September). Visual pollution in historic city centres: Theoretical concepts to develop commercial signage controls in different cultural contexts. *Books of abstracts of IAPS – International Association for people-environment studies – environment, health and sustainable development* (p. 201). Alexandria, Egypt, September.

Rosenthal, R., & Rubin, D. B. (1986). Meta-analytic procedures for combining studies with multiple effect size. *Psychological Bulletins, 99*, 400–406.

Sanoff, H. (1991). *Visual research methods in design*. New York: Van Nostrand Reinhold.

Silverman, D. (2005). *Doing qualitative research: A practical handbook* (2nd ed.). London: Sage.

Sommer, R., & Sommer, B. (2002). *A practical guide to behavioral research* (5th ed.). Oxford: Oxford University Press.

St. John, C., Austin, D. M., & Baba, Y. (1986). The question of community attachment revisited. *Sociological Spectrum, 6*, 411–431.

Stamps, A. E. (2000). *Psychology and the aesthetics of the built environment*. San Francisco: Kluwer.

Stedman, R. C. (2002). Toward a social psychology of place: Predicting behavior from place-based cognition, attitude, and identity. *Environment and Behavior, 34*, 561–581.

Uzzell, D., & Jones, E. (2000). The development of a process-based methodology for assessing the visual impact of buildings. *Journal of Architectural and Planning Research, 17*, 330–343.

Weber, R. (1995). *On the aesthetic of architecture, a psychological approach to the structure and the order of perceived architectural space*. San Francisco: Ashgate.

Zube, E. H., & Pitt, D. H. (1981). Cross-cultural perception of scenic and heritage landscapes. *Landscape Planning, 8*, 69–87.

Zube, E. H., Sell, J. L., & Taylor, J. G. (1982). Landscape perception: Research, application and theory. *Landscape Planning, 9*, 1–33.

The Influence of Environmental Attributes on Social Interaction Between Different Socioeconomic Groups

Paula Silva Gambim and Maria Cristina Dias Lay

School of Architecture/PROPUR – Federal University of Rio Grande do Sul, Brazil

Abstract

This paper presents the results of an investigation of the effects of appearance of buildings and attractiveness of the built environment on the interaction of different socioeconomic groups living in urban areas characterized by shared social or physical changes. The study was conducted in selected areas of the city of Porto Alegre originally occupied by medium- and high-income residents, where low-income residents were inserted through public housing policies and land regularization processes. The procedures consisted of physical survey, interviews, maps, behavioral observations, photographic survey, questionnaires, as well as GIS applications, syntax and urban graphics visibility analysis. The data showed that social interaction among different socioeconomic groups is positively affected by similarity in appearance of the buildings of public housing and buildings in the neighborhood in general, which tends to encourage better use of local streets and identification of a collective image. It is noteworthy that the characteristics of urban areas resulting from project decisions applied to public housing can minimize the effects of heterogeneity between different groups and are more appropriate to the preferences of residents.

Key words: esthetics, public housing, social interaction

Due to the accelerated urbanization process and spatial fragmentation within cities taking place since the last century, there is great concern about violence and segregation that might result from an increasing heterogeneity of populations living in the same urban environment. Nonetheless, evidence has not been provided so far to suggest which variables might affect, positively or negatively, social interaction between different socioeconomic groups. This research empirically addresses the effects of spatial attributes, mainly visual appearance, on social interaction between different socioeconomic groups in local neighborhoods, according to the Brazilian context.

Segregation of Urban Spaces in Residential Areas

Since the 1980s, according to Ribeiro (2005), economic transformations in Brazilian cities have engendered a process of reconfiguration of the nature and composition of urban poverty. Social inequalities have spread due to an increase in the territorial distance between middle- and low-income segments of society, and also to an increase in the differences in their patterns of behavior, which reduce opportunities for informal contact and interaction between the poor and other social groups.

Within this panorama, various public policies have arisen during the last 30 years. For example, in the city of Porto Alegre, South of Brazil, innovative housing policies were developed in the 1980s with the purpose of meeting the demands of the very poor excluded from access to formal housing (Schmidt, Lay, Oliveira, & Horta, 2007). The policies advocate reinsertion and regularization of poor communities in the urban areas they previously occupied illegally, even when they occur in central and consolidated areas of the city. As a result of this policy's implementation, nowadays there are different socioeconomic populations living in the same urban environment. Hence, there are issues such as reducing opportunities for social interaction between groups because of socioeconomic differences, as well as the positive influence on the attitudes of tolerance and coexistence because of the territorial proximity among different populations (Bidou-Zachariasen, 1996 cited in Ribeiro, 2005). Considering the practical results of policy implementation, the need to understand the effects of the built environment in the interaction of different socioeconomic groups living in a common urban environment and to verify the main factors that can help to reduce social conflicts between them is highlighted.

Influence of Environmental Appearance in the Neighborhood for Social Interaction

According to the literature, user perception and environmental evaluation are affected by physical and spatial attributes and users' cultural values. Moreover, it has been argued that attractiveness of a given space is related to its design and physical qualities (Gehl, 1987), and that the level of neighborhood interaction, sense of identity, and sense of community can affect use.

Nasar (1997) contends that the assessment of a place is a consequence of an esthetic response, dependent on an emotional response experienced by individuals with different lifestyles (i.e., occupation, education level, income, and *inter alia*) in a given place and in relation to its attributes. By conveying functional and social structural patterns, the appearance of an urban area can contribute to the social image and to the differentiation or identification process between groups (Rapoport, 1985), which can influence the reputation of a place and its residents (Twigger-Ross & Uzzell, 1996), interfering in social contact regulation. Following these claims, it seems necessary to verify whether there are effects of building characteristics on the level of social interaction among different socio-economic groups living in the same neighborhood.

Safety perception is also related to socioeconomic and physical attributes (Basso, 2001; Perkins, Meeks, & Taylor, 1992). Various studies show that there is a relationship between neighborhood appearance and perception of physical and social disorder (Perkins et al., 1992; Perkins & Taylor, 1996), and that there are effects of safety perception in the use of the environment and in the possibility of social interaction among residents.

Disorder in the community refers to social (e.g., illegal or questionable behavior, social conflicts) and physical (for instance, trash, vandalism, abandoned houses, and lack of maintenance) conditions that exist in a given location (Perkins et al., 1992; Perkins & Taylor, 1996). Studies have shown that the higher the presence of physical and social disorder and the greater the perception of disorder by residents, safety perception among residents tends to decrease, reflecting the decline in activities in the neighborhood (Liska, Sanchirico, & Reed, 1988; Perkins & Taylor, 1996).

Moreover, perception of heterogeneity among residents might be related to issues of maintenance (i.e., in consequence of differences in income, affecting the investment to maintain the residential environment). Empirical studies are needed to verify if characteristics of buildings, especially regarding maintenance, affect safety perception, intensity of use, and the opportunities for social interaction among different socioeconomic populations existing in common urban areas. As different groups can understand residential environments in different ways, places have different meanings depending on each group's lifestyle, even symbols of status and prestige, safety, or life constraint. Some researchers argue that (Sibley, 1988, 1995 as cited in Dixon, 2001) highly classified spaces, because of social behavior or appearance, seem to weaken or limit opportunities for contact among individuals with different lifestyles. For others, cultural differences hinder communication and may raise the bias (Simpson & Yinger, 1965 as cited in Billig & Churchman, 2003). There also is the idea that proximity between different populations can stimulate the interaction and reduce social tensions (Massey, 1985 as cited in Billig & Churchman, 2003). Therefore, there are contradictory points of view about the perception of heterogeneity of the residential environment and its effect on the level of interaction of individuals. Investigating the perception of heterogeneity of the built environment along with appearance and safety perception in a neighborhood seems to allow for a better understanding of implications of these attributes in the identification of residents with their dwelling environment and in the potential for interaction among different socioeconomic groups living in the same urban area.

The above discussion raises the question of whether similarities in the characterization of dwellings according to each socioeconomic group would encourage greater contact (social interaction) among them. To investigate the working hypothesis, this chapter empirically addresses the effects of spatial attributes, mainly related to environmental appearance, on social interaction of different socioeconomic groups in local neighborhoods, in a comparative study (Gambim, 2007) of three central urban areas characterized by high- and medium-income population, where low-income groups were introduced through social housing reurbanization developments.

Method

Physical and compositional attributes related to the interactional process were investigated through the different levels of social interaction, evaluated by residents' attitudes and spatial behavior occurring in the local environment, regarding the type and intensity of simultaneous activities going on and/or the desire of separation among groups. The study was conducted in three areas in the city of Porto Alegre, South of Brazil. The study areas were defined on the basis of preliminary observation of 102 housing estates built by local government (DEMHAB – Municipal Housing Department) between 1989 and 2005. The selection of the areas consisted of residential environments located in the central and consolidated urban areas of the city that had public housing reurbanization developments recently, with significant differences in socioeconomic level between the preexisting groups of residents in the neighborhood and the ones in the public housing. Multiple methods were employed in this study. Data collection comprised physical measurements of the selected areas, interviews (50) with mental maps, questionnaires (194), and behavioral maps. Respondents were divided into two groups: neighborhood residents (original high- and medium-income population) and public housing residents (recently settled low-income population). Data analysis used non-parametric statistics, GIS resources, syntactic analysis, and graphics of visibility analysis. The multiple techniques enhanced the comprehension and the validity of the investigation.

Results

The analysis emphasizes whether similarities or differences between the dwellings of the different socioeconomic groups living in the same neighborhood affect the use of public space and the likelihood of social interaction between both groups.

Places Perceived by Residents in Terms of Appearance or Safety

The places perceived by residents as esthetically attractive, esthetically non-attractive, inadequate to the characteristics of the neighborhood, unsafe, and avoided to use were identified and mapped in ArcGIS.

In Area 1 (Figure 1), Jardim Planetário public housing (p.h.) is the less attractive place (33%) and the less suited to neighborhood characteristics (33%), perceived respectively, by 55% and 31% of public housing and 15% and 36% of neighborhood residents.

Figure 1. Area 1 physical characteristics: Differences and similarities between the neighborhood and the public housing.

Public housing buildings differ greatly from the surroundings, which appears to contribute to the perception of inadequacy and the fact that they are not esthetically appealing. For neighborhood residents, Jardim Planetário p.h. is also the most unsafe place.

The main characteristics of Jardim Planetário p.h. (single family houses, one floor, popular style, low standard of construction, and poor maintenance) in association with heterogeneity of the Area 1 in terms of style, height, and maintenance of buildings highlight the worst conditions of public housing, differentiating residents of the neighborhood and those of the housing estate.

In Area 2 (Figure 2), many locations are identified as attractive, which can be explained by the homogeneity of building use, common building styles, good maintenance, and high construction standards. Among the few non-attractive places identified,

Figure 2. Area 2 physical characteristics: Differences and similarities between the neighborhood and the public housing.

Figure 3. Area 3 physical characteristics: Differences and similarities between the neighborhood and the public housing.

there are Condomínio dos Anjos public housing and Cachorro Sentado (slum area), which were also perceived less desirable than the surrounding characteristics. Some neighborhood residents (8%) also identify the public housing as unsafe.

The high quality of construction of the neighborhood in Area 2, together with homogeneity of style, height, and good maintenance, makes the differentiation of the public housing clear. These differences seem to be increased by the proximity of Condomínio dos Anjos to neighboring lots in very poor maintenance condition.

In Area 3 (Figure 3), there was no replication in the attractive places identified by the residents. Unattractive, inadequate, and unsafe places were also described variably by respondants. Unlike Areas 1 and 2, the relationship between these three aspects is not as clear, especially regarding the perception of attractiveness and safety. In particular, neighborhood residents tend to indicate the Condomínio Princesa Isabel p.h. as inadequate to the characteristics of the neighborhood, suggesting that despite its high quality and proper maintenance and the similarities with the surrounding buildings, there are other factors affecting the perception of adequacy, such as building style (popular) or compositional aspects.

Area 3 shows variation in building styles and uses (popular houses, small factories, warehouses, and multiresidential buildings). The quality of construction in this Area is generally lower than found in Areas 1 and 2: graffiti on the walls, abandoned lots and buildings, a parking area, and poorly maintained houses. Condomínio Princesa Isabel is esthetically identified as public housing, nevertheless, its good maintenance and similarities between the housing estate and the surrounding buildings, as well as the heterogeneity of the area in terms of style, height, and maintenance of buildings, promote the identification of similarities between residents living in the neighborhood and those living in the housing estate. Nevertheless, in all three areas, buildings in public housing tend to be perceived by residents of the neighborhood as non-attractive, inadequate to the characteristics of the area, and unsafe places. The influence of attributes related to satisfaction with neighborhood appearance, safety perception, and perception of neighborhood homogeneity in social interaction between different groups is confirmed from statistically significant relationships and trends (Mann-Whitney test and Kruskal-Wallis and Spearman), as demonstrated by the results below.

Neighborhood Appearance and Satisfaction with the Buildings

It appears that satisfaction with the appearance of neighborhood buildings is influenced by maintenance (Spearman, $c = 0.482$, *Sig.* = .000) and the styles of buildings (Spearman, $c = 0.156$, *Sig.* = .030). Also, the perception of esthetic attractiveness is correlated with satisfaction with neighborhood appearance (Spearman, $c = 0.257$, *Sig.* = .000) and with building maintenance (Spearman, $c = 0.141$, *Sig.* = .000). This suggests that the better the maintenance of buildings and the greater the satisfaction with the different architectural styles in an area, the higher the satisfaction with the appearance of buildings in general, and the greater the identification of attractive places.

The results show that negative perception of neighborhood characteristics is negatively associated with satisfaction with building appearance (Spearman, $c = -0.290$, *Sig.* = .000), maintenance (Spearman, $c = -0.171$, *Sig.* = .000), and styles (Spearman, $c = -0.221$, *Sig.* = .002). It indicates that the lack of building maintenance and dissatisfaction with the architectural styles tends to cause dissatisfaction with neighborhood appearance, leading to the negative identification of inadequate places in the area.

The verification of attributes that most influence perception of building attractiveness (maintenance and style) and the characterization of differences between public housing and neighborhood dwellings corroborate residents' perception regarding the low-income housing: in Area 1, with the poorest maintenance, lowest construction standards, and most dissimilar esthetic attributes (style and high) when compared to other areas, Jardim Planetário p.h. is viewed as different from its surroundings and is identified as non-attractive and inadequate; in Area 2, the uneven surface of the site and the restricted visual accessibility between the two groups tend to constrain evaluation perception of Condomínio dos Anjos p.h. by the neighborhood residents; however, some tend to identify it as inadequate and non-attractive, either because of its formal characteristics or due to poor maintenance of its neighboring lots; in Area 3, due to the great heterogeneity in the area characterization and the good maintenance of Condomínio Princesa Isabel p.h., it has not been perceived as non-attractive, but tends to be identified as inappropriate to the neighborhood characteristics.

Associations Between Safety Perception, Use, and Appearance Satisfaction

Safety perception in the neighborhood is affected by building maintenance (Spearman, $c = 0.161$, *Sig.* = .025). Particularly in Area 2, safety perception is influenced by satisfaction with architectural styles (Spearman, $c = 0.269$, *Sig.* = .028). Among neighborhood residents of the three areas, safety perception is influenced by building appearance

(Spearman, $c = 0.205$, *Sig.* $= .038$). Those results corroborate the literature regarding the influence of appearance and maintenance on safety perception, although it seems that other attributes also may interfere.

Safety perception was further associated with the use of space (Spearman, $c = -0.307$, *Sig.* $= .000$), suggesting that the greater the perceived safety, the less negatively it affects the use of neighborhood places, meaning that a reduced number of places would tend to be avoided by residents. Above all, in each of the study areas, safety perception appears to affect negatively the potential of social interaction among different socioeconomic groups. The tendency of identifying public housing as non-attractive, inadequate, and unsafe (and avoided) suggests the reduction in use of its adjacent places by neighborhood residents, which tends to hamper social interaction between them and public housing residents. A comparison among Areas 1, 2, and 3 demonstrates that where physical differences are more obvious, showing the precarious conditions of social housing in relation to the surroundings, the more the residents tend to indicate that location as unsafe and to be avoided, this occurs most intensely in Area 1, followed by Areas 2 and 3.

Heterogeneity of the Built Environment

The study areas are recognized as homogeneous by 1/3 (64 out of 194) of respondents. Public housing residents, in particular, tend to perceive the built environment a little more homogeneous than neighborhood residents. Among those who see the environment as heterogeneous, three elements in particular are verified more often as influential: types of buildings in the neighborhood (39.7% – 77 out of 194), trees and vegetation in the streets (36.1% – 70 out of 194), and maintenance of the buildings (35.1% – 68 out of 194). Although there are some differences in the amount of heterogeneous elements identified among socioeconomic groups and between the areas, perception of heterogeneity of the built environment appears to be influenced mainly by type and maintenance of the buildings.

Associations Between Appearance, Safety, Homogeneity of the Built Environment, and Social Interaction

Results show that satisfaction with the appearance affects safety perception among neighborhood residents (Spearman, $c = 0.221$, *Sig.* $= .025$), but not among residents from public housing, suggesting differences in the perception of socioeconomic groups and also the existence of other factors besides the influence of appearance.

The built environment heterogeneity is negatively correlated with satisfaction with building appearance (Spearman, $c = -0.221$, *Sig.* $= .025$), implying that great homogeneity perception in the neighborhood increases satisfaction with the residential area. Moreover, while satisfaction with building appearance adversely affects use of other neighborhoods (Spearman, $c = -0.251$, *Sig.* $= .000$), safety perception influences the use of residents' own neighborhood (Spearman, $c = 0.165$, *Sig.* $= .021$). It suggests that place attractiveness and safety encourage use of the neighborhood, promoting appropriation of open public spaces and, as a result, increasing potential for social interaction between neighborhood and public housing residents.

The supportive performance of neighboring lots, in turn, is affected by satisfaction with building appearance (Spearman, $c = 0.163$, *Sig.* $= .023$) and by heterogeneity of the built environment (Spearman, $c = -0.153$, *Sig.* $= .033$), implying that satisfaction and identification with neighborhood residents might be influenced by building attractiveness and the perception of similarities between them, improving social contact among residents.

Moreover, neighbors' relationship and neighborhood attachment are influenced by satisfaction with appearance (Spearman, $c = 0.302$, *Sig.* $= .000$, Spearman, $c = 0.232$, *Sig.* $= .001$, respectively) and with safety perception (Spearman, $c = 0.163$, *Sig.* $= .023$). Safety perception, in particular, affects social ties in the neighborhood (Spearman, $c = 0.206$, *Sig.* $= .004$), reaffirming that attractiveness and safety tend to promote satisfaction with social relationships and with the residential environment, increasing the potential for social interaction among residents.

On the whole, results support the hypothesis that the greater the similarity in appearance of dwellings from neighborhood and of public housing, the greater the likelihood of social interaction (contact) between the residents of the two socioeconomic groups.

Discussion and Conclusion

The study highlights the importance of integration and adequacy of public housing developments in relation to the urban context in which they are developed, and its effects on satisfaction with the neighborhood, reduction in the potential for social conflict and segregation in the use of public space, and increase in the likelihood of social interaction among different socioeconomic groups. In particular, appropriate fit of environmental characteristics to the esthetic preferences of residents in a neighborhood seems to encourage similar behavior and use and avoidance of places among different socioeconomic groups, while the less appropriate environments (according to resident preferences) seem to aggravate differences in the behavior pattern. Therefore, the profusion of similar places in a neighborhood with different socioeconomic groups suggests an increase in the potential of simultaneous use by distinct groups, which implies that lower sociospatial segregation and greater potential to promote equal rights for the use of the city.

Results further corroborate arguments in the literature concerning place attractiveness and its effects on group identity (Twigger-Ross & Uzzell, 1996), enhancement of use of public space (Gehl, 1987; Lay, 1992), and regulation of social contacts (Taylor, 1988). One can conclude that social interaction between different socioeconomic populations is affected by similarities of building appearance between social housing and the neighborhood context, allowing better use of local streets and public places, and the identification of group collective image. Additionally, results indicate that positive evaluation of building appearance, perception of urban security, and homogeneity in the urban environment tend to influence identification and satisfaction with neighbors, enhancing the social relations among them.

Finally, the study provides empirical evidence to support the assumption that physical attributes are relevant to understand and to interfere in social behavior of different groups co-inhabiting in the cities. In addition, it shows that planning and design decisions related to public housing can be improved when concern with physical aspects that might help reduce the effects of heterogeneity on social interaction is taken into account. It is expected that this will stimulate interest in further research on the subject, as well as to promote urban policies congruent with cultural diversity.

References

Basso, J. M. (2001). *Investigação de fatores que afetam o desempenho e a apropriação de espaços abertos públicos: o caso de Campo Grande – MS* [Investigation of factors that affect performance and appropriation of public open spaces: The case of Campo Grande – MS]. M.Phil. Dissertation – Universidade Federal do Rio Grande do Sul. Porto Alegre, Brazil: Faculdade de Arquitetura – PROPUR.

Billig, M., & Churchman, A. (2003). Building walls of brick and breaking walls of separation. *Environment and Behavior, 35*, 227–249.

Dixon, J. (2001). Contact and boundaries. Locating the social psychology of intergroup relations. *Theory & Psychology, 11*, 587–608.

Gambim, P. S. (2007). *A influência de atributos espaciais na interação entre grupos heterogêneos em ambientes residenciais* [Influence of spatial attributes on social interaction between different socioeconomic groups in residential environments]. M.Phil. Dissertation – Universidade Federal do Rio Grande do Sul. Porto Alegre, Brazil: Faculdade de Arquitetura – PROPUR.

Gehl, J. (1987). *Life between buildings. Using public spaces*. New York: Van Nostrand Reinhold.

Lay, M. C. D. (1992). *Responsive site design, user environmental perception and behavior* (unpublished Ph.D. thesis) School of Architecture, Oxford Brookes University, Oxford, UK.

Liska, A. E., Sanchirico, A., & Reed, M. (1988). Fear of crime and constrained behavior specifying and estimating a reciprocal effects model. *Social Forces, 66*, 827–837.

Nasar, J. L. (1997). Urban design aesthetics. In G. Moore & R. Marans (Eds.), *Advances in environmental behavior, and design* (Vol. 4, pp. 149–193). New York: Plenum Press.

Perkins, D. D., Meeks, J. W., & Taylor, R. B. (1992). The physical environment of street blocks and resident perceptions of crime and disorder: Implications for theory and measurement. *Journal of Environmental Psychology, 12*, 21–34.

Perkins, D. D., & Taylor, R. B. (1996). Ecological assessments of community disorder: Their relationship to fear of crime and theoretical implications. *American Journal of Community Psychology, 24*, 63–107.

Rapoport, A. (1985). Designing for diversity. In B. Jidd, J. Dean, & D. Brown (Eds.), *Housing issues n. 1: Design for diversification*. ACT: Raia Camberra.

Ribeiro, L. C. Q. (2005). *Segregação residencial e segmentação social: o "efeito de vizinhança" na reprodução da pobreza nas Metrópoles Brasileiras* [Residential segregation and social segmentation: The neighboring effect for poverty reproduction at Brazilian metropolis]. XI Encontro Nacional da ANPUR [XI National Conference of ANPUR]. Belo Horizonte, Brazil: ANPUR.

Schmidt, C., Lay, M. C. D., Oliveira, C. H., & Horta, E. O. (2007). A Habitação social em Porto Alegre [Public Housing in Porto Alegre]. *RDE – Revista de Desenvolvimento Econômico, 9*, 79–87.

Taylor, R. B. (1988). *Human territorial functioning: An empirical, evolutionary perspective on individual and small group territorial cognitions, behaviors, and consequences.* New York: Cambridge University.

Twigger-Ross, C. L., & Uzzell, D. L. (1996). Place and identity process. *Journal of Environmental Psychology, 16*, 205–220.

A Description of Incongruous Architectures and Related Observations

Paolo Bonaiuto,[1] Valeria Biasi,[2] Gabriele Bonaiuto,[3] and
Anna Maria Giannini[1]

[1]Department of Psychology, Sapienza University of Rome, Italy
[2]Department of Cultural and Educational Studies, University of Rome Tre, Italy
[3]Professional Architect and Department of Psychology, Sapienza University of Rome, Italy

Abstract

Our contribution deals with the classification and description of paradoxical architectures, that is, architectures that contradict the average viewer's expectations. We examined cases of position incongruity, such as leaning buildings; shape incongruity, such as buildings with acute or obtuse corners, fractured constructions, concave facades, phallic and ballistic shapes, etc.; and composition, size, or chromatic incongruities. We list some contrasting views in the specialist literature, such as some favourable opinions by Venturi (1966) and unfavourable comments or severe criticisms by Arnheim (1977), Lo Ricco and Micheli (2003), Silber (2007) and La Cecla (2008). A summary follows of some experimental studies on the perceptual processes involved, such as the exaggeration of the degree of conflict due to the contrast between architecturally incongruous images and normal mental building schemata; or the attenuation of this contrast after appropriate verbal explanations. Our study may contribute, among other things, to demonstrate the dependence of perceptual representations not only on visually stimulating configurations, but also on the perceiver's mental schemata, disposition, and attitudes – which in turn can be influenced by emotional atmospheres that can be experimentally manipulated.

Key words: architecture, Dresden, incongruity, paradox, Prague

Classification and Description of Architectural Incongruities

Over the last 25 years we have collected a great deal of documentation on incongruous architectures, and also have performed several experimental studies in this regard.

The description of the various ways with which visual perception of incongruities in architecture was obtained in various countries, in various periods, and by different builders enables us to integrate a multiform and varied scenario, a conspicuous diversity; and it demonstrates an important iconological and psychological differentiation, a considerable multiplicity of images, construction processes, and visual mechanisms. In this regard, we believe that the review fully satisfies the purposes and criteria underlying the present contribution of environmental psychology.

Firstly, we considered leaning buildings from Medieval or Renaissance periods, where the inclination was due to a partial subsiding of the ground, as is the case with the Leaning Tower of Pisa (Figure 1). Some humorous illustrations were made in an attempt to provide an ironic explanation of tower's inclination. In one example, the Medieval architects say: "We saved money on foundations, but nobody will know it. ..." Moreover, we considered the Garisenda Tower in Bologna and the typical two-storey Tilted House of Bomarzo, near Rome.

Several further examples and different kinds of architectural incongruities were progressively examined, always from the psychological point of view, leading to a systematic classification and to scientific conclusions which considerably distinguish the panorama of this topic with respect to more obvious and generic treatises presented in recent books, such as the richly illustrated ones by Jencks (1979), Papadakis (1994), Thiel-Siling (1999), Cattermole and Westwell (2007), Silber (2007), and Wright (2008). Some authors have made distinctions exclusively on the basis of practical use, that is, residential,

Figure 1. The Pisa tower.

commercial, municipal, and cultural buildings. Other authors have pointed to rationalisations of a philosophical kind, with references to Derrida (Benjamin, 1994; Derrida, 2008) for the so-called "deconstructivism." Our classification was firstly based on the range of phenomenal qualities, which are well known in psychology after contributions by Arnheim (1949), Metzger (1954, 1963), Bonaiuto (1965, 1988), and others. Moreover, we kept in mind the canonic psychological definition of *incongruity*: "A special structural and physiognomic quality due to the contradiction of the average beholder's expectations, for each quality (a variety of psychological conflict)." Each quality is contradicted in each experience of architectural incongruity, with respect to traditions of regularity, order, symmetry, harmony and to preferences for right angles, vertical and horizontal planes, etc., that are aspects proposed and tacitly accepted for centuries, as dominant compositional rules with certain exceptions, which became anomalies attracting tourist interest and curiosity (Bonaiuto, Biasi, Giannini, & Bonaiuto, 2000).

Therefore, we examined cases of architectural *incongruity of position*, such as the aforesaid leaning buildings, to which we may add the almost completely upside-down restaurant in Kurashiki (Japan), the Kino Building, that is the 40-degree tilted UFA Cinema Center, built by Coop Himmelb(l)au in Dresden (Germany; Figure 2), the two symmetrically tilted Towers KYO of the well-known "Puerta de Europa" in Madrid (Spain; designed by architects Philips Johnson and John Burgee), and the Eisenman's House.

We also evaluated cases of *shape incongruity*, such as buildings with vertical obtuse or acute edges: The Farnese Palace in Caprarola (Italy); the modern tower of Den Haag (The Netherlands), with a triangular base and therefore acute corners, which become apparently right when observed frontwise; or the East Building of the National Art Gallery, Washington, DC, by Ieoh Ming Pei: a building made with only acute or obtuse corners. Note that the very

Figure 2. The UFA cinema center (called Kino) in Dresden (Germany).

Figure 3. The very acute marble corner of the East Building, National Art Gallery, Washington, DC.

acute marble corner attracts tourist interest and manipulation, and, in fact, appears dirty at visitor's hand height (Figure 3).

This category also includes, again as shape incongruities, the examples of fractured buildings, such as the "Best Stores" in Sacramento, California (USA), that also refer to the concept and image of ruins after an earthquake. Shape incongruity is also well exemplified by the Flat Iron Building in New York, and moreover by the famous constructions designed by Frank O. Gehry, from the Guggenheim Museum in Bilbao (Spain) to the "Ginger and Fred" Towers in Prague (Figure 4), and to various other buildings (Toledo, Minneapolis, Los Angeles, Seattle, Cleveland, etc.). Even in Tuscany, at Cecina, so to say at the empire periphery, a library was built by local architects in the same style.

Another example is the Twisty Torso Tower in Malmö (Sweden), the second tallest residential tower in Europe, by Santiago Calatrava (completed in 2005). This 190 m building has 95-storey blocks that twist as they rise, with the uppermost being aligned at 90 degrees to the lowest (a progressive rotation). A conspicuous twist may also be appreciated in the Moscow City Wedding Palace, by Architect's Group RMJM and also in the Infinity Tower in Dubai Marina, built after 2006 by Skidmore Owings & Merrill (SOM Studio). Another Calatrava-typical building is the Chicago Spire, built after 2007. This building also shows concave facades and thus, on the whole, constitutes a very conspicuous shape incongruity. The same category also includes the Cobra Hotel-Gateway Building, situated in the Arab Emirate of Ras Al-Khaimah (2007, by the Norwegian group Snohetta), for its strange shape. The same Emirate also sees the typically convex sides of Iris Bay, built after 2006 on plans by W. S. Atkins. Dubai has the Burj Al Arab, which is also characterised by a broad curved surface (designed by W. S. Atkins Design, 1996–1999). We should also include the Transamerica Pyramid in San Francisco, designed by Pereira & Associates (1959–1972), and the Bahrain World Trade Center, with its

Figure 4. The "Ginger and Fred" Towers in Prague, by Frank O. Gehry.

two mirroring pyramid-shaped towers built in Manama, Bahrain, after 2004, on plans by W. S. Atkins. We should also mention the Fountain Place Building in Dallas (USA, by I. M. Pei & Partners, 1986), surmounted by a pyramid-shaped peak.

Other recent examples have a phallic or ballistic shape, such as the Agbar Tower in Barcelona (by Jean Nouvel) or the Swiss Re Building in London (by Norman Forster). We may add some recent Olympic Buildings in China, such as the one with the shape of the Olympic torch, and the National Stadium well known as "The Nest" (by the Swiss architect group Herzog & de Meuron).

Our review also considers *incongruity of composition*, featuring parts which are completely out of context and unexpected, thereby contradicting the common notions of building. Examples range from the Pineapple House in Dunmore (Scotland) to the Le Palais Idéal in Gallure, France. Other examples are the "Shark in a House" in Headington, Oxford (England), and the Chiat/Day Building in Venice, California (USA), created by Gehry with Oldenburg and van Bruggen, including a giant pair of binoculars in the middle. Among the other examples we can mention some buildings with a face physiognomy and also the mechanical composition of the famous Beaubourg in Paris (by Renzo Piano & Richard Rogers).

Different examples concern *incongruity of size*, such as the oversized yellow Caterpillar of the United Equipment Company in Turlock, California (USA) and the Big Duck near Flanders, Long Island, New York. Buildings of exceptional height deserve particular mention, here. The tallest building in the world today is the Burj Dubai, situated in the Arab Emirates. Designed by the SOM Group, it is 819 m tall and has 154 floors. The second tallest building is the 609 m Chicago Spire, which we have already mentioned as regards shape incongruity. Then there is the Lotte Super Tower, 555 m tall (in Seoul,

Figure 5. The Trevi Fountain in Rome, whose water was turned bright red by artist Graziano Cecchini.

South Korea, by the SOM Group, still to be completed), the Taipei 101 with its 509 m (C. Y. Lee, 1999–2004), the International Commerce Centre, in Hong Kong (China), 484 m tall (KPF and Wang & Ouyang, 2005–2010), the Shangai World Financial Center, 492 m (KPF Associates, 1997–2008), and the Petronas Towers complex in Kuala Lumpur, Malaysia, 452 m tall (Cesar Pelli & Associates, 1993–1998).

At this point it is also worth recalling the cases of *chromatic incongruity.* One building is in Warsaw (Poland): Its alarming colouring characterises the Gestapo Building, which, after the war, became the place of the Faculty of Psychology, University of Warsaw. Another typical building is the Medieval Tower in Gdansk, which housed a prison. The incongruity of colour is well exemplified by some modern "graffiti" on building walls, monuments and even bridges, factories, and wagons.

A conspicuous, albeit short-lived example was the Trevi Fountain in Rome (Italy), whose water was recently turned *bright red* by a futurist type action of artist Graziano Cecchini (Figure 5).

Comments For and Against Found in the Specialist Literature

There have been some interesting contrasting views in the specialist literature over the last 40 years. Robert Venturi (1966) wrote in favour of architectural incongruities, quoting even Berlyne (1960). On the other hand, unfavourable comments and severe criticisms were recorded by Rudolf Arnheim (1977). He wrote: "A work of art or of architecture cannot perform its role without order. Contradictions are defects. Venturi defends disorder and confusion, the justapposition of incompatibile elements is an offence to order.

P. Bonaiuto et al.
A Description of Incongruous Architectures and Related Observations

115

The average observer is frustrated by the fights among contradictory elements. Disorderly shapes produce stress, depression and ugliness ….” Recently an Italian anthropologist, Frank La Cecla (2008), wrote a book entitled “Against Architecture,” in which he criticises the current architectural fashion of making bizarre shapes without taking into account more deep functions of buildings: A kind of artistic intent without responsibility. We can find similar comments and criticisms in Lo Ricco and Micheli (2003), and in Silber (2007).

A Summary of Some Experimental Studies

Aims, Methods, Procedures, and Results

Among the psychological processes involved in the perception of these various architectural incongruities, we studied some interesting aspects:

a) The *emphatisation of the degree of conflict* due to the contrast between architecturally incongruous images and normal mental schemata of buildings.
b) The *attenuation of this contrast after using appropriate verbal explanations.*

Moreover, we noted a similar attenuation as a perceptual defence mechanism in the case of conflict overload. Other processes were also identified through systematic psychological research.

We first chose two very incongruous architectural images, reproduced on colour slides, each one projected on a large match-boarded screen (150 × 150 cm), seen in a darkened room by the subject sitting 2 m away. Each large image was presented individually to different subjects, giving rise to two separate experimental sections.

The first slide showed the already mentioned UFA Cinema Palace, the multiscreen entertainment complex built in Dresden. The paradoxical feature is, above all, the overall *lean* to the right: A conspicuous rightward 40-degree inclination with respect to the vertical – an anomaly accompanied by a certain bilateral asymmetry and other irregularities (Figure 2).

The second slide showed the building housing the headquarters of the National Netherland Group, built in Prague on drawings by Frank O. Gehry, and also already quoted. The paradoxical feature is, above all, the conspicuous *inflection* of the right side of one of the two towers, making up the construction. This inflection involves a sinusoidal concavity of the right flank that creates a 7-degree angle with respect to the vertical in the lower section. There is also a series of unaligned windows and other features (Figure 4).

a) The first experiment looked into the phenomenon of the *emphasising of perceptual anomalies* as a contrast with the mental schema of a building, when observed in unambiguous perceptual conditions. When the paradoxical architectural image is observed in such conditions, there is an emphatisation of the incongruity, as was noted in the experiments on leaning buildings by Bonaiuto, Giannini, and Bonaiuto (1989, 1990). An inhibition of this normal emphatisation was then demonstrated when each experimental subject had an appropriate, adequate, and fitting verbal explanation read out to them, which led to reducing or eliminating the conflict between mental schemata and images that would otherwise be very incongruous (Bonaiuto et al., 2000). As a control situation we used an unfitting written narrative, which will be described later.

For this part of the study, the number of participants was extended to 100 subjects per image and per group (experimental and control); that is, a total of 600 participants having the same general features and group distribution: Undergraduates or graduates of various University Faculties in Rome, with ages ranging from 19 to 39 years (mean age: 26.2 years), equally divided for gender and mean age in the various groups. They were blind to the aims and method of the study and none of them had ever seen the images of the buildings under examination.

The dependent variable was the apparent shape of the paradoxical building silhouette projected on the screen. The "limits method" was used for measurement. As soon as the image appeared, the subject had to evaluate the overall configuration by means of two interchangeable 7-step comparison scales (135 × 20 cm), placed below the screen, whose brightness along with the action of an additional spot made the scales completely legible. Each slightly concave scale contained a series of schematic depictions of the profile of the building to be evaluated, with the anomaly increasing or decreasing at regular intervals. They also contained alphabetical letters underneath, with the central one being the letter "D," corresponding to the realistic evaluation. For the experimental subsection focusing on the Dresden Building, the central element (D) realistically showed a 40-degree rightward tilt, while the other elements either increased or decreased this inclination by 3 degrees each time. Each participant made six evaluations and thus used each of the scales three times, in random order.

Two analogous 7-step comparison scales were also used for the Prague Building. The central element (D) presented a sinusoidal inflection from right to left. The sinusoid started below at an angle of 7 degrees with respect to the vertical. The other elements increased or decreased the inflection by one and a half degrees each time. Here, too, each participant made six evaluations by first using one scale and then the other, in random succession, three times.

For both images, the procedure was as follows: Reading a written description (mean duration 2 minutes), or waiting for an analogous short period for the group "Without any explanation," and then performing a visual evaluation of the building shape by means of the same comparison scales.

The results proved the phenomenal accentuation of the structural anomaly, observed frontwise, in that the evaluation without any explanations (no description) gave rise to a significant increase in the apparent perceptual anomaly, with measures clearly higher than the "objective" ones. This experiment was also confirmed by its onsite replications in front of the real buildings (Bonaiuto et al., 2000). Moreover, the significant prevention

P. Bonaiuto et al.
A Description of Incongruous Architectures and Related Observations
117

Table 1. The architectural anomaly (inclination with respect to the vertical) is emphasised by observers examining the Dresden or Prague Building, without any explanation or after unfit explanation. Only after a fitting and appropriate explanation does the perception become more realistic

	Without any explanation	After unfit explanation	After fitting explanation
Dresden Building			
Perceptual anomaly	1° 62	1° 51	0° 14
	($t99 = 5.53$; $p < .01$)	($t99 = 4.74$; $p < .01$)	($t99 = 0.45$; n.s.)
Prague Building			
Perceptual anomaly	2° 45	2° 49	1° 48
	($t99 = 16.24$; $p < .01$)	($t99 = 15.32$; $p < .01$)	($t99 = 8.46$; $p < .01$)

effect (inhibition or great reduction) was demonstrated for the aforesaid emphatisation following the reading of the fitting explanation; there were no effects after the reading of the unfit explanations (Table 1).

b) The subsequent investigation aimed to demonstrate that the fitting explanation also led to reducing or eliminating certain physiognomic aspects like the level of incongruity and the anxiety-generating power attributed to the paradoxical image. The new participants concerned were limited to 20 subjects per image and per group (experimental or control). In other words, two groups of subjects (experimentals and controls), making a total of 80 participants, divided into four groups. They had the same general characteristics and distribution as subjects in the previous experiment.

The fitting *explanation* of each building in question is centred on its nature, history, designers' intentions, and construction materials. The unfitting written narrative was focused on a non-pertinent philosophical description concerning the "soul" concept and had the same number of words and lines as the fitting explanation. In fact, each narrative was printed on a white A4 card (about 40 lines of text, Helvetica font size 14). After entering the very faintly lit room, each participant was asked to sit comfortably in front of the large screen. The subject was allowed to freely view the projected image for half a minute. S/he was given a pen and a sheet containing a total of fifty-six 7-point bipolar scales in order to evaluate the perceptual qualities of the building image. The order and direction of the scales were systematically varied. Filling in the sheet took an average of about 4 minutes. After making the evaluations, each subject was given the suitable description to read. The experimenter said: "Here is some information on the nature and history of the building. Read it carefully." The subject read the text, which took about 2 minutes, from time to time spontaneously looking at the screen to check the image. Then the subject was asked to evaluate the image of the building again, using the same set of scales as before.

At the end of this sequence and before leaving, the participant was given a third short sheet to evaluate certain qualities attributed to the explanatory description itself, read earlier. These qualities concerned clarity, credibility, and relevance.

The data processing started by compiling a detailed sheet for each subject, with the scores given with the first series of evaluations, those given with the second series of evaluations, and the differences between the two series of evaluations. The final evaluations of the explanatory description were also included.

For the different perceptual qualities, the comparisons of the means obtained with the experimental and the control subjects show – for the first evaluations, following the Student t test for each scale used – the absence of any preliminary significant differences between groups. This aspect is very important since it allows us to rule out that the groups were heterogeneous in the first place. Therefore, any changes found after the second series of evaluations can reasonably be ascribed to the sole influence of the experimental condition. In this regard, we may note that the comparisons between the first and second evaluations within each group show conspicuous differences mainly in one direction for the experimental group, while the variations appear weak and two-directional in the control group.

We shall now deal with the structural and physiognomic qualities by defining for each building image the overall size of the *incongruity*, as well as the valences (or bridge qualities, following Metzger, 1954) defining its *anxiety-generating power*. It may also be interesting to report on subjects' behaviour regarding the attribution of *aesthetic qualities*.

In relation to the paradoxical "Dresden Building," the study of the intercorrelations between the scores obtained for each of the aforesaid dimensions led to selecting certain subgroups of bipolar scales as the most representative, as listed below. As regards *incongruity*, we considered the scales contemplating the following pairs of opposite adjectives (Cronbach's alpha = .71; mean correlation between items = .34), since they were seen to have a certain affinity with one another:

1. Incongruent/Congruent
2. Contradictory/Coherent
3. Absurd/Obvious
4. Paradoxical/Reasonable
5. Nonsense/Logical.

As regards *anxiety-generating power*, we considered the following scales (Cronbach's alpha = .87; mean correlation between items = .57):

1. Alarming/Reassuring
2. Anxiety-Inducing/Relaxing
3. Threatening/Comforting
4. Bothersome/Agreeable
5. Irritating/Calming.

In calculating the changes between the series of first and second evaluations, the scores given to the related scales (within each of the aforesaid dimensions) went to make up the mean individual scores which then were used in the analysis of variance.

After reading the suitable explanatory description, and for comparison with the respective control group, we noted the effects reducing the incongruity and the anxiety-generating power, in line with the working hypotheses.

As regards the *aesthetic aspect*, we used a specific scale based on the pair of opposite adjectives: beautiful/ugly (in agreement with Jacobsen & Schröger, 2002). The experimental treatment yielded scores for aesthetic appreciation that turned out to be higher due to the influence of the suitable explanatory description. There were no significant differences or interactions for the participants' gender.

In relation to the paradoxical "Prague Building," the data were collected and the data processing was carried out in the same way. In this case, too, the scale-by-scale comparison of the means of the scores ascribed in the first evaluation by both experimental and control groups usefully revealed the preliminary absence of heterogeneity. The peculiarities of the evaluations replicate those already found in the first section of the experiment and thus have the same meaning. The study of the intercorrelations yielded the following values. For incongruity, for the five bipolar scales considered, we obtained: Cronbach's alpha = .69; mean correlation between items = .32. For anxiety-generating power: Cronbach's alpha = .73; mean correlation between items = .36. Again, the influence of the experimental condition compared with control condition was in the direction predicted by the working hypotheses and was statistically significant.

Table 2 summarises the described results, which confirm that reading a suitable explanatory description can reduce the perception of incongruity and the attributions of anxiety-generating power, while it improves aesthetic appreciation, when the subject is faced with an image of a paradoxical building. There were no differences or interactions regarding gender since both men and women experienced the experimental condition in the same way.

Table 2. Effects of reduction (−) of perceived "Incongruity" and of "Anxiety-Generating Power," attributed to the paradoxical images of the Dresden and Prague buildings, after the relative fitting and appropriate explanations

	Without any explanation	After fitting explanation	Statistical analysis
Dresden Building			
Incongruity level	0.14	−0.93	$F(1, 36) = 12.33; p < .01$
Anxiety-generating power	−0.02	−1.09	$F(1, 36) = 6.97; p < .02$
Prague Building			
Incongruity level	0.14	−0.77	$F(1, 36) = 9.97; p < .01$
Anxiety-generating power	−0.04	−0.65	$F(1, 36) = 6.67; p < .01$

Conclusion and Discussion

The participants' evaluations of the structural and physiognomic qualities of the building image concurred to delineate the paradoxical aspects. In any case our study may contribute, among other things, to demonstrating the dependence of perceptual representations not only on stimulating configurations, but also on the beholder's schemata, dispositions, and attitudes. These are in turn influenced by precise emotional experiences and atmospheres that can be experimentally manipulated. The study can also contribute to proving continuity, at a psychological level, between the full-colour projected images of new paradoxical buildings and the tridimensional building models used in our previous experiments which in turn can be linked to the cases of real paradoxical buildings, some of which were mentioned in the beginning of the present work.

References

Arnheim, R. (1949). The Gestalt theory of expression. *Psychological Review, 56*, 156–171.

Arnheim, R. (1977). *The dynamics of architectural form*. Berkeley, CA: University of California Press.

Benjamin, A. (1994). Derrida, Architecture and Philosophy. In A.C. Papadakis (Ed.), *Deconstruction in Architecture. Architectural Design Profile 72* (pp. 8–11). London: Academy Group.

Berlyne, D. E. (1960). *Conflict, arousal and curiosity*. New York: McGraw Hill.

Bonaiuto, P. (1965). Tavola d'inquadramento e di previsione degli "effetti di campo" e dinamica delle qualità fenomeniche [Table to frame and foresee the "field effects" and dynamics of phenomenal qualities]. *Giornale di Psichiatria e Neuropatologia, 93*(4 Suppl.), 1443–1685 (reprint: Rome, Kappa).

Bonaiuto, P. (1988). Processi cognitivi e significati nelle arti visive [Cognitive processes and meanings in the visual arts]. In L. Cassanelli (Ed.), *Linguaggi Visivi, Storia dell'Arte, Psicologia della percezione* [Visual languages, history of art and psychology of perception] (pp. 47–79). Rome: Multigrafica.

Bonaiuto, P., Biasi, V., Giannini, A. M., & Bonaiuto, G. (2000). *Effects of narratives on perception when looking to paradoxical building images*. Rome: Università "La Sapienza".

Bonaiuto, P., Giannini, A. M., & Bonaiuto, M. (1989). Maximizers, minimizers, acceptors, removers and normals: Diagnostic tools and procedures. *Rassegna di Psicologia, 6*(3), 121–129.

Bonaiuto, P., Giannini, A.M. & Bonaiuto, M. (1990). Piloting mental schemata on building images. In A. Fusco, F. M. Battisti, & R. Tomassoni (Eds.), *Recent experiences in general and social psychology in Italy and Poland* (pp. 85–129). Milan: Angeli.

Cattermole, P., & Westwell, I. (2007). *Bizarre buildings*. Richmond Hill: Firely Books.

Derrida, J. (2008). *Maintenant l'architecture,* Succession Derrida 2008 (posthumous), tr. en. by F. Vitale and H. Scelzo, *now the architecture,* books Scheiwiller, Milan 2008.

Jacobsen, T., & Schröger, E. (2002). *A primacy of beauty: On describing the aesthetics of objects*. Paper presented at the XVII Congress, International Association of Empirical Aesthetics, "Art and Environment", Takarazuka.

Jencks, C. (1979). *Bizarre architectures*. New York: Rizzoli International.

La Cecla, F. (2008). *Against architecture*. Turin: Bollati Boringhieri.

Lo Ricco, S., & Micheli, S. (2003). *Lo spettacolo dell'architettura. Profilo dell'archistar* [The show of architecture. Profile of the archistar]. Milan: Mondadori.

Metzger, W. (1954, 1975). *Psychologie*. Darmstadt: Steinkopf.

Metzger W. (1963). *I fondamenti dell'esperienza estetica* [Foundations of Aesthetic Experience]. Paper presented at the *Second International Colloquium on Expression*, Bologna. Publ. in G. Maccagnani (Ed.), *Psicopatologia dell'espressione* [Psychopathology of Expression] (pp. 767–780). Imola: Galeati, 1966.

Papadakis, A. C. (Ed.). (1994). *Deconstruction in architecture. Architectural design profile 72*. London: Academy Group.

Silber, J. (2007). *Architecture of absurd. How "Genius" disfigured "Practical Art"*. New York: The Quantuk Lane Press.

Thiel-Siling, S. (Ed.). (1999). *Icons of architecture. The 20th century*. Munich: Prestel.

Venturi, R. (1966). *Complexity and contradiction in architecture*. New York: Museum of Modern Art.

Wright, H. (2008). *Skyscrapers. Reaching for the sky*. London: Paragon Books.

Diversity in Urban Green Spaces and Well-Being

Green Areas and Housing's Habitability

A. Maritza Landázuri,[1] Terence R. Lee,[2] Alejandra Terán,[1] and Serafín J. Mercado[3]

[1]Facultad de Estudios Superiores Iztacala, UNAM, Mexico
[2]School of Psychology, University of St. Andrews, Scotland
[3]Facultad de Psicología, UNAM, Mexico

Abstract

The purpose of this study was to explore people's emotional reactions in terms of Merhabian and Russell's (1974) states of pleasure, arousal, and dominance, in relation to the existence or not of natural green areas and flowers in the environment. Additionally, the specific reactions to vegetation were explored, using another scale designed for this project. The sample was non-probabilistic intentional, consisting of 220 inhabitants of Mexico City and St. Andrews, Scotland (100 from Mexico City and 120 from St. Andrews), with ages ranging between 16 and 85 years. An explanatory, co-relational, ex post facto multivariate design was used. The instruments used were 59 Likert scale items (green areas and housing inhabitability) and Mehrabian and Russell's (1974) Semantic Differential Scales of Emotional State. A descriptive analysis and a multivariate linear regression were carried out to analyze the effect of people's interactions with greenery with regard to the habitability of the house as measured through their emotional states. It was found that the variables pleasure and activation were significant in relation to perception toward greenery, which implies that for the two scales and the two variables there is a direct relationship between green areas and psycho-emotional variables related to pleasure and activation.

Key words: green areas, housing, habitability

In undeveloped countries, asphalt predominates in cities. In some ways green areas are thought to be of no value for people. It is necessary to highlight the importance of greenery for human beings, because there is evidence that green areas and flowers in one's immediate internal and external environments provide daily pleasure and tranquillity. There is a significant amount of scientific support for this which will be detailed in the first part of this chapter. This research is important as in Mexico, there are no studies on this issue.

Mercado et al. (Landázuri & Mercado, 2004; Mercado, Ortega, Luna, & Estrada, 1994, 1995) stated that housing is a behavioural setting, in which the individual and the basic group (the family) find safety and shelter, are able to socialize, fulfil their basic physiological needs, and maintain their strength and health. There is empirical support for green areas in the interior and exterior of dwellings being a source of satisfaction and peace. The aim of our research was to explore the relationship between people's emotional reactions to residential environments and the effect of green areas and flowers in one's interior and immediate external environments on their perception of their dwellings. Specifically, we focus on the environment that is perceptible from the inside, regarding green areas: grass, shrubs, foliage, trees, and flowers, all of them natural should be possible to see outside vegetation through the windows and doors of the house.

Our contention is that inhabitants who enjoy their natural spaces more have a more positive emotional reaction to their home; the ways in which they are pleased about their natural ambience permit them to have more positive emotions about it. The results support the view that greenery within and surrounding a dwelling has a significant pleasant and a relaxing effect over inhabitants' perceptions of their homes.

Importance of Natural Areas

Wilson (1984) proposed the biophilia hypothesis (love of life) to point out that human beings are attached genetically to the landscape by the process of evolution, and now the preference for natural environments is coded in our genes. The research team in the ACES (Human-Environment Research Laboratory), under the leadership of Frances Kuo and Bill Sullivan (Prow, 2007), Atlanta, USA, is challenging the viewpoint that favours cities with little green spaces, accumulating data that show that trees are an integral part of quality of life and may alleviate some costly social ills.

In general, the findings sustain the notion that natural areas are an important part of our living condition. Green spaces and natural ambience not only give us aesthetic pleasure, they also have the function of stimulating positive effects on health. In addition to their natural beauty and potential as a food source, plants may provide restorative experiences that allow people to recover from day-to-day stress (Kaplan & Kaplan, 1987). There is ample anecdotal backup and a growing empirical literature regarding windows being favoured in diverse settings, including residential environments.

Views about nature play a substantial role in participants' satisfaction with their residential context. In the residential context, the role of the view from the window is reflected in economic indicators such as rent, price of housing, and even hotel rates. The view is also likely to be mentioned as an amenity in advertisements for both temporary and permanent housing.

Tennessen and Cimprich (1995) studied the possible restorative benefits of a natural view from college dormitory windows. Dormitory views ranged from all natural to all built. Controlling for the geographical location of the buildings, undergraduates with more nature in their dormitory view scored significantly higher on tests of directed attention than undergraduates with built views. Those with more natural views also tended to rate themselves as functioning more effectively in daily life activities and having more directed attention, than those with more buildings in their view.

Nature as a Restorative Experience

Both Kaplan and Kaplan (1989) and Ulrich (1986) hypothesize that restorative environments are settings that facilitate the reduction of stress. The empirical research also has shown that the restorative influence of environments manifests itself in human emotional, physiological, and cognitive responses (Ulrich et al., 1991).

The contact with certain types of nature creates what are called restorative responses. Settings that foster these responses are termed restorative environments. Restorative responses may include reduced physiological stress, reduced aggression, and a re-establishment of energy and health (Bell, Greene, Fisher, & Baum, 2001).

Restoration can proceed when four factors characterize the person-environment interaction (e.g., Kaplan & Kaplan, 1989):

- *Being away,* involves getting psychological and possibly geographical distance from one's usual context, including the work one ordinarily does and the pursuit of particular goals and purposes. For an environment to be restorative, one must feel a sensation of "being away" due to a change of scenery as well as an escape from some aspects of life that are ordinarily present, such as distractions, obligations, and pursuits of purposes and thoughts.
- *Fascination* or effortless attention. When functioning is supported by fascination, efforts at avoiding distractions can be easygoing and directed attention capacity can be restored. Fascination can be engaged by environmental features such as water or by the processes of exploring and making sense of an environment. Fascination is essential for restoration according to Kaplan and Kaplan (1989).
- *Extent* refers to the capability for immersion in a coherent physical or conceptual environment that is of sufficient scope to sustain exploration and interpretation. Here the two properties, connectedness and scope, are important. Scope refers to the environment that is extended in time and space, so that it is perceived to allow entering and spending time in it (Kaplan, 1983). The environment must also be sufficiently connected to constitute a part of a larger whole.
- *Compatibility* refers to a match between the environment, the individual's inclination, and the actions required by the environment (Kaplan, 1983). Compatibility is, for instance, fostered if there is a match between the individual's purposes for action and the demands imposed by the environment (Kaplan & Kaplan, 1989).

All of these findings form the basis of our scale. We propose a form of housing that incorporates such features as nature views and gardens in which family members can "restore" themselves.

The Transactional Perspective

In examining the interdependence of people and their surroundings, an understanding of the dynamics of behavioural responses is relevant. This is important for many recreational activities. It is, in fact, central for person-environment transactions in many domains of activity, not just leisure and recreation; people merely pass by many environments they experience in daily life. Deeper understanding of the human-environment transactions that occur along the way requires research into the dynamics of those transactions.

According to Little (1991), the main areas of the physical environment that have impact upon human personality are: the sense of meaning, environmental structure, and a sense of community. They are, in an important sense, the places that we inhabit (Cooper, 1971; Little, 1991). Developing a sense of belonging to our physical surrounds appears to be important. Conversely, when there is little opportunity to establish a bond with the environment or to develop a place meaning, abnormal development can occur (Little, 1991).

The study of habitability emerged from the need to improve the design of homes. It is now recognized that the quality of housing directly affects the quality of life (Ávalos, 2003; Monsalvo & Vital, 1998).

A house's internal habitability affects the quality of social processes in family life because it provides the requirements for the bonding of many kinds of links within the central nucleus that we call family.

Housing and Emotions

Numerous theorists state the need for a psychosocial perspective in psychological research because environmental psychology should be concerned not only with the physical environment, but with the emotional setting of human beings as well. There is strong evidence that features of a physical setting can affect the emotions and behaviour of people occupying that space (Finlay, Kanetkar, Londerville, & Marmurek, 2006).

We propose that it is fundamental to have green areas at home, which should be a restorative environment in which people avoid stress and are extracted from daily problems, and develop pleasant moods. We are interested in how the green areas affect these emotional responses and how now people react to green areas inside and outside of the home.

Emotional Dimensions and Housing's Habitability

Mehrabian and Russell (1974) proposed the theory that physical or social stimuli in the environment directly affect the emotional state of a person, thereby influencing his/her behaviour in it. These emotional reactions to situations may be defined in terms of three basic dimensions: pleasure, arousal, and dominance. They created a *Scale of Emotional State* that evaluates these variables. In a general approach to understanding man's interaction with various environments, it is essential to identify those responses that are the immediate result of stimulation and that occur in varying degrees in all environments. They point out that these emotional reactions can be used in different combinations to personalize any individual experience, time, and setting that is going to influence different behaviours related to the environments.

Dominance

Also called control, dominance is defined as an individual sensation with which it is possible to act freely and without restriction in such ways that it makes an individual to feel free and with a sensation of dominance over his own territory. The feeling of control has a cognitive nature in dominion that generates an emotional reaction; therefore, it is considered part of an evaluative-emotional system (Mercado et al., 1994).

This concept has been established empirically and articulated through research, in Rotter's (1966) "Attribution Theory" and Seligman's (1975, 1980) "Learned Helplessness Theory" which focuses on the behavioural effect that aversive circumstances have upon the perception of control and with the attempt to cope with them.

Another aspect of control is privacy; control also is lost when privacy is affected by views from the bedroom windows of houses at the bottom of gardens. Where there is sufficient space, the planting of even small growing trees can make a substantial impact by creating some screening without totally cutting off the view.

Pleasure

Different levels of emotion are associated with pleasure, this is a feeling state that can be assessed readily with self-report, such as semantic differential measures, or with behavioural indicators, such as smiles, laughter, and, in general, positive versus negative facial expressions (Mehrabian & Russell, 1974).

The ways in which inhabitants relate to their plants, gardens and flowers, and how they use housing green areas reflect pleasure because they can restore and block out the demands and stresses of daily work and urban living. Natural settings are pleasurable, they "restore" because they produce activation without mental effort. Not only are pleasant images aesthetically satisfying, they are also psychologically refreshing.

Cheeck, Field, and Burdge (1976) found in their study that home was clearly the space where most leisure time was spent, alone or with friends. Bechtel (1989) found the same thing, not only for residential, but for all environments. However, home designs are the least focused on recreation (Bechtel, 1997). In general terms, the relation between leisure and housing has a direct effect on an individual's satisfaction; this will depend on the general contribution of the physical environment as well as its specific characteristics (Mercado et al., 1995).

In this study we expect that pleasure would be linked to a number of variables related to restoration and the natural settings. Well-organized green areas as decoration would be judged satisfying, suggesting that settings that have more grass, flowers, and greenery are more pleasurable and indeed more preferred.

Arousal

Arousal acts as a modulating variable of a wide variety of kinds of behaviour; this has helped to explain the influence of the environment on behaviour, especially its activity level.

In the sense in which Mehrabian and Russell (1974) have used activation (along with pleasure and dominance) to describe any environment is that awakening induces us to search information about our internal state and thus we try to interpret the nature of activation and its raison d'être, that could be pleasure-displeasure. They propose that the emotional state that a person experiences in a setting is directly influenced by stimuli around the person, his emotional states, and the person's affective inclinations related to his personal individual traits.

Mehrabian and Russell focus on the variety of correlations between individual characteristics of physical stimuli in an environment (light, colour, sound, and temperature) and their two emotional dimensions of pleasure and activation. They, nonetheless, explain that the environments usually have stimuli available which activate a number of sensorial receptors simultaneously and in complex combinations and that the effects of the stimuli vary in time.

From the literature reviewed we can emphasize that it is consistent that there is a close relationship between greenery and positive emotions, the possibility of health preservation and recovery due to it, and the influence of greenery on restorative environments and over inhabitant's welfare and quality of life. The evidence points to a relationship between how people feel about greenery and the way they evaluate their house.

Finally, the findings in the literature, empirical as well as experimental research, point out that all the beneficial effects of greenery over emotions (which at the same time gives better quality of life) justify the investigation about greenery just inside housing. Our goal is to generate better quality spaces in housing for better living.

A. M. Landázuri et al.
Green Areas and Housing's Habitability

131

Method

Participants

A non-probabilistic intentional sample of 220 participants (100 from Mexico City and 120 from St. Andrews) ranging in age from 15 to 75 years took part in this study. Among the interviewed subjects there was an equivalent proportion of gender, social class, and marital status who lived in owned, rented, or borrowed houses or flats.

Instruments

A Likert scale of 59 questions was designed to measure the importance of green areas for the habitability of the inner and immediate external environments of dwellings, called "The Green Areas and Housing Scale." In the first phase, and according to the reviewed literature, we identified 70 open questions. Items were rewritten in a five-option Likert scale. The scale was validated by seven judges and reduced to 59 items. This scale was evaluated by a language expert. For its application in Mexico, it was translated in Spanish. The categorics evaluated by the questionnaire were: fascination, being away, place attachment, no place attachment, homocentric, participation, restorativeness, pleasure, dominance, activation, emotions, and general information. Items measuring demographic variables were included as well.

The questionnaire was administered to the sample participants, who after reading the instructions, had to select from five options in a Likert scale, choosing the response they believed described their feelings better about inside and in the immediate external environment they perceived from the inside of their homes. Both reliability and validity of the instrument were determined by Cronbach's alpha.

Mehrabian and Russell's (1974) Semantic Differential Scales of Emotional State, which measure pleasure, arousal, and dominance, were used to assess the emotional segment of housing's habitability. This complex variable has been shown to have substantial influence upon a family's quality of life and social relations (Ávalos, 2003; Monsalvo & Vital, 1998). The second phase was the administration of The Semantic Differential Measures of Emotional State Scale elaborated by Mehrabian and Rusell, which provided participants clear instructions.

We attempted to provide a clear and convincing explanation of the nature of this research to the interviewers to obtain the best collaboration.

Procedure

We approached the participants at their home. Stressing the importance of the research project, we asked the respondents to answer the scale. They were handed the questionnaire and interviewers waited for participants to fill it out. Any questions were answered. The same procedure was carried out both in St. Andrews and in Mexico City.

Results

A Multidimensional Scaling Analysis was completed using all items. Through multivariate multiple linear regression analysis, we assessed the effect of the response to green areas and housing (GAH) with regard to the three variables of emotional state.

Multidimensional Scaling Analysis

We performed the first Multidimensional Scaling Analysis with all the items and we discovered that we had only one homogeneous factor. The items that were not attached to the central configuration were eliminated. With that system we obtained a homogeneous configuration, which denotes that the GAH Scale is a single factor, helping to establish its construct validity.

For the second run, we used Kruskal's Monotonic Multidimensional Scaling Analysis of the correlations among items. Data were analysed as similarities, minimizing Kruskal's Stress (form 1) in two dimensions. The final configuration stress was 0.204 and the proportion of explained variance (RSQ) was 0.793.

In Table 1, the Multidimensional Scaling Analysis functioned as a factor analysis procedure, and we found very high internal consistency, obtaining a Spearman-Brown coefficient of 0.982, a Guttman (Rulon) coefficient of 0.981 and a Cronbach's alpha coefficient of 0.975.

As we can see in the configuration from Figure 1, there is considerable homogeneity. These are not separate groups, meaning that in fact we have just one factor. The items closer to the centroid have a larger factor load, thus we have very good reliability as shown by all the calculated indexes, meaning that our scale is very reliable.

Multiple Linear Regression Analysis

As can be seen from Tables 2–4, in the multivariate multiple linear regression analysis, we found significant results between the scale of "Green Areas and Housing" regressed to the "Semantic Differential Scales of Emotional State." In Table 2, the variables pleasure and arousal were specifically significant in relation to perception of greenery, which indicates that the relations between both scales and both variables is positive. Green areas and psychoemotional

Table 1. Internal consistency data of the GAH scale items

Spearman-Brown coefficient	0.982
Guttman (Rulon) coefficient	0.981
Cronbach's alpha coefficient	0.975

A. M. Landázuri et al.
Green Areas and Housing's Habitability

133

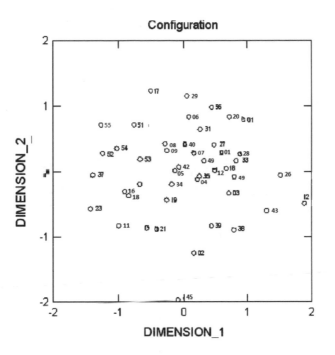

Figure 1. Multidimensional scaling graph of GAH Scale. The numbers correspond to items in the GAH (Green Areas and Housing) Scale.

Table 2. Dependent variable means

Pleasure	Arousal	Control
2.382	4.780	3.453

Table 3. Regression coefficients

Factor	Pleasure	Arousal	Control
Constant	3.529	3.760	2.834
GAH	0.325***	−0.289*	0.175

* = .05 and *** = .001

Table 4. Adjusted R^2

Pleasure	Arousal	Control
0.030	0.015	0.002

variables are related to pleasure and activation. We see in Table 3 that pleasure has a direct effect, implying that this variable increases slightly as people have a more positive perception of their green areas. With the arousal variable, the relationship is negative (Table 4).

Discussion and Conclusion

We found significant results on the scale of "Green Areas and Housing" and the "Semantic Differential Scales of Emotional State." The variable pleasure was highly significant in relation to perception of greenery. Pleasure has a direct effect, implying that pleasure increases slightly as people have a more positive perception of their green areas. With arousal, the relationship is negative, meaning that as people have a more positive perception of green areas, they feel more relaxed in the house.

In general terms, the relation between leisure and housing has a direct effect on the individual's satisfaction; this will depend on the general contribution of the physical environment as well as its specific characteristics (Mercado et al., 1995).

Since natural settings may tend to have lower levels of complexity and other arousal properties than urban environments (Wohlwill, 1966), arousal theory implies that nature should have comparatively restorative influences on stress. Mehrabian and Russell (1974) propose that the emotional state that a person experiences in a setting is directly influenced by stimuli around the person, his or her emotional states, and the person's affective inclinations related to his or her personal individual traits.

The house is a source of activation. In fact, houses should be a source of adequate internal activation. Stimuli come from sources such as natural and artificial lighting, colour, plants, and windows.

However, there were not significant results with the control variable (dominance).

Acknowledgments

We would like to express our sincere gratitude to the School of Psychology at the University of St. Andrews, Scotland for the opportunity for a sabbatical research stay. We also want to thank the General Direction of Faculty Affairs (DGAPA), UNAM, México City, which provided the grant that made it possible to carry out this research project.

References

Ávalos, L. (2003). ¿Interviene la habitabilidad de la vivienda en la calidad de vida familiar [Does housing habitability affect the quality of family life]? Tesis de Licenciatura en Psicología, Facultad de Psicología, Universidad Nacional Autónoma de México.

Bechtel, R. (1989). Behavior in the house: A cross-cultural comparison using behavior-setting methodology. In S. Low & E. Chambers (Eds.), *Housing, culture and design*. Philadelphia: University of Pennsylvania Press.

A. M. Landázuri et al.
Green Areas and Housing's Habitability

135

Bechtel, R. B. (1997). *Environment and behavior. An introduction*. London: Sage.

Bell, P. A., Greene, T. C., Fisher, J. D., & Baum, A. (2001). *Environmental psychology*. USA: Hartcourt College.

Cheeck, N., Field, D., & Burdge, R. (1976). *Leisure and recreation places*. Ann Arbor, MI: Ann Arbor Sciences.

Cooper, C. (1971). *The house as symbol of the self*. Berkeley: University of California, Institute of Urban and Regional Development.

Finlay, K., Kanetkar, V., Londerville, J., & Marmurek, H. C. (2006). The physical and psychological measurement of gambling environments. *Environment and Behavior, 38*, 570–581.

Kaplan, R., & Kaplan, S. (1987). The garden as a restorative experience. In M. Francis & R. T. Hester Jr. (Eds.), *Meanings of the garden*. Davis, CA: University of California.

Kaplan, R., & Kaplan, S. (1989). *The experience of nature: A psychological perspective*. New York: Cambridge University Press.

Kaplan, S. (1983). A model of person-environment compatibility. *Environment and Behavior, 15*(3), 311–332.

Landázuri, A. M., & Mercado, S. J. (2004). Algunos factores físicos y psicológicos relacionados con la habitabilidad interna de la vivienda [Some physical and psychological factors linked to housing's internal inhabitability]. *Medio Ambiente Y Comportamiento Humano, 5*(1–2).

Little, B. R. (1991). Personality and the environment. In D. Stokols & I. Altman (Eds.), *Handbook of environmental psychology*. Malabar, Florida: Krieger Publishing.

Mehrabian, A., & Russell, J. A. (1974). *An approach to environmental psychology*. Cambridge, MA: MIT Press.

Mercado, S., Ortega, P., Luna, G., & Estrada, C. (1994). *Factores psicológicos y ambientales de la habitabilidad de la vivienda* [Psychological and environmental factors of housing habitability]. México, DF: Facultad de Psicología, UNAM.

Mercado, S., Ortega, P., Luna, G., & Estrada, C. (1995). *Habitabilidad de la Vivienda Urbana* [Habitability of urban housing]. México, DF: Facultad de Psicología, UNAM.

Monsalvo, J., & Vital, A. T. (1998). *Habitabilidad de la vivienda y calidad de vida* [Housing habitability and quality of life]. Tesis de Licenciatura en Psicología, Facultad de Psicología, Universidad Nacional Autónoma de México, Mexico.

Prow, T. (2007). The Power of Trees. Trees Atlanta. *Protecting & improving our urban environment by planting & conserving trees*. Available from http://www.treesatlanta.org/health.html.

Rotter, J. B. (1966). Generalized expectancies for internal versus external control of reinforcement. *Psychological Monographs, 80*, 1.

Seligman, M. (1975). Behavioral and cognitive therapy for depression form a learned helplessness point of view. In L. P. Rehm (Ed.), *Behavior therapy for depression: Present status and future directions*. New York: Academic Press.

Seligman, M. (1980). *Human helplessness*. New York: Academic Press.

Tennessen, C. M., & Cimprich, B. (1995). Views to nature: Effects on attention. *Journal of Environmental Psychology*, 77–85.

Ulrich, R. S. (1986). Human responses to vegetation and landscapes. *Landscape and Urban Planning, 13*, 29–44.

Ulrich, R. S., Simons, R. F., Losito, B. D., Fiorito, E., Miles, M. A., & Zelson, M. (1991). Stress recovery during exposure to natural and urban environments. *Journal of Environmental Psychology, 11*, 201.

Wilson, E. (1984). *Biophilia*. Cambridge, MA: Harvard University Press.

Wohlwill, J. F. (1966). The physical environment: A problem for a psychology of stimulation. *Journal of Social Issues, 22*(4), 29–38.

Green Spaces, Vegetation, and Well-Being in the Housing Environment

Antônio Tarcísio da Luz Reis[1] and Alexandra Barcelos[2]

[1]School of Architecture/PROPUR, Federal University of Rio Grande do Sul, Brazil
[2]School of Engineering, Federal University of Rio Grande do Sul, Brazil

Abstract

This paper investigates the relationship between green spaces and vegetation and residents' well-being in housing environments for low-income people, characterized by distinct urban densities and dwelling types, as well as distance to city centre. Questionnaires were distributed among residents to reveal satisfaction levels regarding the housing estate, quality of views from the living-room, and use and appearance of open spaces. Structured interviews were used to understand better residents' attitudes regarding the importance of vegetation. Green spaces' attributes, such as area and number of trees, were registered through physical measurements. Among the main results is the importance of green spaces and vegetation for residents of social housing. Moreover, vegetation and green spaces are perceived as aesthetically pleasant, thereby improving the use of open spaces and the level of satisfaction with the housing environment as a whole and increasing residents' well-being and self-esteem.

Key words: green spaces, housing environment, resident well-being, vegetation

Green spaces and vegetation generally are understood as helpful in urban drainages, improving the quality of air and thermal comfort in urban spaces, and as contributing to create aesthetically pleasant urban environments. The Millennium Ecosystem Assessment (MA) report (2005) included in cultural services the "... nonmaterial benefits people obtain from ecosystems through spiritual enrichment, cognitive development, reflection, recreation, and aesthetic experiences ..." (p. 40) and emphasizes that in urban areas, green spaces and vegetation may provide a number of these services, but the diversity and complexity of processes demand innovative ways to manage and maintain these services.

Moreover, aesthetics has been an important aspect of satisfactory environments for users (Cooper Marcus & Sarkissian, 1986). The importance of aesthetics has also been reflected in legal judgements, being used as a criterion by American courts for determining the adequacy of physical interventions (Sanoff, 1991). The importance of aesthetic quality of views from buildings has been identified in studies in homes, offices, hospitals, and prisons (Kaplan, Kaplan, & Ryan, 1998). Aesthetically pleasant views have the tendency to be characterized, apart from large and organized visual fields with some variation, by the presence of natural elements (Lynch, 1960; Nasar, 1998). On the other hand, aesthetically unpleasant views tend to have the presence of parking, blind walls, buildings very close to each other, and monotonous facades (Lang, 1987; Nasar, 1992). Aesthetically pleasant views from the living-room and from the kitchen are important for residents of social housing (Cooper Marcus & Sarkissian, 1986). Views including vegetation tend to have positive effects on peoples' health and well-being. For example, views of nature in offices generate a better work environment promoting positive attitudes and behaviour of workers concerning their job activities and even regarding their own lives (Kaplan et al., 1998). Views of nature in hospitals reduce patients' recovery time (Ulrich, 1984). Green spaces and vegetation are among the environmental physical characteristics mentioned as important elements for the environments to be considered aesthetically satisfactory (Kaplan et al., 1998).

This information normally originated from Anglo-Saxon cultural and socioeconomic realities appears to be replicated in the Brazilian context according to a study carried out in housing estates characterized by four-storey blocks of flats in the metropolitan region of Porto Alegre (Reis, Ambrosini, & Lay, 2004). Nonetheless, it is necessary to investigate further how in urban areas, specifically in housing environments for low-income people, the existing green spaces and vegetation relate to the built environment and how they affect residents' well-being. It is essential to describe and analyse better the amount and location of green spaces and vegetation in the open spaces of housing estates. More research is also needed in Brazil, specifically, in social housing, regarding the importance and the elements characterizing pleasant and unpleasant views. Therefore, the purpose of this chapter is to investigate the relationship between green spaces and vegetation and residents' well-being in housing environments for low-income people, taking into consideration urban diversities, the biosphere, and people's well-being in the design of our common environment.

Method

The object of study is 12 housing estates for low-middle income people in the metropolitan area of Porto Alegre, characterized by semi-detached, detached, and row houses (Costa e Silva, Restinga, and Guajuviras), terraced houses (Vale Verde, João Vedana, São Jorge, and Santo Alfredo), and four-story blocks of flats (Loureiro, Angico, Cavalhada, Guajuviras, and Sapucaia). Data related to residents' attitudes and the existing vegetation were collected through 374 questionnaires and physical measurements conducted in the estates. Structured interviews were used to understand better residents' attitudes regarding the importance of vegetation. The data obtained through the questionnaires were analysed quantitatively using the statistical software SPSS/PC by means of non-parametric statistical tests like Kruskal-Wallis and Spearman rank correlation.

In the communal open spaces of four estates, constituted by four-story blocks of flats (Loureiro, Angico, Guajuviras, and Sapucaia), an analysis, using the GIS software IDRISI, of isovist areas, amount of green areas, trees, and open spaces was carried out. Moreover, in estates with blocks having different satisfaction levels in relation to the appearance of open spaces, namely Sapucaia and Loureiro/Angico, the degree of visualization of green spaces and vegetation (trees) was analysed through its integration levels in Depthmap. Higher integration levels mean that the vegetation is more visualized in the estate, and lower levels of integration (or higher levels of segregation) mean that the vegetation is less visualized. In two estates (São Jorge and Restinga) isovists were produced from the window of the living-room of each selected housing unit, using the Spatialist software. The boundary of housing estate area, the perimeter of buildings, the points representing the windows of living-rooms, as well as the isovists were imported in the ArcGIS software, where the physical attributes of each visual field (i.e., green spaces represented by polygons and trees represented by points) were included and the calculations of areas and distances were performed, making possible the identification of location of such attributes according to the following bands of visualization: band 1 (B1) – up to 12 m; band 2 (B2) – up to 24 m; band 3 (B3) – up to 140 m; and band 4 (B4) – beyond 140 m.

Results

Importance Attributed by Residents to the Existence of Vegetation

The analysis of the importance of having trees planted in the streets and open spaces in each estate indicates that this aspect is important to 96.3% of the total sample of residents in the 12 estates and to more than 90% of the residents in each one of the estates, with no statistically significant difference among them (Table 1). In the estates of Cavalhada, São Jorge, and João Vedana, some residents (1.3% of the general sample) did not find the existence of trees in the estate important. Therefore, the existence of trees has been confirmed as an important aspect, independently of the architectural type or the estate layout configuration where the resident lives. Correlations were not found between the importance attributed by the respondents to the existence of trees in the streets and open spaces of the housing estates and degree of satisfaction with the estates as well as with the places where they live. Hence, independent of the residents' attitudes in relation to their housing estates and places where they live, the existence of trees in the open spaces is an important aspect of the estate. Moreover, it was reinforced by several interviewees in the estates with blocks of flats and in those with houses that a good amount of trees is an essential element for a good appearance of the open spaces of the estates. These results confirm the

Table 1. Importance of the existence of trees in the estate according to the residents

Housing estates	Not important	Indifferent	Important	Mean rank values	Total
Loureiro da Silva – blocks of flats	0	0	45 (100%)	194.50	45
Guajuviras – blocks of flats	0	0	32 (100%)	194.50	32
Costa e Silva – detached and row houses	0	0	32 (100%)	194.50	32
Restinga – semi-detached houses	0	1 (2.8%)	35 (97.2%)	189.38	36
Guajuviras – detached houses	0	1 (3.1%)	31 (96.9%)	188.73	32
Angico – blocks of flats	0	1 (3.3%)	29 (96.7%)	188.35	30
Sapucaia – blocks of flats	0	1 (3.3%)	29 (96.7%)	188.35	30
Vale Verde – terraced houses	0	1 (3.3%)	29 (96.7%)	188.35	30
Santo Alfredo – terraced houses	0	1 (4.2%)	23 (95.8%)	186.81	24
Cavalhada – blocks of flats	2 (6.1%)	1 (3%)	30 (90.9%)	177.30	33
João Vedana – terraced houses	1 (3.3%)	2 (6.7%)	27 (90%)	175.82	30
São Jorge – terraced houses	2 (10%)	0	18 (90%)	175.35	20
Total	5 (1.3%)	9 (2.4%)	360 (96.3%)	374 (100%)	374 (100%)

Note. Mean rank values were obtained through Kruskal-Wallis non-parametric statistical test and indicate the mean of ordinal values attributed by the respondents of the questionnaires; the estates are ordered based on percentage of residents who consider the existence of trees in the estate more important to those who consider it less important.

importance of including vegetation, specifically trees, in the architectural design of social housing, at least, in the urban areas of the investigated housing estates.

Adequacy of the Amount of Vegetation

The inadequacy of the amount of vegetation is related, according to the residents interviewed in the 12 estates, to the non-existence or insufficient vegetation in the pedestrian circulation paths, mainly in the estates with blocks of flats. In the case of the estates with terraced houses, the presence of vegetation of medium and large size is obstructed by the reduced dimensions of the open spaces. The existence of a narrow sidewalks also creates difficulty or impedes the planting of vegetation, as in the estate Costa e Silva characterized by houses, or forces the occupation by the vegetation of a large part of the sidewalk, getting in the way of the pedestrian circulation. This occurs in parts of a some estates with blocks (Loureiro and Angico) where the pedestrian circulation path is narrowed due to its partial occupation by grass that forms a small garden for the trees. The lack of vegetation in the vehicles' circulation routes was mentioned by some residents interviewed in several estates, independently of the existent architectural type in the estate, but mainly in

Loureiro and in Angico. The nonexistent or insufficient vegetation in other open spaces also was reported, fundamentally, by the interviewees in the estates with blocks of flats.

Satisfaction Levels Regarding Quality of View From the Living-Room

The levels of satisfaction with the views from the windows of the living-rooms are significantly higher in the semi-detached houses in Restinga (11.1% – 4 of 36 – poor or very poor; 52.8% – 19 of 36 – good) than in terraced houses in São Jorge (70% – 14 of 20 – poor or very poor, 10% – 2 of 20 – good) (Reis et al., 2004). The importance of the aesthetic quality of view from the living-room to the general satisfaction with the housing unit in the two housing estates is supported by correlations found in houses in Restinga (Spearman, $c. = .3765$, $Sig. = .024$) as in terraced houses in São Jorge (Spearman, $c. = .4773$, $Sig. = .033$).

Satisfaction Levels Regarding the Use and the Appearance of Open Spaces

The degrees of satisfaction with the appearance of open spaces in the estates are significantly different among the residents of the 12 housing estates analysed (K-W, $\chi^2 = 67.6607$, $Sig. = .0000$). The most satisfied are the residents of Vale Verde, followed by those in Sapucaia, the only estates to have half or more than half of the respondents finding the open spaces beautiful or very beautiful. The most dissatisfied are the residents of São Jorge, followed by those in João Vedana, with a minimum of 65% finding the open spaces ugly or very ugly. The existence of vegetation was an aspect frequently related to the positive appearance of the open spaces for residents of all the estates. Explanations included the presence of the nature, the promotion of a more pleasant landscape, and the provision of a better environmental comfort due to the possibility of shade, as evidenced by the existent vegetation in Vale Verde, where the residents are the most satisfied with the appearance of the open spaces. However, in the residents' opinions, all the estates are in need of more vegetation in the communal open spaces and streets, mainly, in Angico and São Jorge, where the residents are among the most dissatisfied with the appearance of the open spaces. The lack of vegetation and/or the existence of inadequate vegetation are part of the explanations given for negative evaluations of appearance of open spaces in São Jorge (30% of respondents) and in João Vedana (46.7% of respondents), where levels of dissatisfaction with the appearance of the open spaces are the highest among all the estates.

Isovists in the Open Spaces of the Housing Estates, Existent Vegetation, and Areas of the Open Spaces

The identification and analysis through IDRISI of the isovists in the open spaces of four housing estates with blocks of flats, of the existence of vegetation in such spaces, of the relationship between these and the areas of the open spaces, and of the degrees of the residents' satisfaction with the appearance of the open spaces reveals that: the Sapucaia estate, the one with the largest percentage (35.16%) of green areas in relation to the area of the open spaces and with the largest percentage (33%) of green areas in relation to the area of the isovists (visualized area on the way to the access of blocks of flats), is where the residents are the most satisfied with the appearance of the open spaces among the four estates with blocks. Additionally, Sapucaia is the estate that presents the highest density of trees in the open spaces (0.0147 trees/m^2), the highest density (0.0152 trees/m^2), and percentage of trees (93.71%) in the isovists. Therefore, these results suggest that as much the amount of green areas as the amount of existent trees in the open spaces, visualized from the main pedestrian circulation paths, tends to promote a positive aesthetic sense on the part of the users in relation to the appearance of the open spaces.

Integration Levels of Position of Trees and Polygons Defining Green Areas in the Visual Fields in the Open Spaces

The analysis of integration levels of position of polygons defining green areas and of position of points representing existing trees, in Sapucaia and Loureiro/Angico estates (Figure 1), where the residents are, respectively, more and less satisfied with the

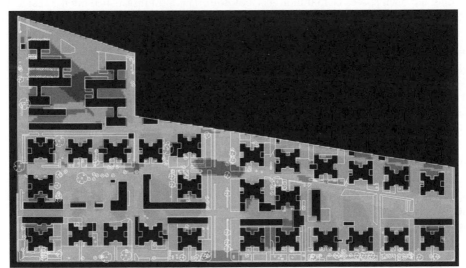

Note: the surfaces in black colour inside of the limits of the estates represent the built areas (buildings, garages, additions); the lines in white colour represents the limits of the built areas (around the black areas), the green areas (polygons) and trees; different shades of grey indicate more to less integrated visual fields, according to analysis carried out in Depthmap.

Figure 1. Integration levels of the isovists in Loureiro/Angico housing estates.

appearance of the open spaces, reveals that: Although the integration levels of the points representing 10% of the trees with the most integrated positions in the isovists are higher in Sapucaia 1 than in Loureiro/Angico, in Sapucaia 2 they are lower than in Loureiro/Angico; Sapucaia 1 presents a larger number of trees than Loureiro and Angico, all of them in much more integrated positions than in these last ones; with regard to integration levels of the points representing 10% of the trees with more segregated positions (or less integrated) in the isovists, these are quite similar in Loureiro/Angico and in Sapucaia 1, being more segregated in Sapucaia 2; similar situation to that of trees with more integrated positions happens with the polygons representing 10% of the most integrated green areas, the polygons of Sapucaia 1 being more integrated than the ones of Loureiro/Angico, and the polygons of Sapucaia 2 being less integrated; with regard to polygons representing 10% of the most segregated (or least integrated) green areas, although the values are similar, the polygons in Sapucaia 2 are the most segregated, followed by those in Sapucaia 1 and in Loureiro/Angico.

Hence, this initial analysis of integration values of positions of trees, bushes, and grassy areas in Loureiro, Angico, and Sapucaia estates reveals that expressive part of the vegetation is in more integrated positions (and so is more visualized) in Sapucaia (specifically, in Sapucaia 1) than in the other two estates. This helps to explain why residents of Sapucaia are much more satisfied with the appearance of the open spaces than the residents of Loureiro/Angico.

Number and Distance of Vegetation in the Visual Fields From the Housing Units

Residents satisfied with the view from the living-room tend to visualize areas with vegetation and trees in B4 (beyond visual range of 140 m) while the dissatisfied residents do not visualize such views, revealing the positive impact of more distant views with natural elements. Both in São Jorge and in Restinga, the average quantities of vegetation (in m^2) in three bands (B1, B2, and B3) are clearly superior for the residents satisfied with the view from the living-room than for those dissatisfied. Moreover, while in São Jorge, the number of trees is similar in the three bands for the residents satisfied and those dissatisfied with the view from the living-room, in Restinga the number of trees in the B3 and B4 is significantly higher for the residents satisfied than for those dissatisfied with the view from the living-room. From the window of the living-room of the houses in Restinga it is possible to visualize greater areas with vegetation and with far greater number of trees, especially after 24 m of views span (B3 and B4).

With regard to the distances of trees to the living-room of each housing unit, they tend to be higher for the satisfied residents of São Jorge and Restinga than for those dissatisfied with the view from the living-room, suggesting that the presence of more distant trees tends to produce a more positive effect than the presence of more nearby trees that can become an obstacle to broader and distant vistas. This is evidenced by the fact that the average minimum distances in São Jorge are much smaller for dissatisfied (5.53 m) than for those satisfied (8.24 m) with the view from the living-room. The minimum and average distances of visualized trees are much larger in Restinga than in São Jorge. The existence of views with blind walls is expressive in bands 1–3 in São Jorge, where residents tend to be dissatisfied, and absent in Restinga, where the residents tend to be satisfied with the views. Regarding views with the presence of walls with openings, with one exception, residents satisfied with the view do not visualize walls with openings within a distance of 12 m (B1), while many dissatisfied residents visualize such walls. The presence of walls with openings in more distant bands (B2–B4) does not seem to affect the quality of views. Supporting these results, the reasons given by the residents in terraced houses in São Jorge to justify their dissatisfaction tend to be related to the view from the living-room that has been characterized by buildings (60%) and to views blocked by walls without opening or backs of garages (40%).

Discussion and Conclusion

Independently of the architectural type and estate configuration where the resident inhabits, and regardless of the residents' attitudes in relation to their housing estates and places where they live, the importance of green spaces and vegetation for residents of social housing was revealed. Apart from its perceived positive impact on thermal comfort of open spaces, vegetation and green spaces are perceived as aesthetically pleasant, thereby improving the use of open spaces and the level of satisfaction with the housing environment as a whole, and increasing residents' well-being and self-esteem. On the other hand, the lack of vegetation and/or the existence of inadequate vegetation were related to a negative appearance of the open spaces of the estates. These results seem to be even more important for the design of open spaces of estates with blocks of flats. Additionally, the results suggest that as much as the amount of green areas, the amount of trees and existent bushes in the open spaces visualized from the main pedestrian circulation paths and in the most integrated positions, tends to promote a positive aesthetic response on the part of the users in relation to the appearance of the open spaces. The positive impact of visualization of vegetation, as well as the negative impact of nearby visual barriers, confirms the results for the views from ground-floor flats in the metropolitan region of Porto Alegre (Reis et al., 2004), and supports the results found in the international literature with regard to the positive impact promoted by vegetation and broad vistas (Kaplan et al., 1998; Nasar, 1998). Considering the importance for low-income residents of the aesthetic quality of view from the living-room to the general satisfaction with the housing unit, these results indicate how to include pleasant views from the living-rooms in the design of social housing (Table 2).

Hence, this study allowed a better understanding of the aesthetic impact of views from different types of housing units (semi-detached and terraced houses) on residents' satisfaction, contributing to the characterization of more and less attractive views and to more aesthetically pleasing, and thus more qualified, housing design. Moreover, the use of methods

Table 2. Positive and negative aspects according to the depth of visual fields

Positive aspects			Negative aspects		
Visual field longer than 140 m					
Vegetation	Trees	Larger and longer visual fields			
Visual field longer than 24 m					
Greater areas with vegetation	Greater number of trees	Larger and longer visual fields			
Visual field not longer than 24 m					
Vegetation	Trees		Blind walls		
Visual field not longer than 12 m					
Vegetation	Trees		Blind walls	Walls with openings	Shallow and reduced visual fields
Visual field not longer than 8 m					
Vegetation			Blind walls	Walls with openings	Shallow and reduced visual fields and trees

which incorporate GIS, Spatialist, and Depthmap software, that help to describe and analyse visual fields and vegetation attributes and their relationships to the open spaces and buildings, has shown to be relevant. Therefore, results confirm that vegetation has an important role in planning for health promotion and well-being in urban areas, specifically, in residential environments for those less well-off in society, in southern Brazil. Further research may include the exploration of the impact of different vegetation types and attributes in urban areas, according to distinct cultures and climates.

Acknowledgments

This investigation was undertaken with financial support from CNPq (National Council of Scientific and Technological Development), a Brazilian governmental institution sponsor of Scientific and Technological Development, and from CEF (Federal Economical Bank).

References

Cooper Marcus, C., & Sarkissian, W. (1986). *Housing as if people mattered*. Berkeley: University of Califórnia Press.

Kaplan, R., Kaplan, S., & Ryan, R. (1998). *With people in mind: Design and management of everyday nature*. Washington, DC: Island Press.

Lang, J. (1987). *Creating architectural theory: The role of the behavioural sciences in environmental design*. New York: Van Nostrand Reinhold.

Lynch, K. (1960). *The image of the city*. Cambridge, MA: MIT Press.

Millennium Ecosystem Assessment. (2005). *Ecosystems and human well-being: Synthesis*. Washington, DC: Island Press.

Nasar J. (Ed.). (1992). *Environmental aesthetics: Theory, research, and applications*. Cambridge: Cambridge University Press.

Nasar, J. (1998). *The evaluative image of the city*. Thousand Oaks, CA: Sage.

Reis, A., Ambrosini, V., & Lay, M. C. (2004). Qualidade de campos visuais, SIG e percepção dos residentes de habitação de interesse social [Quality of visual fields, GIS and social housing residents' perception]. *Revista Ambiente Construído, 4*, 67–77.

Sanoff, H. (1991). *Visual research methods in design*. New York: Van Nostrand Reinhold.

Ulrich, R. (1984). View through a window may influence recovery from surgery. *Science, 224*, 420–421.

Soundscapes Within Urban Parks

Their Restorative Value

Sarah R. Payne

International Digital Laboratory, WMG, The University of Warwick, UK

Abstract

Restorative environments are important to help alleviate attentional fatigue and stress as well as to improve people's general well-being. Urban parks visually include the natural elements that can support restoration, yet the sounds heard within urban parks can vary from birds singing to background traffic. The effect of the juxtaposition of these natural and urban sounds on individuals' restorative experiences is unknown. Through a series of studies, the role of urban park soundscapes in psychological restoration was explored. Firstly, an examination of the conceptualisation of urban park sounds identified variations between people who perceived high and low levels of restoration from visiting an urban park. Secondly, a perceived restorativeness soundscape scale was developed to assess people's perception of a soundscape as having the potential to be restorative. The scale differentiated between the perceived restorativeness of an urban, an urban park, and a rural soundscape. Thirdly, an *in situ* study examined the relationship between perceived urban park soundscapes and the park visitors' perceived restoration, while accounting for other factors. A summary of these studies and their implications for planning urban environments is presented.

Key words: attention restoration, soundscapes, urban parks

Nature and green spaces in urban environments are important components in helping to provide a healthy, sustainable human population. Research has shown that views of natural elements, in contrast to urban elements, provide positive benefits in terms of people's physical health (Ulrich, 1984), ability to cope with poverty (Kuo, 2001), cognition (Tennessen & Cimprich, 1995), and well-being (Kaplan, 2001). In general, natural environments are more restorative than urban environments (Hartig, Mang, & Evans, 1991), providing recovery from attentional fatigue, as well as enabling reflection (Herzog, Black, Fountaine, & Knotts, 1997; Kaplan & Kaplan, 1989). Access to natural, restorative environments is therefore important to help reduce urban dwellers' stress and alleviate cognitive fatigue (Grahn & Stigsdotter, 2003).

Attention Restoration Theory (ART; Kaplan & Kaplan, 1989; Kaplan, 1995) lists four components that are important in producing restorative environments: Fascination (use of involuntary, effortless attention), Being-Away (a physical or cognitive relocation of one's self from everyday activities), Compatibility (a match between the individual's desired activity/behaviour and the environment), and Extent (the scope and connectedness of the environment). In general, natural environments are considered as having higher levels of each of the four ART components than urban environments (Hartig, Korpela, Evans, & Garling, 1997; Kaplan, 1995). Urban parks contain many natural elements, which imply they are also likely to have higher levels of ART components than the built urban environment. Urban parks therefore provide the opportunity of a restorative environment for people living and working in cities. However, it is not just the type of environment that is important, but it is also what the person does in a place, the time they have available (Scopelliti & Giuliani, 2004), and who they are with (Staats & Hartig, 2004), as these elements affect the perception of a place as restorative. Therefore, a restorative environment is one that facilitates a restorative experience.

People's experiences of environments are not just visually based but are multi-sensorial, and as such, the sonic environment could be important in providing a restorative experience. Urban parks may provide a visual respite from the built environment, yet the soundscape (sonic environment) may contain a mix of both natural and "urban" sounds. In addition, within a large urban park, a number of diverse soundscapes can be identified, of which some may contain more natural elements than others (Ge & Hokao, 2004). Currently though, the restorative impact of soundscapes, in particular those that contain a mixture of natural and urban elements, is unknown.

There is a growing body of research considering soundscapes and the cultural and individual meaning associated with perceived environmental sounds. Similar to visual elements, this has identified a general preference for natural sounds over mechanical sounds (see review by Kang, 2007). Physical and cognitive health issues derived from living with a poor (noisy) soundscape are also well documented (World Health Organization, 2000). These include hypertension and reduced cognitive performance, which are the same types of problems that visits to restorative environments can help alleviate (Hartig et al., 1991). Yet attention restoration and soundscape research has barely been combined, although support for this research direction is growing. ART was suggested as a potential method of interpreting and understanding results about the positive benefits of nearby green areas and perceptions of residential noise, such as reduced long-term noise annoyance (Gidlöf-Gunnarsson & Öhrström, 2007). Additionally, similar terms as the four ART components were used by blind people when describing natural environments (Shaw, Ungar, & Gatersleben, 2005), which they experience partly through its soundscapes, thereby implicating soundscapes' restorative potential. The process by which restorative soundscapes could be implemented into urban designs has also been suggested (Graham, 2004).

This research therefore aimed to extend the theoretical and practical research into restorative environments and green spaces by focusing on the potential role of soundscapes in providing a restorative experience. The combination of natural and urban sounds, along with the importance of enabling restorative experiences for urban dwellers and workers, made urban parks the ideal contextual focus for this research. Specifically, the research aimed to understand the categorisation and description of urban park sounds; develop a reliable measure that differentiates between soundscapes' perceived restorativeness levels; and start establishing the contribution of soundscapes in providing a restorative experience. An overview of the series of sequential studies conducted for the research is presented.

Study 1: Categorisation and Semantics of Urban Park Sounds

In order to understand the restorative value of urban park soundscapes, it was first considered necessary to discover what sounds people perceive within urban parks, as well as how people describe and categorise these sounds. This first study therefore aimed to understand people's categorisation and semantics of urban park sounds.

Method

Data from a prior urban park study identified sounds people heard in 15 green spaces in Sheffield, UK (part published in Irvine et al., 2009). From this, 31 representative urban park sounds were ascertained. These were written on cards and presented to 38 laypeople (55% male) within Sheffield, UK for a multiple card sort. Participants imagined being in a familiar urban park, before sorting the cards in any way they chose. For each group of sounds the participant identified, they were asked to provide a category label and an affective label. The results were interpreted using content analysis and multi-dimensional scaling (NewMDSX). Participants were also asked to rate how much they agreed with four statements measuring their general perceived restoration after having spent some time in their familiar urban park (using adapted items from Staats, Kievet, & Hartig, 2003; Hartig et al., 1998; and Herzog et al., 1997). For further detail, see Payne, Devine-Wright, and Irvine (2007).

Results

Sounds heard in the parks were described in terms of their sources rather than as onomatopoeias or physical characteristics. The most frequently provided label for each sound was

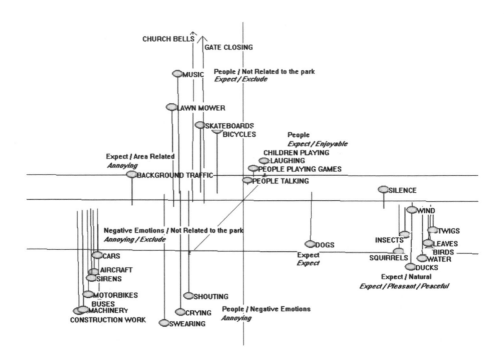

Figure 1. Participants' categorisation of urban park sounds represented in a three-dimensional plot. Category labels are in upper and lowercase, above the Affective Overall Impression labels are in italics.

identified. These labels were then used to define the collective clusters of sounds which were produced by combining all the participants' results (Figure 1). The groups of sounds had category labels that involved affective terms (e.g., negative emotions) as well as cognitive terms (e.g., people). The distance between the sounds and clusters of sounds is considered a representation of the conceptual distance between them; the closer the sounds the more similar they are considered to be. Expectation played a role in differentiating between the groups of sounds, as did affect, with a clear negative to positive progression across the sound clusters. Participants affectively rated natural sounds highly compared to construction work and cars.

Separate analyses of the card sort results created by participants with the lowest perceived levels of attention restoration ($n = 13$) and the highest perceived levels of attention restoration ($n = 10$) after visiting urban parks were conducted. This illustrated that the two different groups of participants conceptualised urban park sounds differently (Figure 2). Participants with low levels of perceived attention restoration showed little differentiation between the sounds, while those with high levels considered natural sounds as a very distinct group of sounds.

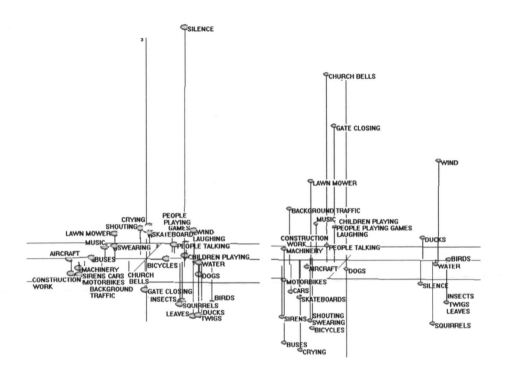

Figure 2. The categorisation of urban park sounds by participants with the lowest (left image) and highest (right image) perceived levels of attention restoration, after visiting urban parks.

In total, eight urban park sound types were identified. These were loosely based on the results of the cluster solution (Figure 1); the category and affective terms used to define the clusters; and the need for the categorisation system to be transferable to, and understood by, other people. The categories were: Natural, Dogs, Happy People, Sad and Angry People, Object sounds from People in the park, Sounds from the surrounding Buildings, Individual Vehicles and Aircraft, and Background City sounds.

Study 2: A Perceived Restorativeness Soundscape Scale

To ascertain if urban park soundscapes vary in their perceived restorativeness levels, a measure needed to be developed and tested. As soundscapes are likely to be involved in the assessment of environments, it was assumed that perceived restorativeness levels of natural and urban soundscapes would vary in a similar manner as they do for natural and urban environments in general. Therefore, the developed measure would be partially validated by comparing soundscapes from urban and rural environments, before using it to assess different urban park soundscapes.

Method

Scales assessing the perceived restorativeness of environments in general, via the four ART components (Hartig, 2007; Laumann, Gärling, & Stormark, 2001), were adapted to become sound specific, to develop a 19-item Perceived Restorativeness Soundscape Scale (PRSS). For example, "my attention is drawn to many interesting things here" (Hartig, 2007) was adapted to become "my attention is drawn to many of the interesting sounds here."

Continuous 2.5-minute clips were made using a handheld video camera and microphone in an urban environment (Sheffield city centre, UK), an urban park (in Sheffield, UK), and a rural environment (stream and forest in the Peak District, UK). These were presented to three groups of University of Manchester undergraduate students in lecture theatres ($n = 123$, 48% male) in a variety of orders. Their perceived affective and behavioural fatigue levels were first evaluated (using items by Hartig & Staats, 2006). Participants watched and listened to a clip, and then answered the 19 PRSS items while the audio segment was replayed. The familiarity and typicality of each environment was rated. The perceived spatial sound quality was also assessed to control for the lack of professional recordings and playback facilities. This process was repeated for each audio-visual clip.

Results

The attentional fatigue, familiarity, typicality, and spatial sound quality results from the three groups of participants were similar, thus the three groups' results were combined. Preliminary principal axis analyses determined the success of the individual items in the PRSS, which led to the removal of five items. Another principal axis analysis was then conducted on the remaining 14 PRSS items, with a forced two-factor solution (as determined by principal component analysis). This resulted in the final factor structure and factor scores.

The first factor contained items relating to the ART components of Fascination, Being-Away-From, Compatibility, and Scope (Extent). The second factor contained the items for Being-Away-To and Coherence (Extent). The two factors both produced a reliable scale for the urban park and rural audio-visual clip ($\alpha > .7$ or $.2 < \bar{X}r < .4$), but only the first factor was reliable for the urban audio-visual clip. There were significant differences ($p < .001$) between the PRSS median scores for each audio-visual clip for Factor 1 and for Factor 2; the urban soundscape was perceived as less restorative than the urban park soundscape which was in turn perceived as less restorative than the rural soundscape.

Overall, similar results to Perccived Restorativeness Scales for environments in general were found, thus partially validating the newly developed PRSS.

Study 3: Restorative Soundscapes in Urban Parks

This final study aimed to examine the restorativeness of potentially diverse soundscapes within urban parks and to establish their role in providing a restorative experience within urban parks. It uses the results of Studies 1 and 2 to determine perceived soundscapes within urban parks and their perceived restorativeness levels. This information, along with the combination of other factors that can influence an individual's experience within an urban park, is assessed to start to understand the restorative value of urban park soundscapes.

Method

People leaving two medium-sized urban parks (around 5 and 7 Ha) in Sheffield, during the summer of 2007, were asked to participate by completing an on-the-spot questionnaire ($n = 395$, 50/50 gender split). The questionnaire involved the free recall of sounds heard in the park and open-ended questions, including what activities they had carried out, how long they had been there, and with whom they had been there with, if anyone. Participants' perceived restoration was assessed with semantic differential scales (using items adapted from Staats et al., 2003). The urban park sound types, as defined by Study 1, aided the identification of the perceived soundscape by participants rating what proportion of their park visit they had heard each of the eight sound types (0–100% of the time) and its general volume (quiet to loud, 7-point scale). Half the participants responded to the PRSS developed in Study 2, while the other half rated how fatigued they had been before they entered the park (using adapted items from Hartig & Staats, 2006). Open-ended questions were coded by two raters and factor/component analyses produced reliable scales to measure perceived restoration and further develop the PRSS.

Results

Participants freely listed sounds similar to those that formed the database for Study 1. These were coded into the newly defined eight categories. Similar affective ratings were ascertained with Natural sounds rated as more pleasant than sounds from the Background City. The majority of the participants perceived Natural, Happy People, and Background City sounds. Over a third of the participants perceived Objects in the Park and Individual Traffic/Aircraft sounds. The perceived volume of a sound type (excluding Sad and Angry People) related to its perceived duration ($.39 < r < .65$, $p < .01$); the louder the sound, the longer it was perceived. The combination of these variables (percentage of time the sound type was heard for multiplied by its perceived volume) indicated that Natural and Happy People sounds were the predominant sound types in the two parks.

Five different types of soundscapes were identified using cluster analysis on the varying predominance levels of each of the sound types. This identified that some urban park soundscapes were specific to one type of park, while others could be heard in either park. A chi-square analysis found a significant relationship ($\chi^2 = 38.77, p < .000$) with a medium effect size (Cramer's $V = .32$) between the type of soundscape heard and the perceived restorativeness of the soundscape, as rated by the PRSS factor scores. In particular, the participants who perceived the soundscape type consisting of strong Natural sounds with Happy People and Object sounds were more likely to rate the soundscape as high in perceived restorativeness, than to be expected by chance. In contrast, participants who heard the soundscape type consisting of strong Building/Construction sounds with Background City/Traffic, as well as Natural and Happy people sounds, were more likely to rate the soundscape as low in perceived restorativeness, than to be expected by chance.

On average, participants leaving the park were slightly recovered and had been able to reflect slightly. Initial analyses suggest that only a small amount of the perceived restoration variance (10–15%) is explained by the significant contextual, personal, and experiential variables, as they had very small effect sizes. This is thought to be due to the large interaction between all the variables, which cannot be controlled, given the type of study (in situ) and sample size (for more detail, see Payne, 2008). Importantly, one significant contributor to the restorative experience was related to the sonic environment – the participant's awareness of the soundscape. The more aware the participants were of the soundscape, the more restored they felt. Those more aware were also more likely to recall hearing a Natural sound and less likely to recall hearing Background City sounds than to be expected by chance ($\chi^2 = 27.27, p < .05$). These relationships suggest there are links between having a restorative experience within urban parks and being aware of its soundscape, in particular its natural components.

Discussion

Associations between restorative experiences and soundscapes have been identified throughout these studies. First, sounds were identified, described, categorised, and assessed in urban parks, before relating soundscapes directly with attention restoration, via a developed scale and the experiences people have within urban parks. The collective studies suggest that soundscapes play a role in generating restorative experiences within urban parks. Therefore, soundscapes are an important aspect to consider when reflecting upon and intending to improve urban workers' and dwellers' well-being.

In line with prior research, sounds were described by their sources, not their physical characteristics (Dubois, 2000) and natural sounds were rated positively while traffic sounds were rated negatively (Kang, 2007). Finer levels of sound categorisation were identified, resulting in eight sound types, rather than three broader categories (e.g., Natural, Human, and Mechanical), that are often used by researchers (e.g., Rozec, 2003). This included the separation of human sounds into enjoyable (Happy People) and annoying (Sad and Angry People) sounds. Affective terms and expectation were frequently used in laypeople's sound categorisations, highlighting the meaningful nature of sounds, rather than "objective" assessments involving sound level measurements. Natural sounds in particular were considered as a distinctly separate sound category by those who had higher levels of perceived restoration after visiting urban parks compared to those with lower levels. This suggests that natural sounds in urban parks may be important for those who have restorative experiences, as they might be a contributory factor to restoration. These subjective aspects should be considered when trying to maintain "environmental noise quality where it is good," as part of European directives on environmental noise (European Parliament and Council, 2002), instead of a reliance on noise maps, that are based solely on sound pressure levels.

The development of a PRSS was partly validated and deemed successful. Although there was no clear factor separation of the four ART components in the developed PRSS, the scales developed for assessing environments in general also had similar problems at the outset (Hartig et al., 1997). The scale was able to differentiate between soundscapes heard in urban, urban park, and rural environments in the same manner that Perceived Restorativeness Scales do for environments in general (Hartig et al., 1997; Laumann et al., 2001); the more natural the environment, the more its soundscape was perceived as restorative. This result coincides with the distinct separation in the categorisation of natural sounds by people who perceive visiting urban parks as restorative (Study 1). Therefore, just like the visual scenery of natural environments (Hartig et al., 1991), natural sounds may be just as important in producing a restorative experience.

The PRSS was also able to differentiate between soundscapes within the same type of place (in this case, urban parks), thus identifying the diversity of soundscapes that are perceived within green spaces (Study 3). The quality of these diverse soundscapes in terms of perceived restoration both within and across different parks was also assessed with the PRSS. Further analysis on the relationship between PRSS scores and the predominance level of individual sound types may help identify the role of certain sound types in providing a restorative experience. The presence or absence of these sound types or the interaction between different sound types would therefore contribute to the perception of a soundscape as restorative. Such findings would be useful in the design and development of restorative environments, so that certain features could be enhanced and others removed or masked. Maintaining diverse positive soundscapes is also likely to be important for the enjoyment of different spaces by different people, rather than the production of similar soundscapes within every similar place type.

The studied urban parks were generally perceived as predominating in Natural and Happy People sounds. The expectation of hearing these sounds though within urban parks may have played a role in their recall, considering expectation was an important aspect in the conceptualisation of sounds. Similarly, the contributory role of soundscape awareness in restorative experiences (Study 3) again reflects the distinct conceptualisation of natural sounds, from all other sounds, by those who state they have a good restorative experience in urban parks (Study 1). Those who have restorative experiences appear to have been more aware of natural sounds, although they may be more inclined to recall perceiving natural sounds, due to the importance given to them. Either way, the ability to hear natural sounds may be just as important as views of natural elements, in the provision of a restorative environment that facilitates a restorative experience. Therefore, when planning and designing urban parks and other urban green spaces, their soundscapes need to be carefully considered. In addition, the layout and management of the surrounding buildings should also be regarded, as they can impact upon and influence urban green spaces' soundscapes and their restorative qualities.

Conclusions

These studies have highlighted the ability to integrate attention restoration and soundscape research. Associations between these two areas suggest that soundscapes may be an important aspect of an individual having a restorative experience. Although limitations exist with each of the studies (experimental control, acoustic facilities, and complexity from numerous variables), the array of methods has helped build support for the important associations between soundscapes and attention restoration. With growing concerns about the acoustic environment and its effect upon human beings, the consideration and future management of soundscapes are likely to become an important aspect in enabling well-being and successful sustainable communities. Urban green spaces and parks, in particular, can therefore help contribute to the development of necessary restorative places, by providing both visual and acoustic restorative experiences.

Acknowledgments

The author would like to thank the EPSRC, University of Manchester, UK, and De Montfort University, UK for the funding provided for this doctoral research, as well as Professor P. Devine-Wright.

References

Dubois, D. (2000). Categories as acts of meaning: The case of categories in olfaction and audition. *Cognitive Science Quarterly, 1*(1), 33–66.
European Parliament and Council. (2002). Directive 2002/49/EC of the European Parliament and of the Council of 25th June 2002, relating to the assessment and management of environmental noise. *Official Journal of the European Communities, L189*, 12–25.

Ge, J., & Hokao, K. (2004). Research on the sound environment of urban open space from the viewpoint of soundscape – A case study of Saga Forest Park, Japan. *Acta Acustica United With Acustica, 90*, 555–563.

Gidlöf-Gunnarsson, A., & Öhrström, E. (2007). Noise and well-being in urban residential environments: The potential role of perceived availability to nearby green areas. *Landscape and Urban Planning, 83*(2–3), 115–126.

Graham, C. S. R. (2004). *Designing landscapes for psychological restoration: Adding considerations of sound*. Canada: Master of Landscape Architecture Thesis for the University of Guelph.

Grahn, P., & Stigsdotter, U. A. (2003). Landscape planning and stress. *Urban Forestry and Greening, 2*(1), 1–18.

Hartig, T. (2007). *Personal communication An extension of:*

Hartig, T., Korpela, K., Evans, G. W., & Gärling, T. (1997). A measure of restorative quality in environments. *Scandinavian Housing and Planning Research, 14*, 175–194.

Hartig, T., Kaiser, F. G., & Bowler, P. A. (1997). *Further development of a measure of perceived environmental restorativeness (Working Paper #5)*. Gävle, Sweden: Institute for Housing Research, Uppsala University.

Hartig, T., Korpela, K., Evans, G. W., & Gärling, T. (1997). A measure of restorative quality in environments. *Scandinavian Housing and Planning Research, 14*, 175–194.

Hartig, T., Lindblom, K., & Ovefelt, K. (1998). The home and near-home area offer restoration opportunities differentiated by gender. *Scandinavian Housing and Planning Research, 15*, 283–296.

Hartig, T., Mang, M., & Evans, G. W. (1991). Restorative effects of natural environment experiences. *Environment and Behavior, 23*(1), 3–26.

Hartig, T., & Staats, H. (2006). The need for psychological restoration as a determinant of environmental preferences. *Journal of Environmental Psychology, 26*(3), 215–226.

Herzog, T. R., Black, A. M., Fountaine, K. A., & Knotts, D. J. (1997). Reflection and attentional recovery as distinctive benefits of restorative environments. *Journal of Environmental Psychology, 17*, 165–170.

Irvine, K. N., Devine-Wright, P., Payne, S. R., Fuller, R. A., Krausse, B., & Gaston, K. J. (2009). Green space, soundscape and urban sustainability: An interdisciplinary, empirical study. *Local Environment, 14*(2), 155–172.

Kang, J. (2007). *Urban sound environment*. London: Taylor & Francis.

Kaplan, R. (2001). The nature of the view from home. Psychological benefits. *Environment and Behavior, 33*(4), 507–542.

Kaplan, R., & Kaplan, S. (1989). *The experience of nature: Towards an integrative framework*. New York: Cambridge University Press.

Kaplan, S. (1995). The restorative benefits of nature: Toward an integrative framework. *Journal of Environmental Psychology, 15*(3), 169–182.

Kuo, F. E. (2001). Coping with poverty. Impacts of environment and attention in the inner city. *Environment and Behavior, 33*(1), 5–34.

Laumann, K., Garling, T., & Stormark, K. M. (2001). Rating scale measures of restorative components of environments. *Journal of Environmental Psychology, 21*(1), 31–44.

NewMDSX series of multidimensional scaling programs (2008, June). http://www.newmdsx.com (last accessed October 2, 2010).

Payne, S. R. (2008, June). *Are perceived soundscapes within urban parks restorative?* Paper presented at Acoustics' 08 in Paris, France.

Payne, S. R., Devine-Wright, P., & Irvine, K. N. (2007, August). *People's perceptions and classifications of sounds heard in urban parks: Semantics, affect and restoration*. Paper presented at Inter-Noise in Istanbul, Turkey.

Rozec, V. (2003). The influence of a specific urban planning on sonic environment. In G. Moser, E. Pol, Y. Bernard, M. Bonnes, J. A. Corraliza, & M. V. Giuliani (Eds.), *People, Places and Sustainability* (pp. 209–219). Seattle, USA: Hogrefe & Huber.

Scopelliti, M., & Giuliani, M. V. (2004). Choosing restorative environments across the lifespan: A matter of place experience. *Journal of Environmental Psychology, 24*(4), 423–437.

Shaw, B., Ungar, S., & Gatersleben, B. (2005, September). *Represented in a glittering array: An understanding of blind people's perceptions of natural environments.* Paper presented at Royal Geographical Society with IBG conference in London, UK.

Staats, H., & Hartig, T. (2004). Alone or with a friend: A social context for psychological restoration and environmental preferences. *Journal of Environmental Psychology, 24*(2), 199–211.

Staats, H., Kieviet, A., & Hartig, T. (2003). Where to recover from attentional fatigue: An expectancy-value analysis of environmental preference. *Journal of Environmental Psychology, 23*(2), 147–157.

Tennessen, C. M., & Cimprich, B. (1995). Views to nature: Effects on attention. *Journal of Environmental Psychology, 15*(1), 77–85.

Ulrich, R. S. (1984). View through a window may influence recovery from surgery. *Science, 224*(4647), 420–421.

World Health Organization. (2000). B. Berglund, T. Lindvall, & D. H. Schwela (Eds.), *Guidelines for community noise.* Geneva: WHO.

Are "Attractive" Built Places as Restorative and Emotionally Positive as Natural Places in the Urban Environment?

Ferdinando Fornara

Department of Psychology, University of Cagliari, Italy

Abstract

Many studies have shown that natural environments are more preferred and have higher restorative power than built environments, but there is a substantial lack of studies examining "attractive" built areas in comparison with natural ones. Typically, research literature on restorativeness and related issues has included experiments or field studies where participants had to rate the restorative potential of places represented in images (photographs, pictures, video, etc.) of natural and built environments. The general aim of this study is to compare the restorative power and the affective qualities attributed to attractive natural and built urban environments by people who are using them, thus catching the "actual" *in situ* experience of the places. Participants (N = 157) were recruited in three kinds of urban places of the city of Cagliari (Sardinia, Italy), i.e., one natural (an urban park) and two built (a shopping mall and a panoramic and historical site), where they had to fill in the Perceived Restorativeness Scale and the Scale of Perceived Affective Qualities of Places with reference to the place they were experiencing. On the whole, the attractive built setting including panoramic and historical features emerged as equally restorative and positively connoted as the urban park.

Key words: affective qualities, historic-panoramic places, leisure places, natural versus built environments, restorativeness

Research on restorativeness of places has its roots in Kaplan's Attention Restoration Theory (Kaplan, 1995; Kaplan & Kaplan, 1989) and has investigated which environmental features promote individual "restoration" (Hartig & Staats, 2003), that is recovery from stress and cognitive fatigue, and retrieval of directed attention. Restorativeness is not only associated with feelings of relaxation, but with enjoyment and excitement as well (Korpela, Hartig, Kaiser, & Fuhrer, 2001).

The Attention Restoration Theory (Kaplan, 1995; Kaplan & Kaplan, 1989) indicated four components of restorativeness, that is (1) Being-away, which refers to a change of scenery and experience from everyday life, (2) Fascination, which refers to the capability of environments to catch one's attention involuntarily (not demanding mental effort), (3) Compatibility, which refers to the degree of fit between the characteristics of the environment and the individual's purposes and inclinations, and (4) Extent, which refers to the properties of coherence and scope in the environments.

Most studies on this field have shown that natural environments have higher restorative power than built environments (e.g., see Laumann, Gärling, & Stormark, 2001). Typically, research designs of these studies have been experiments or field studies in which participants had to rate the restorative potential of places represented in images (photographs, pictures, video, etc.) of natural and built environments.

Recent studies (e.g., Scopelliti & Giuliani, 2004; Staats & Hartig, 2004) revealed the influence of social factors (being alone versus being in company), stage of lifespan, and time available for restoration on the restorative potential of natural and built environments, moving the attention to the "real" places as they are experienced by people. In this direction, Korpela et al. (2001) found that the choice of favourite places usually is made on the basis of place experience. Thus, the focus should be put on places (as intersection of spatial-physical aspect, users, and behaviours; see Canter, 1977) and actual experiences that people judge as restorative.

Regarding psychological responses that presented a relationship with restorativeness, there is empirical evidence on the role of the need of restorativeness as an antecedent to environmental preference (Hartig & Staats, 2006) as well as on the influence of aesthetic features on the restorative potential of places (Hernandez, Hidalgo, Berto, & Peron, 2001). In particular, natural environment was rated as both more attractive and more restorative than urban environment, but there is a substantial lack of studies assessing the impact of unattractive natural environments and attractive urban places, as noted by Hartig and Staats (2003).

Galindo and Hidalgo (2005) identified five kinds of urban places that are distinguishable in terms of aesthetic preference, that is, three attractive ones (cultural-historical places, recreational places for leisure and/or walking, and panoramic places) and two unattractive ones (housing areas and industrial places). As mentioned by Hidalgo, Berto, Galindo, and Getrevi (2006), the preference for and the higher restorative power of natural settings emerged in the comparison of natural versus urban environments could be due to the choice of the (built) urban settings depicted in most studies, that is, streets, buildings, and industrial areas that are typically unattractive. On the contrary, in the literature there is a substantial lack of historical, recreational, and panoramic sites as (built) urban places

F. Fornara 161

Are "Attractive" Built Places as Restorative and Emotionally Positive as Natural Places in the Urban Environment?

to put in comparison with natural ones. For example, there is empirical evidence on the assessment of historical buildings as high-quality and highly restorative places (Galindo & Hidalgo, 2005; Scopelliti & Giuliani, 2004). Dimensions such as architectural style and type are key dimensions in orienting our aesthetic preferences (Nasar, 1994, 1997). Regarding panoramic sites, by definition they express the characteristic of openness (one of the aesthetic attributes in the typology of Nasar, 1994, 1997) and can also favour the exposition to natural scenes, thus promoting restorativeness (Hartig, Korpela, Evans, & Gärling, 1996). Hence, there is the need to take into account pleasant built urban places in order to confirm the supremacy of natural environments over built urban environments.

A specific indicator of environmental preference is represented by the affective qualities that a target place evokes in our mind. Ittelson (1973) claimed that the first level of response to the environment is affective, since the emotional impact drives the following directions of the relationship person/environment. Russell and colleagues (Russell & Lanius, 1984; Russell & Pratt, 1980) developed a circomplex model (Environmental Emotional Reaction Indices) of the perceived affective qualities (PAQs) of places. Such a model is based on two principal bipolar axes (pleasant-unpleasant and arousing-sleepy) and two secondary bipolar axes (relaxing-distressing and exciting-gloomy).

Objective and Hypotheses

The general aim of this study is to compare the restorative power and the affective qualities attributed to attractive natural and built urban environments by people who are using them, thus focusing on the "actual" in situ experience of the places. The degree of congruence between different kinds of assessments of the same targets of natural and built environments is tested.

A more specific research goal concerns the analysis of how built environments including particular qualities of historical and panoramic nature can be placed along the continuum of built/natural in the assessment of users.

The main hypotheses are:

H1: The natural environment is perceived as more restorative than the built environment.

H2: The (built) historical/panoramic environment is perceived as more restorative than the built environment and as restorative as the natural environment.

H3: The natural environment receives higher positive affective ratings than the built environment.

H4: The (built) historical/panoramic environment receives higher positive affective ratings than the built environment and is rated as positive as the natural environment.

Method

Places and Participants

Three places included in the city of Cagliari (Region of Sardinia, Italy) were chosen as samples of the types of urban environments under analysis. In particular, the natural environment was represented by an urban park ("Monte Claro" park); and the built environment was represented by a modern shopping mall (Le vele); and the built environment with historical and panoramic characteristics was represented by the terrace of the ancient stronghold of the city (Bastione di San Remy), which presents a wide view on the sea, on the port, and on various parts of the city. The choice of the two built places was made on the basis of their potential pleasantness, since they refer to the categories of attractiveness found by Galindo and Hidalgo (2005), that is, recreational (both the shopping mall and the terrace), historical, and panoramic (the terrace).

All the three places are used by people for leisure activities and include benches where people spend time to relax or to have a chat. They were selected as target places where it was easier to attract volunteers for the study.

One hundred fifty-seven residents of Cagliari (or its hinterland) represented the sample of participants, which was composed as follows: 54 participants (34.4%) were recruited in the urban park, 61 (38.8%) in the historical-panoramic terrace, and 42 (26.8%) in the shopping mall; 88 (56.1%) were female and 69 (43.9%) were male, they ranged in age from 16 to 68 years (mean age = 33.19). Regarding education, 31 (19.9%) had a junior high school education, 89 (57.0%) had a senior high school education, and 36 (23.1%) had a degree. No one of the participants used the location where they were contacted for work related activities.

Participants assessed the specific environment (the urban park versus the historical-panoramic terrace versus the shopping mall) they were experiencing at that moment.

Data were collected from March to May 2007.

Tools and Data Analysis

Participants were contacted by trained interviewers (two students of Psychology) and then asked to complete in a self-administered questionnaire including the following tools:

1. Perceived Restorativeness Scale (PRS), which measures the components related to restorative environments (i.e., being-away, fascination, compatibility coherence, and scope) of 26 items (see Hartig et al., 1996). The response scale was a 7-point Likert-type in which participants rated how well each sentence described their feelings about and experience in the place (from 1 = not at all to 7 = at all).
2. The scale of PAQs of places, which is based on the circomplex model of affective quality attributed to places (Russell & Lanius, 1984). The Italian version of this

scale (Perugini, Bonnes, Aiello, & Ercolani, 2003) consists of a list of 48 adjectives in four bipolar dimensions (12 items each) of PAQs (i.e., Relaxing versus Distressing, Exciting versus Gloomy, Pleasant versus Unpleasant, and Stimulating versus Sleepy). The response scale was a 7-point Likert-type scale in which participants rated how well each adjective suitably described the place (from 1 = not at all to 7 = at all).

The final part of the questionnaire included the usual items on sociodemographics and two items on social aspects of the place experience (the first concerning being alone versus being in company, the second concerning which kind of company).

Principal Component Analyses were run on both the PRS and each bipolar dimension of the PAQs to obtain more reliable factorial solutions. Cronbach's alphas were calculated to test each factors' internal consistency. After reversing negative-sense items, for each dimension aggregate scores were computed and then used as DV for the following one-way ANOVAs, where the type of environment (urban park versus historical-panoramic terrace versus shopping mall) was the IV. Gender, age, and education were inserted as covariates in the analysis. Bonferroni's alpha ($p < .05$) was used as the index in the post hoc tests.

Results

All the Principal Component Analyses (PRS and PAQs) produced monofactorial solutions. Cronbach's alpha was .92 in PRS, .92 in Relaxing versus Distressing PAQ, .93 in Pleasant versus Unpleasant PAQ, .84 in Exciting versus Gloomy PAQ, and .80 in Arousing versus Sleepy PAQ.[1]

The ANOVAs with the three places as IV and PRS and PAQ dimensions as DV (controlling for gender, age, and education[2]) produced the following outcomes:

PRS (see Figure 1). The effect of place was significant ($F_{2,150} = 7.20$, $p < .01$). The urban park ($\bar{X} = 4.63$; $DS = .85$) was perceived as restorative as the historical-panoramic terrace ($\bar{X} = 4.59$; $SD = .89$), but both scored significantly higher than the shopping mall ($\bar{X} = 3.94$; $SD = 1.12$).

Relaxing versus Distressing (see Figure 2). The effect of place was significant ($F_{2,150} = 29.75$, $p < .001$). The urban park ($\bar{X} = 5.07$; $DS = .85$) was perceived as more relaxing than the historical-panoramic terrace ($\bar{X} = 4.06$; $SD = 1.32$), while the shopping mall scored lower than the other two places ($\bar{X} = 3.28$; $SD = 1.38$).

Pleasant versus Unpleasant (see Figure 3). The effect of place was significant ($F_{2,150} = 18.41$, $p < .001$). The urban park ($\bar{X} = 5.75$; $DS = .72$) was perceived as more

---

[1] Two items were eliminated from this PAQ because their factor loading in the PCA was $< .30$.
[2] In only one of the ANOVAs one of the covariates showed a significant weight on the *DV*: It was the case of the effect of gender on the Relaxing versus Distressing PAQ (males rated the places as more relaxing than females, $p < .01$).

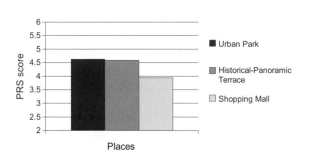

Figure 1. PRS mean scores related to the three urban places.
Note. Range from 1 = not at all to 7 = at all.

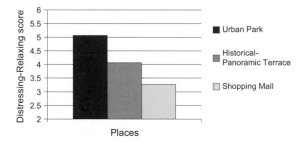

Figure 2. "Relaxing versus Distressing" mean scores related to the three urban places.
Note. Range from 1 = highest Distressing score to 7 = highest Relaxing score.

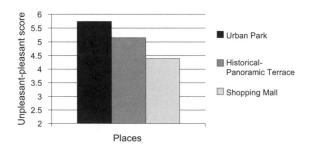

Figure 3. "Pleasant versus Unpleasant" mean scores related to the three urban places.
Note. Range from 1 = highest Unpleasant score to 7 = highest Pleasant score.

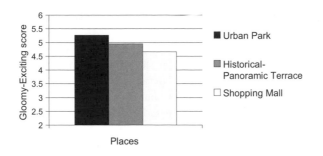

Figure 4. "Exciting versus Gloomy" mean scores related to the three urban places.
Note. Range from 1 = highest Gloomy score to 7 = highest Exciting score.

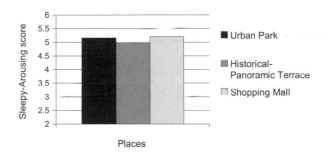

Figure 5. "Arousing versus Sleepy" mean scores related to the three urban places.
Note. Range from 1 = highest Sleepy score to 7 = highest Arousing score.

pleasant than the historical-panoramic terrace ($\bar{X}$ = 5.16; SD = 1.06), while the shopping mall was perceived as the least pleasant among the three places ($\bar{X}$ = 4.39; SD = 1.42).

Exciting versus Gloomy (see Figure 4). The effect of place was significant ($F_{2,150}$ = 5.97, $p < .01$). The urban park ($\bar{X}$ = 5.27; DS = .78) was perceived as more pleasant than the shopping mall ($\bar{X}$ = 4.66; SD = 1.08), whereas the historical-panoramic terrace ($\bar{X}$ = 4.95; SD = .63) was as pleasant as the other two places.

Stimulating versus Boring (see Figure 5). There was no significant effect of place ($F_{2,150}$ = 1.39, p = ns).

Discussion and Conclusion

These empirical outcomes, which are based on the actual (*hic et nunc*) place experience, confirmed both H1 and H3, that is, people value the natural environment as, respectively, more restorative and more positive in terms of affective qualities than the built environment.

This result is rather expected for H1, since the targeted built environment (i.e., a shopping mall) could be judged as a distressing place, with little or no ability to restore attention. Nevertheless, the PRS score for this environment was much greater than the mean of the response scale, thus our data suggest that even a shopping mall can be perceived as restorative in absolute terms (at least for those who use that place for spending time and for leisure, as did most of our study participants).

Regarding H3, it is not as obvious that a built environment like a shopping mall evokes fewer positive affective qualities than a natural environment like an urban park. Being also a recreational place, the shopping mall is included in one of the three attractive kinds of built urban places found by Galindo and Hidalgo (2005). Furthermore, we need to consider that in our times, the shopping mall typically is viewed (and used) as a place to spend time for leisure, socialization, and relaxing (as discovered in some open ended responses to a questionnaire item investigating the motivations underlying participants' presence in the place). In spite of that, the natural environment is perceived as more relaxing, pleasant, and exciting than the built environment, while no difference emerged between the two places in the degree of arousal. Thus, the natural environment seems to evoke positive affective qualities, indicating both excitement and relaxation. This is consistent with our restorativeness outcomes as well as with the restorativeness construct (Korpela et al., 2001).

Regarding the position of a historical and panoramic built environment along the continuum natural/built environment in the assessment of restorative power and affective qualities, H2 received empirical evidence, whereas H4 was proven only partially. As foreseen by H2, the historical and panoramic place was perceived as restorative as the natural place, and both places were assessed as more restorative than the built place. This outcome seems to confirm that not only natural environments possess a restorative potential. Thus, even some kinds of built environment can support recovery from stress and cognitive fatigue, and elicit focalized attention (Hartig & Staats, 2003). In particular, the "historic" and the "panoramic" properties were just shown to be potentially restorative (Hidalgo et al., 2006). The effect of the first property can be explained in the light of the symbolic meaning of historic landmarks as key components of the urban identity (Lalli, 1992) and important parts of our place identity (Proshansky, 1978). Regarding the second property, openness is a spatial aspect that influences our aesthetic preference (Nasar, 1997). Furthermore, the panoramic view from the location selected for the study included natural spots (e.g., the sea, a headland, a close hill, and some hills in the distance) and it was found that a "natural" view can influence health and well-being positively (Ulrich, 1984).

The historic-panoramic place appears as more relaxing and pleasant than the built environment (H4), but at the same time was less relaxing and pleasant than the natural environment. In other words, the primacy of the natural environment in terms of pleasantness (that can be viewed as a pattern of global preference) and induced relaxation seems to be confirmed especially if we take into account the nice targets of built environment. Conversely, in the attribution of positive affective qualities indicating arousal (i.e., exciting-gloomy and arousing-sleepy) no differences emerged among the historic-panoramic place and the other two places.

On the whole, these findings corroborate the supremacy of natural over built environments in both restorative potential and perceived quality, but at the same time some kinds of built environments seem to elicit similar positive assessments as natural environments. In other words, the green space confirmed its "healthy" nature in comparison to built spaces in the urban context, but the latter showed also clear differences among users' perception. Further, some differences emerged between restorativeness and PAQs responses regarding the position of the historic-panoramic place along the continuum built/natural environment. This result mirrors the distinctiveness of perceived restorativeness with reference to similar psychological responses as the PAQs of places.

At this point questions arise. Is it the "historic" or the "panoramic" element that makes the environment restorative? Is the natural environment more pleasant and relaxing than the built environment? Or is there a multiplicative effect of the two elements? Further research should verify the unique effect of each property by disaggregating panoramic and historical qualities. This can be carried out by adding samples of panoramic *but not* historical, and historical *but not* panoramic places.

One of the initial aims of this study was to verify the relationship between places and their different restorative components. This was not achieved as PRS emerged as mono-factorial.[3] It would be interesting to study this point in the future.

A clear limit of this study is related to self-selection of participants. It is likely that volunteers accepting to collaborate were those with more time to spend among all users. Such dimensions have proven to be influential on the restorativeness pattern (Scopelliti & Giuliani, 2004), but it is likely that the inclusion of users having less time to spend would not have provided a very different picture. Furthermore, lower internal validity can be counterbalanced by the higher ecological validity that field research expresses. In fact, it is to recall that participants' responses about the place were recorded exactly while they were experiencing the place itself.

Regarding the role of social factors (being alone versus being in company) for restorative experiences (Staats & Hartig, 2004; Scopelliti & Giuliani, 2004), unfortunately the low number of participants experiencing the place without any company did not permit to verify this point.

Future field research should also address the impact of motivations underlying the presence-in-the-place on the restorative potential attributed to a place.

---

[3]   We tested also four- and five-factor solutions, but most factors presented a mix of loading items included in two or three restorative components.

Acknowledgements

I wish to thank Dr. Renato Troffa for his help in the ideation of the research, and Giovanna Bua and Loredana Vargiu for the collection of data.

References

Canter, D. (1977). *The psychology of places*. London: Architectural Press.

Galindo, M. P., & Hidalgo, M. C. (2005). Aesthetic preferences and the attribution of meaning: Environmental categorization processes in the evaluation of urban scenes. *International Journal of Psychology, 40,* 19–27.

Hartig, T., Korpela, K., Evans, G. W., & Gärling, T. (1996). Validation of a measure of perceived environmental restorativeness. *Göteborg Psychological Reports, 26* (7).

Hartig, T., & Staats, H. (2003). Guest Editors' introduction: Restorative environments. *Journal of Environmental Psychology, 23,* 103–107.

Hartig, T., & Staats, H. (2006). The need for psychological restoration as a determinant of environmental preferences. *Journal of Environmental Psychology, 26,* 215–226.

Hernandez, B., Hidalgo, M. C., Berto, R., & Peron, E. (2001). The role of familiarity on the restorative value of a place: Research on a Spanish sample. *IAPS Bulletin of People-Environment Studies, 18,* 22–24.

Hidalgo, M. C., Berto, R., Galindo, M. P., & Getrevi, A. (2006). Identifying attractive and unattractive urban places: Categories, restorativeness and aesthetic attributes. *Medio ambiente y comportamento humano* [Environment and Human Behaviour], *7,* 115–223.

Ittelson, W. (1973). *Environment and cognition*. New York: Academic Press.

Kaplan, R., & Kaplan, S. (1989). *The experience of nature: A psychological perspective*. New York, Cambridge: University Press.

Kaplan, S. (1995). The restorative benefit of nature: Toward an integrative framework. *Journal of Environmental Psychology, 15,* 169–182.

Korpela, K. M., Hartig, T., Kaiser, F. G., & Fuhrer, U. (2001). Restorative experience and self-regulation in favorite places. *Environment and Behavior, 33,* 572–589.

Lalli, M. (1992). Urban-related identity: Theory, measurement, and empirical findings. *Journal of Environmental Psychology, 12,* 285–303.

Laumann, K., Gärling, T., & Stormark, K. M. (2001). Rating scale measures of restorative components of environments. *Journal of Environmental Psychology, 21,* 31–44.

Nasar, J. L. (1994). Urban design aesthetics: The evaluative qualities of building exteriors. *Environment and Behavior, 26,* 377–401.

Nasar, J. L. (1997). New developments in aesthetics for urban design. In G. T. Moore & R. W. Marans (Eds.), *Advances in environment, behavior, and design,* (Vol. 4, pp. 149–193). New York: Plenum Press.

Perugini, M., Bonnes, M., Aiello, A., & Ercolani, A. P. (2003). Il modello circonflesso delle qualita affettive dei luoghi. Sviluppo di uno strumento valutativo italiano [The circomplex model of affective qualities of places. Development of an Italian assessment tool]. *Testing Psicometria Metodologia* [Testing, Psychometrics, & Methodology], *9,* 131–152.

Proshansky, H. M. (1978). The city and self identity. *Environment and Behavior, 10,* 147–169.

Russell, J. A., & Lanius, U. F. (1984). Adaptation level and the affective appraisal of environments. *Journal of Environmental Psychology, 4*, 119–135.

Russell, J. A., & Pratt, G. (1980). A description of the affective quality attributed to environments. *Journal of Personality and Social Psychology, 38*, 311–322.

Scopelliti, M., & Giuliani, M. V. (2004). Choosing restorative environments across the lifespan: A matter of place experience. *Journal of Environmental Psychology, 24*, 423–437.

Staats, H., & Hartig, T. (2004). Alone or with a friend: A social context for psychological restoration and environmental preferences. *Journal of Environmental Psychology, 24*, 199–211.

Ulrich, R. S. (1984). View through a window may influence recovery from surgery. *Science, 244*, 420–421.

Diversity in Lifestyles and Urban Sustainability

A Room with a View

Nancy H. Blossom[1] and Elizabeth L. Blossom[2]

[1]Interdisciplinary Design Institute, Washington State University, Spokane, WA, USA
[2]Integrated Design Laboratory, Washington State University, Spokane, WA, USA

Abstract

Based on the findings of an integrated inquiry this paper argues for sustainable design strategies that reflect cultural and social traditions as well as achieve specific energy goals in the construction of modern housing. Substantial research supports a prescription of passive design strategies that aim to reduce dependency on fossil fuels in third world countries. However, little is known about the impact of these strategies on more intangible aspects of culture such as traditional personal and public relationships. The intent of this discussion is to consider critically contemporary views of green architecture and sustainability as well as the notion that historically vernacular buildings naturally respond to the environment. How do these reflect on the one hand, and shape, on the other the inherent cultural and symbolic meanings imbedded in the qualities of interior space? To test the notion that there are unique light qualities in a vernacular Tibetan interior, three tactics were used to collect and analyze data. These yielded metrics that are compared to daily use patterns of interior rooms. The findings suggest that there are traditional strategies used in Tibet to both exploit and mitigate sunlight. Further, these strategies influence tangible and intangible aspects of the interior that reflect functional and symbolic traditions. These aspects should be valued and protected as we move forward to develop new integrated approaches to passive design solutions.

Key words: architecture, culture, daylight, interiors, Tibet, vernacular

The room is . . . where life is lived inseparably from its context; it is daily life's link to the world. Marked by changes in attitude toward personal conduct society and the world, the room is also an image of the contemporary world (Benzel, 1997, p. 4).

At face value the relationship between a room and the complexities of the biosphere is not apparent. Nevertheless, a postmodern perspective of the world has increased our awareness of the multiple scales in which people of the planet operate simultaneously.

The initial emphasis of this thinking in disciplines such as architecture, landscape architecture, or urban planning was to recognize the importance of a surrounding neighborhood, town, city, or region, for example to the design or interpretation of a building. However by the end of the 20th century scholars posited that all inhabited spaces, despite scale, can be thought of as interwoven spatial environments. Benzel (1997), for example, demonstrates the relationship of regional and urban scales and a room. As the awareness increases of the limited resources of the earth and the impact of modernization and/or industrialization, the relationship between local action and global affect is apparent. Thus a holistic philosophy emerges that links each element of the environment to the next – the room to the building, to the urban and peri-urban, and finally the all-encompassing world around it (Benzel, 1997; Frampton, 2002). Our study is grounded in this framework exploring the collective symbols, patterns, ideals, and ideas of social living represented in aspects of the interior of Tibetan homes. Our intent is to critically consider contemporary views of green architecture and sustainability as well as the notion that historic vernacular building approaches naturally respond to the environment. How do these reflect, on the one hand, and shape, on the other, the inherent cultural and symbolic meanings imbedded in qualities of interior space?

Lhasa

The capital of the Tibet Autonomous Region, Lhasa, demonstrates cultural, symbolic, and environmental affinity to both premodern and postmodern worldviews. Historically isolated and remote, Lhasa remained a preindustrial city of moderate size (300,000 until the mid-20th century). By the end of the century it had grown into a modern urban environment covering almost the entire Lhasa valley. In premodern Lhasa the traditional town plan focused on the major religious, cultural, and public buildings with traffic routes used for religious processions and for daily activity. Centers of commerce were separated by pastoral interludes creating within the city boundaries an atmosphere of the contemporary peri-urban environment whose characteristics tend to be part urban and part rural.[1] By the end of the century Lhasa, like many other cities in China, had become increasingly urban with large pockets of land being turned over to industrial production, competing with schools, government buildings, and housing. Lhasa in the larger context of China provides a micro view of the macro environmental changes in both the urban and rural fabric of the country. These changes have been outpaced only by accelerated economic growth in the

---

[1]   According to Larsen and Sinding-Larsen (2001), before Lhasa developed a dense townscape, areas of the city turned into tent towns accommodating thousands of pilgrims and visitors at festival times. This practice was evident as late as the 1980s in areas that have now been taken over by city. As the city grows, the pilgrims are pushed further and further into the periphery.

last decade. Lhasa's relative isolation has protected it from more aggressive urbanization thus far, but as the larger country turns to the TAR's abundant resources for exploitation, the region is challenged to balance the positive and negative impacts of modernization on the environments of the region. Lhasa is situated in the alluvial plain of a valley at 3,650 m above sea level. The climate belongs to the half drought plateau area. The annual rainfall, which occurs mostly at night, is between 200 mm and 500 mm, and concentrates from June to September. Strong winds characterize the dry seasons of winter and spring. Temperatures range from 14 to 28 °C fluctuating dramatically from day to day. There are only 100–120 days without frost annually. Lhasa is the least polluted city in China, surrounded by a region of abundant blue sky, clean water, and fresh air. The sun shines on average 3,000 hours annually. It is recognized as a cultural and environmental factor that has influenced traditional architecture as well as an abundant natural resource.

It is important to note that architecture in general is not considered to be of great importance when compared with other aspects of Tibet's rich material, intellectual and religious culture. The vernacular house form thus is even lower on the list. There is limited scholarship on the architecture of Tibet and that scholarship focuses primarily on religious centers, monasteries, and palaces. Two seminal works, *The Lhasa Atlas* (Larsen & Sinding-Larsen, 2001) and *Lhasa* (Barnett, 2006), inform this study as scholarly views of the contemporary political, social, and cultural tensions that are influenced by the cityscape of Lhasa. Larsen and Sinding-Larsen offer a comprehensive analysis of vernacular architecture of Tibet. Focusing primarily on what they call the old town, the authors document and describe the rapidly disappearing ethos of the traditional Tibetan urban environment.[2] The authors describe the vernacular of Lhasa as buildings that are simple, meeting normal habitat needs, are native to the place, and importantly reflect the material and immaterial components of cultural traditions, building traditions, and the natural environment. Of particular value to this study is the documentation of dwelling types in the old town of Lhasa representing the "typical" vernacular of native Tibetans.

Vernacular House Forms as Ecological Response

It is a commonly held notion that a vernacular house form in any part of the world will demonstrate best practices in passive environmental building techniques. The logic of this argument is that the primary goals of the builders are functional environmentally appropriate solutions. These goals are reached by considering carefully the life, climate, topography, locally available materials, and traditional building technology. As Larsen and Sinding-Larsen (2001) demonstrate and we observed in field research, there are key components of the vernacular Tibetan house that can be identified as representative of the

---

[2]   Despite Lhasa's antiquity as a regional center, urban culture only developed in Lhasa during and after the 5th Dalai Lama (1682) when wealthy rural families were encouraged to relocate to the city.

regional vernacular. It does not matter if the house is extant in the middle of contemporary Lhasa or is currently under construction in an adjacent village.[3]

Historically the Tibetan habitat whether located in village, town, or city demonstrated a strongly rural character. The traditional house in Lhasa modeled all Tibetan architecture in characteristics of protection, orientation, and oneness with the landscape. For purposes of our field research, we looked closely at the interiors of two rural houses to test ideas about the quality of light in interior spaces and its impact on qualities of space. Nearly 88% of the Tibetan population of the TAR is found in the rural areas today. Because of the large percentage of population in rural homes, one can posit that these houses are most highly representative of Tibetan tradition both in form and function. Investigation of the characteristics of these rural homes provides the discussion for climatic considerations. In old Lhasa, the larger early homes were built on the same plan as a rural farmstead. As the city grew, the courtyard became less dominant and the houses more rectangular. Finally as density overcame the city, a smaller narrower house without any courtyard but with openings to the street evolved (Larsen & Sinding-Larsen, 2001) (see Figure 1).

In Tibet a room needs fresh air, daylight, and warm sunshine because typically the traditional buildings are not artificially heated or cooled.[4] There are many other examples of purposeful vernacular response to the surrounding environment in the exterior. Traditional looking decorative overhangs protect from rain and mitigate direct sun exposure. The exterior penetrations are treated with dark paint around the trim and within the doorway that absorbs direct sun. In contrast, the bulk of the traditional adobe brick material is whitewashed reflecting the intense heat of summer. In the rural setting the gate that defines the interior courtyard serves not only to pen animals but also acts as a buffer for the exposed house against the harsh western wind. The exterior walls are often treated with what superficially appears as decorative vertical waves running the height of each story. Upon further investigation, these prove to be rainwater run-off channels to combat the heavy deluge of water during the rainy season and prevent excessive erosion of the adobe.

These strategies that moderate and protect from the climate have created a unique interior light quality that is inherently imbedded with cultural meaning. What will happen when modern interventions alter that quality of light? Can and should the quality be protected?

---

[3]   This is not to suggest that current building practices in Lhasa uniformly represent traditional Tibetan approaches. Much of the traditional vernacular architecture of the city has been destroyed since the Chinese occupation. In its place is either a modern building representing postmodern building materials, practices, and thinking, that outwardly conforms to components of the traditional approaches, for example in color and scale, but structurally is a modern building, using new building methods such as concrete block.

[4]   The traditional Tibetan building was built out of earth bricks in double rows to provide insulation against the cold and to retain warmth; low, timber-framed ceilings and smaller windows also contributed to heat retention. The modern approach to building with concrete blocks sacrifices these attributes (Barnett, 2006).

Figure 1. Sun fills the courtyard spaces of urban Lhasa houses. Viewing clockwise, the first photograph shows a house built with postmodern materials. The next two photographs are of a house built in the traditional vernacular. The courtyard plays an important role in supporting daily activities of the occupants (photographs by Aaron Pasquale).

The Green Architecture Research Center Project

These questions were posed in response to the goals established by Dr. Liu Jiaping, the Director of the Green Architecture Research Center (GARC) of Xian University of Architecture and Technology, Xi'an, China. A leader in the field of sustainable architecture in China, Dr. Liu and his team are working to establish green building standards in the Tibet Autonomous Region. A focus of the project is the potential that exists for exploiting the abundant solar resources of Tibet in the development of modern urban and rural housing types while at the same time honoring the traditional Tibetan house form. The premise of Dr. Liu's work, particularly in housing, is "the combination of traditional vernacular elements with reflective external intervention" (Liu, Wang, & Yang, 2002, p. 8). The point being that with sensitive interpretation of local values and studied expert intervention (in this case with an emphasis on sustainability as well as modernization) a successful outcome can serve both the past and the future of communities. This approach has been successfully demonstrated in Dr. Liu's previous work in north-central China working with the vernacular of the yaodong cave dwelling. In that project passive design interventions focused on solar heat collection and air circulation.[5] These interventions primarily exploit orientation through greenhouse additions and in some cases also include the addition of a second floor to increase living space and signify modernization. They appear (as viewed in postoccupancy photographs) to significantly alter the original ambience and daylight levels of the traditional single cavernous vaulted interior. Observation of these postoccupancy photographs prompted the question of what impact these types of interventions might have on tangible and intangible aspects of interior space.

Methods

In order to test the idea that there are unique light qualities in a vernacular Tibetan interior, three tactics were used to collect and analyze data. First, field data were collected in two vernacular Tibetan houses during a trip to Tibet with the GARC team. Standard for qualifying as vernacular Tibetan included location and orientation, ownership, layout, building method, materials, and documented decorative characteristics such as those described by experts (Barnett, 2006; Larsen & Sinding-Larsen, 2001). One house was randomly selected. It represented the dwelling of a family described as of moderate means (see Figure 2).

The second house represented the dwelling of a family of status within a rural village.[6] Light level data points in the residences were collected using a light meter at work surface

---

[5]   The GARC interventions are consistent with an unpublished graduate study at MIT of passive solar interventions on different housing types in the urban environment of Beijing. For more recent MIT case studies, see Glicksman and Lin (2006).

[6]   As an indicator of status, Dr. Liu referenced the fact that the village bore the family name.

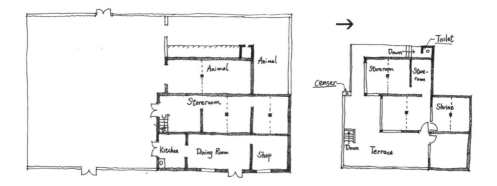

Figure 2. Field sketch of first Tibetan courtyard house. This house was randomly selected by the research team as a data collection site (drawing provided by He Quan).

level across a $2'' \times 2''$ grid. The interior daylight level readings were compared with the available exterior daylight level conditions. In addition to the light meter testing, photographic documentation recorded the nuances of the interior spaces: decorative details, furniture, textiles, uses as well as capture the perception of the occupant in the space and the relative layers of light.

Next scale models of the first house were built in order for the daylight levels to be analyzed in a skybox. This analysis allowed comparison with the field data. The skybox is a mirror-box artificial sky that meets the International Overcast Sky standard of being three times brighter at the zenith than it is at the horizon. There are two methods of testing in the skybox: photocell measurement readings and photography. The photocells measure daylight levels within the space. The photocell readings are then divided by the available exterior daylight levels to find the daylight factor (percentage of available daylight in the space). To record the daylight levels a control cell is placed above the model to absorb the available exterior light. The remaining cells are placed within the model and the readings provide a measure of the daylight performance of the space.

Finally the models were photographed using high dynamic range (HDR) technology to capture all available light levels. HDR imaging produces a set of tonal analysis that allows for a greater range of exposures than just one photograph alone. HDR is used to capture the total range of light levels that exist in the space from brightest daylight to the darkest shadows. The photographer takes a range of exposures and then inputs them into a software program to analyze for perception and daylight levels present as well as for surface luminance quality.

The interior readings collected in the field were multiplied by a factor of 0.604.[7] The data were then overlaid on top of each house plan to depict the daylight zones in the

---

[7] This is a standard calculation used in the Integrated Design Lab that incorporates the typical opacity of glace and the interference of mullions.

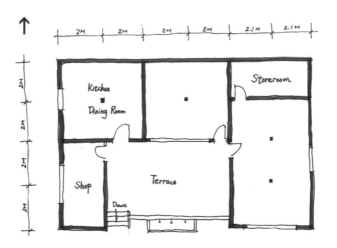

Figure 3. Field drawing of a traditional Tibetan house demonstrating the grid pattern of pillar placement that regulates interior space. In this layout, circulation between rooms is through the terrace, space less protected from climatic elements (drawing provided by He Quan).

interior. These zones were compared to the typical way these spaces are used according to occupants' descriptions, Larsen and Sinding-Larsen (2001),[8] and photographic evidence gathered on site. Data from skybox testing and HDR analysis were compared to field data to confirm the zone patterns.

Findings

A modular grid determined by pillar placement regulates interior Tibetan space. The grid is dependent on the length of timber beams, typically 2–2.2 m. The basic domestic unit of space is a one-pillar room. As a house grows, the rooms are typically arranged in a pass-through style from an entrance point (usually located in the south or east wall) to an innermost north wall, so occupants travel through one space to get to the next. This stacking of space creates a layering of interior volumes. However, it is not unusual for the exterior courtyard or terrace area to be used as circulation from one part of the house to another.

---

[8]   We were unable to verify data gathered verbally from the occupants of either home due to language barriers. Any anecdotal data gathered were through the interpretation of the Chinese team; it was unclear if the Tibetan women in the homes were speaking Chinese or if assumptions were being made about how the rooms were used. Thus the documentation found in Larsen and Sinding-Larsen is important to the analysis.

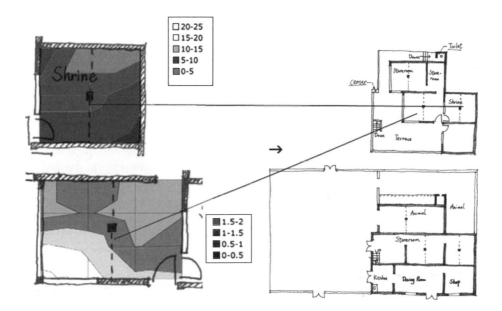

Figure 4. This drawing demonstrates the daylight level as recorded in the field and confirmed through testing in the laboratory. The detail on the lower left is the first tier of daylight entering the house. The upper detail represents the second and most remote layer of daylight.

The courtyard and/or terrace serve as buffer spaces that mitigate sun and wind in the rural setting. In the more dense urban settings modifications to the traditional courtyard placements increase access to the sun; wind is mitigated by the surrounding city. Rooms that support activities of daily living that engage the courtyard, for example, the kitchen and frequented storeroom spaces are located toward this public side of the house.[9]

In the interior, decoration is restricted to the wooden pillars, brackets, and main beam. These are usually carved and elaborately painted. The lower part of the pillar is smooth to support the function of the space, but the upper part supporting the small square capital is decorated and carved. The two horizontal brackets, the "short" and the "long" bow, on top of the pillar are more elaborately carved and generally taper toward the end. The forms are often stylized clouds to give the impression of weightlessness, combined with floral motifs. Woodwork is painted in intense saturated hues.[10]

---

[9] In fact, much of the food preparation is done on the terrace and in the courtyard; the Chinese government requires the use of solar ovens as a main source of heat for cooking in the TAR. Even in two- and three-story apartment style complexes, the solar ovens line the common spaces on the grounds.

[10] As in most cultures any use of color in Tibet is based on a system of symbolism grounded primarily in Buddhism and Bon.

A field drawing of one of the two village homes demonstrates function and arrangement of spaces as shown in Figure 4.

Details representing the analysis of data (Figure 4) demonstrate the layers of the interior and the relative daylight levels in two interior spaces. The detail on the lower left represents the first tier of interior space. This is a communal bedroom/living space on the upper level of the house. The shaded areas represent daylight levels; the level in the lower left corner (southeastern exposure) is approaching a daylight factor of 3–4. By comparison, a recommended daylight factor for an office work plane is 2. The second detail represents daylight levels in the shrine room. All daylight readings in this space are well below a daylight factor of 2. In fact, many of the most interior rooms perform at a daylight factor between 0 and 1. By western standards the room is inadequately lit for most tasks. Further, compared to the brightness of the room in front, this space will experientially seem even darker.

Photographic documentation demonstrates that penetrations to the exterior, entrances, and windows are protected with at least one and sometimes two layers of fabric to diffuse the power of direct sunlight.[11] Windows within the interior walls, that seem like relights, were also covered with gauze to mitigate the ambient light in the front space and dampen the light levels even further in the most interior spaces. The rooms along the north wall, the deepest spaces in the home, have little or no openings.

The data demonstrating the layering of light correlate with what we know about the way the interior spaces are used. In the first place, most typical Tibetan interior spaces are viewed as multifunctional so it is difficult to name areas by function as we would in a more western setting. In the two home studies, the progress of space from the entrance to the most remote location suggests a transition from functionally practical, public spaces to more private spaces that are reserved for family and/or ceremonial, and it is opened only to monks who may visit at the invitation of the family for the purpose of spiritual activities. For example, the shrine room is considered private space for the sole use of the family and as seen in Figure 3 was located deep in a receding layer.[12] It is opened only to monks who may visit at the invitation of the family for the purpose of spiritual intervention.

Discussion

It is apparent that in the vernacular Tibetan tradition strategies are employed that both exploit and mitigate sunlight and that these strategies influence tangible and intangible aspects of the interior. If these aspects are valued and to be protected, a studied strategy of passive solar intervention that integrates both interior and exterior intervention is

---

[11]   In the more affluent home, the windows were also tinted.
[12]   Traditionally the house is fortified against the malevolent forces outside of it from the beginning of construction. A typical Tibetan house would have a number of seats for the male god (pho lha) that protects the house. The female god has a special seat in the kitchen, usually at the top of the structural post in the center of the room. The shrine room typically houses statues of Buddha.

merited. The testing of preliminary methods, as reported by Blossom and Blossom (2008) and outlined above, suggests that such strategy is possible. It seems paramount that to be true to the traditional atmosphere of layering of light and spatial volumes in the residential interior, any passive design intervention will need to acknowledge and understand the current daylight levels and their cultural relevance. Any interventions that focus on modern passive sustainable strategies (e.g., greenhouse, skylights, daylight monitors, or the introduction of north light)[13] need to be weighed against the intrinsic values of the current qualities. These adaptations tend to flood direct sun into interior spaces. How does that weaken the perception and understanding of the traditional house as a fortress against malevolent outside forces? While the energy goals may be successful, what will be lost when the increases in light levels significantly change the nature of the vernacular Tibetan interior?

It is easy to overromanticize the notion of filtered, layered light throughout the interior volumes of a Tibetan home. Any balanced discussion must acknowledge the broader question this study raises. How does the introduction of modern views alter or impede a traditional cultural understanding of the environment, social, and worldviews? And what are the trade-offs? If indeed a room is an image of the contemporary world that represents cultural and social attitudes, then the room is an important measure of the broader question. What we observed is a specific pattern of layout, function, and decorative detail in the interior volumes that signify the nuances of the nomadic rural traditions of Tibet, such as diverse family structures, the Tibetan sense of place, the sacred, the social and economic collaboration, to name a few. The nomadic rural tradition is the Tibetan claim to a civilization that represents a coherent sustainable worldview that is somewhat indifferent or disinterested in the modern prescription of production and consumption as sources of human wellbeing.[14]

On the other hand, what we also observed are aspects of an interior that represent a subsistence lifestyle dependent on quality of life standards that many would find unacceptable: Light levels that are too low to support many standard activities of daily living such as reading or cooking most hours of the day, and inadequate heat sources and sanitation. As Wang (2003) points out, the introduction of modern ideas through rapid urbanization represents the realities of predominantly western, postindustrialist cultures and the resulting impact of unsustainable lifestyles. Imbedded in these notions, however, is a basic standard of living that humanitarians agree should be available to all people. Our position is that with careful and thoughtful acknowledgment of details such as the layered volumes and light qualities of a room, new sustainable interventions can be introduced in the design process that honor the tangible and intangible qualities of the interior, and at the same time, improve standards of living and support a lifestyle that honors the relationship

[13]   There appears to be a deliberate choice not to use north light in the interior spaces of the home. The choice not to use north light is in contrast to western and sustainable notions that take advantage of it as an abundant source of ambient light, escaping the direct sun penetration problems of the southern direct sun (Blossom & Blossom, 2008).

[14]   The splitting of people and nature into categories is alien to the Tibetan outlook as claimed by Tibetans in exile. For a compelling critical discussion of the Green Tibetan worldview, see the works of Huber (1997), Huber and Pedersen (1997), and Korom (1997).

between human beings and the biosphere as well as the cultural and social traditions of the city and the people who inhabit it.

Acknowledgments

The authors wish to acknowledge the contribution of research team assistants Stacey DeKoekkoek, Jaclin Kingen, and Aaron Pasquale of Washington State University, and He Quan, of Xian University of Architecture and Technology, as well as our colleague Dr. David Wang, Professor of Architecture, Washington State University.

References

Barnett, R. (2006). *Lhasa: Streets with memories*. New York: Columbia University Press.

Benzel, K. (1997). *The room in context: Design without boundaries*. New York: McGraw Hill.

Blossom, N., & Blossom, L. (2008). The vernacular of Tibet: Harnessing panoramic sunshine. In G. Broadbent & C. A. Brebbia (Eds.), *ECO-architecture: Harmonization between architecture and nature* (pp. 27–36). Southampton: WIT Press..

Frampton, K. (2002). Towards a critical regionalism: Six points for an architecture of resistance. In H. Foster (Ed.). *The anti-aesthetic: Essays on postmodern culture* (pp. 16–30). New Press..

Glicksman, L., & Lin, J. (2006). *Sustainable urban housing in China: Principles and case studies for low-energy design*. Dordrecht: Springer.

Huber, T. (1997). *Green Tibetans: A brief social history*. Wien: Verlag der Osterreichischen Akademie der Wissenschaften.

Huber, T., & Pedersen, P. (1997). Meteorological knowledge and environmental ideas in traditional and modern societies: The case of Tibet. *Journal of the Royal Anthropology Institute, 3*(3), 577–597.

Korom F. J., (Ed.) (1997). *Tibetan culture in the diaspora*. Papers presented at a panel of the 7th seminar of the International Association for Tibetan Studies, Graz 1995. Verlag der Österreichischen Akademie der Wissenschaften, Wien.

Larsen, K., & Sinding-Larsen, A. (2001). *The Lhasa atlas: Traditional Tibetan architecture and townscape*. London: Serindia.

Liu, J., Wang, D., & Yang, L. (2002). An instance of critical regionalism. *Field Report TDSR, 13*(2), 8.

Wang, W. (2003). Sustainability is a cultural problem. *Harvard Design Magazine, 18*, 3.

Consumption and Electric Power at Home

Its Relationship with the Socio-Demographic Level

Claudia García-Landa and María Montero

School of Psychology, National Autonomous University of Mexico, Mexico

Abstract

An austere consumer's lifestyle is characterized by moderation in the acquisition and use of economic goods and services in such an inventive way that long-term goals are achieved (Lastovicka, et al. 1999). From a social-ecological perspective, and within the Mexican context, electric power (EP) consumption represents a problem which has been scarcely studied and which requires a multidisciplinary approach to determine viable and efficient options. The objective of this study was to document austere household EP consumption and how it relates to low and medium socioeconomic levels. The scale generated, "Rational Electric Power Consumption – CREE" (using its acronym in Spanish), is based on the social satisfaction curve proposed by Domínguez and Robin (1992). The scale has five factors (luxury, squander, consumption due to ignorance, efficient consumption, and pollution) with an alpha value of .67 or greater; it was applied to a sample of 104 housewives living in two apartment complexes in Mexico City from medium and low socioeconomic classes. The results show that EP consumption was different between groups of medium and low income on luxury, overconsumption, and unaware consumption.

Key words: lifestyle, low income, luxury, social satisfaction

The lifestyle of human beings is determined by income, education, and social class (Degenhardt, 2002) thus implying the consumption styles of different goods and services makes for different lifestyles. Today, consumers' pursuit of comfort appears to be increasing every day. Thanks to technological progress that has been made, consumers have greater access to comfort in all their daily activities at home, in the office, and regarding transportation. However, all these amenities have a considerable environmental cost, specifically in the consumption of electricity, gas, and food, etc., which can cause environmental harm.

Austere consumption is a means of consuming without excessive waste of the Earth's resources. An austere consumer's lifestyle is characterized by moderation in the acquisition and use of economic goods and services in such an inventive way that long-term environmental goals are achieved (Lastovicka, Bettencourt, Shaw, & Kuntze, 1999). It is useful to understand consumer behavior, both those with an austere lifestyle and those who live a life of luxury.

From a social-ecological perspective, and within the Mexican context, electric power (EP) consumption represents a problem that scarcely has been studied and which requires a multidisciplinary approach to obtain viable and efficient outcomes.

Currently in Mexico City, the average use of EP is 270 kW h bimonthly per household, equivalent to $450 Pesos ($37 USD approximately) (Gobierno del Distrito Federal, 2007; Luz y Fuerza del Centro, 2007). The economic impact derived from EP services varies from household to household. Thus, this value may represent between 15% and 30% of the family income (Gobierno del Distrito Federal, 2007). Therefore, controls implemented by users can range from using a "*diablito*" (irregular EP outlets) (Comisión Federal de Electricidad, 2007) to using, to a lesser extent, EP-saving light bulbs or appliances (Comisión para el Ahorro de Energía, 2007). From a social-ecological point of view and within the Mexican scenario, the consumption of EP in households represents a rarely studied problem that requires a multidisciplinary approach to develop feasible and efficient options.

In Mexico City, there is a household EP consumption pattern expressed as a function of equipment, weather, habits, and time of day. Lighting accounts for 35% of EP consumption in households, 30% for refrigeration, 25% for entertainment, and 10% for miscellaneous purposes (Ramos, 1998, 2003). The EP consumption pattern in households depends on daylight (Ramos, 1998) and users' lifestyle (Leonard-Barton, 1981; Reddy, 2004). The lifestyle of EP consumers is characterized by the use of lighting, intense energy devices, and energy-conservation devices (Reddy, 2004).

To best understand consumption patterns for environmental-protection purposes, Pro-Environmental Behavior (PEB) has been studied. PEB means a "set of conscious, focused and effective actions exerting an influence to meet individual social requirements resulting from the protection of the environment" (Corral, 2001, p. 40). PEB studies include such variables as values (Corraliza & Martín, 2000; González, 2002), motivation (Corral, 1996; De Young, 1996), competence (Corral, 1996), skills (Bustos, 2004), and austerity (Corral & Pinheiro, 2004; De Young, 1996), among others that may help partially to explain PEB in matters such as water, waste recycling, and energy in general.

Research conducted on lifestyles demonstrated that people with austere characteristics tend to take actions in favor of the environment (Corral & Pinheiro, 2004; De Young, 1996; Iwata, 1999, 2006; Lastovicka et al., 1999). In six studies showed by Lastovicka et al. (1999), a significantly negative relationship between frugality and compulsive consumption ($r = -.25, p < .05$) was found. Corral and Pinheiro (2004) noticed a positive relationship between austerity and water consumption ($r = .18, p < .005$). In addition, Iwata (2006) found a positive and significant correlation between environmentally friendly consumption and an austere lifestyle ($r = .33, p < .05$). Empirical evidence shows that austere consumption is a relevant variable for PEB regarding water consumption, the purchase of goods, and consumption reduction.

The curve of social satisfaction proposed by Domínguez and Robin (1992) explains the relationship between spending and satisfaction experienced by consumers as derived from a good or service. They analyze four stages:

(1) *Survival*: The belief that consumption is necessary to meet basic, psychological, and spiritual needs. Minimum consumption necessary for life.
(2) *Comfort*: The belief that there is a positive relationship between money and satisfaction seeking for basic comfort.
(3) *Luxury*: Belief that no comfort is enough, so consumers try to gain satisfaction with "small" perquisites involving sumptuosness.
(4) *Overconsumption*: Belief that discomfort may be relieved with external goods and services using things indiscriminately.

This curve shows that consumption fits within the framework of comfort where the individual restrains his or her consumption of goods and services without compromising comfort. A lifestyle based on simplicity and the frugal consumption of resources allows individuals to consume to achieve comfort, mitigating environmental harm (Constanza, Daly, & Bartholomew, 1999; Johnson, 1978).

"Enough" consumption may provide a way to consume without abusing natural resources. Austere consumers' lifestyles are characterized by moderate acquisition and use of economic goods and services in a way appropriate to meet long-term goals (Lastovicka et al., 1999). Thus, PEB is a long-term goal as individuals, in most cases, will not reap the advantages of their actions immediately. This is true with respect to the benefits to the environment as a result of a restrained EP consumption in households without compromising comfort. Enough EP consumption in households will be reflected in both the acquisition and usage of electric appliances, and the performance of specific actions. For example, turning the light off each time one leaves the room and unplugging devices that use EP while turned off (i.e., microwave, television, and stereo).

The goal to achieve in sustainable consumption patterns of goods and services should be efficient consumption. To learn if consumers will act in a favorable manner for the environment is one goal of PEB experts. Further, we must understand the patterns that characterize both consumers who lead an austere lifestyle and those who lead a life full of luxury and excesses. Some variables that could have influenced electrical consumption in households are: lifestyle, values, knowledge, beliefs, demographic, and situational. The present study has documented household EP consumption and how it relates to people of low and medium socioeconomic levels in Mexico City.

Method

The sample was comprised of 104 housewives having their residence in Mexico City, ages ranging between 20 and 81 years old (median age = 37.3). With respect to education, 16% completed elementary school, 28% junior high, 17% a technical career, 22% high school, and 17% graduate studies. The housewives surveyed with low monthly family income for less than USD $273 were 58% and with monthly family income of more than USD $546 were 42%. Most housewives interviewed earned an average bimonthly salary of $225 Pesos, equivalent to $18 USD.

The "Scale of Electric Power Consumption" (CREE) of 69 items (5 factors) about rational EP consumption in households was used. These 69 items used a 5-point scale (1 = *never*, 5 = *always*). CREE was developed based on the fulfillment curve proposed by Domínguez and Robin (1992) to explain the relationship between spending and satisfaction experienced by consumers from goods or services.

This instrument was administered individually to subjects meeting inclusion criteria (housewives living in apartment complexes). The participants were asked to answer as truthfully as possible. A meeting was held with the managers of the UH to obtain their consent to access the premises prior to administering the survey.

Results

The CREE scale is composed of five factors. Table 1 includes the names of all five, an example of items grouped within each factor, and evidence that the mean of unaware consumption is slightly above that of efficient and excessive consumption. Further, unaware consumption displays more dispersion. The alpha values were $\geq .66$.

Table 2 shows the mean and standard deviation by income group for each factor. The group had an average median income highest in relation to luxury consumption (1.91), overconsumption (1.75), and unaware consumption (1.67), compared to the low-income group luxury (1.30), overconsumption (1.43), and unaware consumption (1.24).

Table 3 shows that only luxury, overconsumption, and unaware consumption showed significant differences among the groups of low-income and medium income. With regard to income level, differences were found in the level of consumption related to luxury ($t = -6.000$, $df = 48$, $p < .05$), overconsumption ($t = -2.458$, $df = 43$, $p < .05$), and unaware consumption ($t = -3.622$, $df = 55$, $p < .05$) among the groups of low income and medium income. In addition, no differences were found in the level of consumption related to efficient consumption and pollution among the groups of low income and medium income.

Table 1. Mean, standard deviation, and internal consistency of factors constituting the CREE scale

Factor	Mean	SD	α
Luxury (e.g., "I use the coffee machine to prepare coffee or tea")	1.61	0.697	.79
Overconsumption (e.g., "I am used to going to bed with the TV set turned on")	1.75	0.763	.66
Unaware Consumption (e.g., "at home, all the electric appliances are permanently plugged in")	3.01	1.24	.78
Efficient Consumption (e.g., "I am well aware of closing the fridge each time I take something out")	1.96	0.891	.67
Pollution (e.g., "I leave the fridge open until I arrange everything inside it")	1.95	0.761	.67

Table 2. Average and standard deviation by income group for each factor

Factor	Income group	N	Median	SD
Luxury	1	30	1.30	0.466
	2	24	1.91	0.282
Overconsumption	1	37	1.43	0.502
	2	20	1.75	0.444
Unaware consumption	1	29	1.24	0.435
	2	28	1.67	0.475
Efficient consumption	1	33	1.36	0.488
	2	21	1.52	0.511
Pollution	1	24	1.33	0.481
	2	23	1.60	0.499

Discussion and Conclusion

In this sample, EP consumption was different between groups of medium and low income on luxury, overconsumption, and unaware consumption. Efficient consumption was found in both the medium-income and the low-income groups, indicating that it is more related

Table 3. Differences in the level of consumption among the group of low income and medium income

Factor	t	df	Sig.
Luxury	−6.000	48.767	.000
Overconsumption	−2.458	43.391	.018
Unaware consumption	−3.622	55	.001
Efficient consumption	−1.153	52	.254
Pollution	−1.925	45	.061

to austere lifestyle (Lastovicka et al., 1999) and values (Aguilar, Monteoliva, & García, 2005; Guagnano, 2001) than to monthly income.

Consumption-related pollution occurs in the two income groups because consumption is the erosion and destruction of things to satisfy human needs (OECD, 2002). In the case of electricity, consumption of products (bulb) and service (lighting) involves pollution (CONAE, 2006).

To avoid overconsumption of EP at home, it is necessary to focus on psycho-educational interventions to the two income groups in conjunction with government programs to save energy at home. In addition, consumption, from a multidimensional approach, allows us to be aware of consumers' social satisfaction and, to a certain extent, understand the proposal by Lastovicka et al. (1999) regarding general satisfaction with life.

Acknowledgments

This chapter was supported partially by CONACYT through doctoral Grant No. 201439 awarded to Claudia García-Landa, under the supervision of Doctor María Montero. We are indebted to all the housewives for their participation and time, to Edith Bello, Yesica Soto, and Male Nava for their assistance in data collection.

References

Aguilar, M., Monteoliva, A., & García, J. (2005). Influencia de las normas, los valores, las creencias pro ambientales y la conducta pasada sobre la intención de reciclar [Influence of norms, values, pro environmentel beliefs and the last conduct on the intention to recycle]. *Medio Ambiente y Comportamiento Humano, 6*, 23–36.

Bustos, M. (2004). *Modelo de conducta pro ambiental para el estudio de la conservación de agua potable* [Pro-environmental behavior model for studying the conservation of water]. Tesis de Doctorado. Facultad de Psicología, UNAM.

Comisión Federal de Electricidad. (2007). Preguntas más frecuentes [Frequent questions] Recuperado el 10 de octubre de 2007, de http://www.cfe.gob.mx.

Comisión Nacional para el Ahorro de Energía [CONAE] (2006). *Ahorra Energía Desde el Hogar* [*Save Energy at Home*]. Retrieved from www.conae.gob.mx/wb/distribuidor.jsp?seccion=2045.

Comisión para el Ahorro de Energía. (2007). Cómo ahorrar energía [How to save energy]. Recuperado el 10 de octubre de 2007, de http://www.conae.gob.mx/ahorroenergia.

Constanza, R., Daly, H., & Bartholomew, J. (1999). Goals, agenda and policy recommendations for ecological economics. In *Ecological Economics*. New York, USA: Columbia University.

Corral, V. (1996). Un modelo estructural de reuso y reciclaje en México [A structural model of reuse and recycling in Mexico]. *La Psicología Social en México, VI*, 423–437.

Corral, V. (2001). *Una introducción al comportamiento pro ambiental* [An introduction to the pro-environmental behavior]. España: Resma.

Corral, V., & Pinheiro, J. (2004). Aproximaciones al estudio de la conducta sustentable [Approaches to the study of sustainable behavior]. *Medio Ambiente y Comportamiento Humano, 5*, 1–26.

Corraliza, J., & Martín, R. (2000). Estilos de vida, actitudes y comportamientos ambientales [Lifestyles, attitudes and environmental behavior]. *Medio Ambiente y Comportamiento Humano, 1*, 31–56.

Degenhardt, L. (2002). Why do people act in sustainable ways? Results of an empirical survey of lifestyles pioneers. In P. Schmuck & W. Schultz (Eds.), *Psychology of sustainable development* (pp. 123–148). Massachusetts: Kluwer Academic.

De Young, R. (1996). Some psychological aspects of reduce consumption behavior. *Environment and Behavior, 28*, 358–409.

Domínguez, J., & Robin, V. (1992). *Your money or your life*. USA: Penguin Books.

Gobierno del Distrito Federal. (2007). *Programa de energía* [Energy program]. Recuperado el 02 de octubre de 2007, de http://www.gdf.gob.mx/.

González, A. (2002). Valores, actitudes y conductas pro ambientales en estudiantes peruanos [Values, attitudes and behaviors in friendly Peruvian students]. In V. Corral (Coord.), *Conductas Protectoras del Ambiente. Teoría investigación y estrategias de intervención* [Environmental protective behavior. Theory research and intervention strategies] (pp. 165–183). México: CONACYT RM Editores. Unison.

Guagnano, G. (2001). Altruism and market-like behavior: An analysis of willingness to pay for recycled paper products. *Population and Environment, 22*, 425–438.

Iwata, O. (1999). Perceptual and behavioral correlates of a voluntary simplicity lifestyle. *Social Behavior and Personality, 27*, 379–386.

Iwata, O. (2006). An evaluation of consumerism and lifestyle as correlates of a voluntary simplicity lifestyle. *Social Behavior and Personality, 34*, 557–567.

Johnson, W. (1978). *La era de la frugalidad o la alternativa ecológica a la crisis* [The era of frugality or the ecological alternative to the crisis]. Barcelona, España: Editorial Kairos.

Lastovicka, J., Bettencourt, L., Shaw, R., & Kuntze, R. (1999). Lifestyles of the tight and frugal: Theory and measurement. *Journal of Consumer Research, 26*, 85–98.

Leonard-Barton, D. (1981). Voluntary simplicity lifestyles and energy conservation. *Journal of Consumer Research, 8*, 243–252.

Luz y Fuerza del Centro. (2007). *Tarifas uso doméstico* [Domestic rates]. Recuperado el 03 de octubre del 2007, de http://www.lfc.gob.mx/tarifas/domestico.

Organisation for Economic Co-operation for Development OECD (2002). *Towards Sustainable Household Consumption?* Trends and Policies in OECD Countries. Paris, France: OECD.

Ramos, G. (1998, enero-febrero). Modelado de la curva de usuarios domésticos para la implementación de medidas de administración por el lado de la demanda [Modeling curve home users to implement management measures for the demand side]. Boletín del Instituto de Investigaciones Eléctricas. Recuperado el 16 de septiembre del 2007, de http://www.iie.org.mx/publica/bolef98/aplief98.htm.

Ramos, G. (2003, julio-septiembre). Variables que influyen en el modelado del consumo de energía en usuarios domésticos, para la implementación de medidas de ADL [Variables that influence the modeling of energy consumption in households, to implement ADL measures]. *Energía Racional, 48,* 1–11.

Reddy, A. (2004). *Energy and social issues.* In World Energy Assessment: Energy and the challenge of sustainability. Cambridge: University Press.

Collective Motivation for Managing Our Common Environment

Carmen Tabernero[1] and Bernardo Hernández[2]

[1]Department of Psychology, University of Córdoba, Spain
[2]Department of Social Psychology, University of La Laguna, Campus de Guajara, Spain

Abstract

The role of collective motivation to explain collective environmentally responsible behaviour (CERB) is the main topic of this chapter. The authors explore the internal motivation that leads communities to adopt certain lifestyle and environmental behaviours. One of the challenges facing applied psychology today is to explain and predict the environmentally responsible behaviour of individuals, groups, and collectives. This chapter first presents a reflection upon the different theoretical approaches to the study of CERB motivation. Secondly, it analyses the effects of high shared levels of intrinsic satisfaction and collective efficacy in terms of developing CERB. And finally, from the previous theoretical point of view, the authors present research carried out with a large sample of the population. The results show that the majority of pro-environmental behaviours are carried out due to intrinsic motivation and the desire to accomplish self-transcendent goals. Data show that smaller communities have a greater belief in their collective efficacy to develop pro-environmental action than do larger communities. Results also show that populations with higher belief in their collective capacity recycle to a greater extent.

Key words: collective efficacy, environmentally responsible behaviour, intrinsic motivation

This chapter analyses the role of collective motivation in collective environmentally responsible behaviour (CERB). The purpose of this chapter is to determine the internal motivation that leads communities to adopt certain lifestyle and environmental behaviours. We show the theoretical framework that contributes to understanding the motivation for lifestyle diversity. One of the challenges facing applied psychology today is to explain and predict the motivations of individuals, groups, and collectives to engage in environmentally responsible behaviour (ERB) and share their resources for the good of the common environment.

As a result of growing interest in this subject, in recent years an increasing number of researchers have attempted to identify the variables that predict environmentally responsible behaviour (e.g., Geller, 2002). Almost all psychosocial processes have been put forward at some point as antecedents or motives for carrying out some kind of ERB. The aim of this chapter is to present a reflection upon the different theoretical approaches to the study of CERB motivation. Specifically, this chapter analyses the effects of high shared levels of intrinsic satisfaction and collective efficacy in terms of developing CERB.

Intrinsic Satisfaction

When a person engages in a certain form of behaviour purely for reasons of intrinsic satisfaction, the satisfaction produced is associated more with personal interest in the behaviour than with ecocentric or anthropocentric interest; they simply feel satisfied at carrying out the action. Intrinsic satisfaction can be related in some ways to altruism, in the sense that these actions are freely engaged in by the person, entail a certain amount of sacrifice, but provide a high level of personal satisfaction. Kasser and Ryan (1996) have analysed the content of goals people set for themselves, drawing a distinction between intrinsic and extrinsic motivations. The first category refers to motivations that directly aim to satisfy the psychological needs of relatedness, autonomy, and competence, such as self-acceptance, affiliation, community feeling, and community health. Deci and Ryans' (2000) "Theory of Self-Determination" proposes that all these psychological needs as relating to motivation. Extrinsic motivation refers to obtaining some kind of social reinforcement or recognition such as economic success, a good image, or popularity.

De Young (2000) has presented a review of articles that consider the intrinsic satisfaction experienced when engaging in some kind of ERB to be a source of motivation. As a result of this review, he drew a distinction between three types of motivating factors: (a) the satisfaction of having certain *competences* to carry out specific actions, (b) the satisfaction of *engaging in responsible consumption* even if it is not long lasting, and (c) the satisfaction of maintaining a *feeling of community* by helping to sustain the environment. The articles reviewed highlight the multidimensional nature of intrinsic satisfaction.

For this reason, taking the context into account, Grouzet et al. (2005) proposed the need for a more complex model that, in addition to the "intrinsic-extrinsic" dimension, would also include an orthogonal dimension to encompass more values, namely those proposed by Schwartz (1992). Hence, they establish four types of goals. The first is based on the need to conform; according to Schwartz's theory, people adapt to social norms created by a collective of people that does not necessarily have to be very large. The second goal is based on the need for security, the need to feel safe and to know that survival is likely. The third goal is based on our "need for hedonism," and the fourth is based on spirituality. The last two can form an orthogonal dimension of expectations or self-transcendent goals as opposed to physical goals, an addition that complements the intrinsic-extrinsic division. Therefore, there are two dimensions: intrinsic goals (acceptance and affiliation) versus

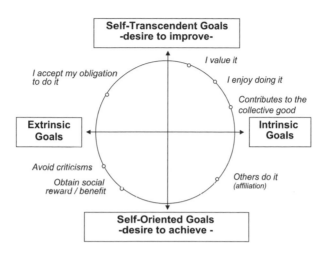

Figure 1. Representation of the motives for carrying out ERB according to SDT (Deci & Ryan, 2000) and the model proposed by Grouzet et al. (2005) to represent the cross-cultural consistency of goals.

extrinsic goals (economic satisfaction and image) and self-transcendent goals (spirituality) versus physical goals (hedonism). The cultural differences that exist in relation to the organisation of goals can vary when taking the economic level of the reference cultures into account, although the actual differences found are few. Figure 1 represents an adaptation of the circular model proposed by Grouzet et al. (2005) to analyse the motives put forward when carrying out recycling ERB. The figure represents motives in accordance with the circular model of Grouzet et al. (2005), together with the intrinsic and extrinsic motivations as described by Deci and Ryan (2000) in Self-Determination Theory. Drawing on all these ideas, the present study aims to analyse goals shared by communities in relation to their recycling habits.

Collective Efficacy

Among the different self-regulating mechanisms of behaviour, Bandura (2002) maintains that self-efficacy is the best predictor of actions in which we choose to get involved and for which a greater level of personal effort is required. Self-efficacy can be defined as the belief in one's own capacity to organise and direct the courses of action required to cope with certain situations in the near future (Bandura, 1997). Therefore, self-efficacy is a self-regulating mechanism that motivates the course of action required to mobilise high levels of effort, persistence in the face of adversity, and achievement of the expected results. Along the same lines, Bandura (1997) presents collective efficacy or perceived group efficacy as a construct that can respond to questions raised about collective motivation. Perceived collective efficacy refers to people's judgements or beliefs regarding their competence to successfully accomplish specific tasks of the collective community to which they belong. The level of confidence generated about collective efficacy determines the perception of the group goal or purpose; the intensity of commitment acquired by the group or community toward the goal it aims to accomplish; the mutual understanding and empathy within the group to achieve satisfactory results and the persistence of the group in the face of adversity (Bandura, 1997). Although the concepts of *self-efficacy* and *perceived group efficacy* might be related, they are independent constructs. We know that judgements about individual efficacy influence group and collective judgements, both directly and indirectly (Bandura, 1997).

However, self-efficacy does not act in isolation; motivation is explained by the relationship between this cognitive judgement of capacity and the situation, emotional state and certain personality variables such as locus of control. For example, in the dynamic

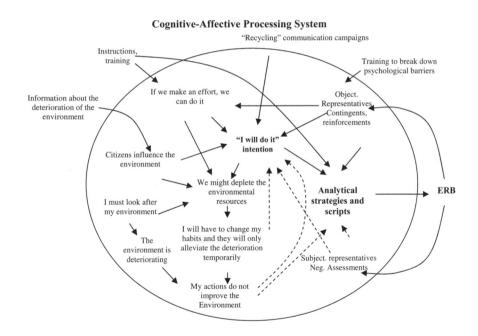

Figure 2. Representation of the social construction generated by an individual in the face of certain stimuli that activate their coding, and the links between the self-regulating mechanisms of the CAPS that explain intention and ERB dynamically. The relationship between the different elements of the CAPS can be positive (continuous lines) or negative (dashed lines). Focusing on these relationships allows a stable framework within which to place explanations of behaviour. Adapted from Shoda and Mischel (2006, Figure 2, p. 445).

cognitive-affective model of personality regarding motivation (Shoda & Mischel, 2006), the elements present are activated, change from trait to state, and interact in accordance with the characteristics of the situation. A representation of this model applied to the explanation of different behaviours is provided below in Figure 2. In the figure this dynamic system has been adapted to apply to recycling behaviour, focusing on mental representations of the psychological significance of situations, representations of self, of others, of the development of events in the future, goals, the affective state, beliefs, expectations, as well as the different ERB chosen. Following the order presented in the figure, the networks established between cognitions and emotions are grounded in past experience and provide a stable framework within which to place explanations of behaviour. The aim of this chapter is to analyse the effect of a shared judgement capacity – "I can do it" – regarding CERB among a specific group of people.

Certain circumstances may foster an increase in or loss of confidence among members of a group or collective that their group will be capable of carrying out a certain action. Analysing the effect of perceived group efficacy on individual behaviour in social dilemmas, Kerr (1989) demonstrated that even though the size of the group was objectively irrelevant to determine the level of the results obtained, the members of small groups experienced a higher level of self-efficacy than the members of larger groups. Furthermore, analysing the effect of group size on perceptions of "collective" efficacy, Kerr (1989) found that when a high proportion of group members in his study demonstrated their contribution to the behaviour required to achieve a common goal (67%), the size of the group did not have a significant effect on perceived collective efficacy. Therefore, the perception of group efficacy directly determined group performance. Hence, one aim of this chapter is to analyse how smaller communities present a greater belief in their collective efficacy to develop pro-environmental action than do larger communities with a weaker perception of collective efficacy.

Method

Participants

Given that the intention of this study was to analyse collective behaviour, a representative sample was taken from the 55 localities that make up the province of Cordoba. The sample was selected at random and proportionally from a population of 360,000 inhabitants (120,000 homes) residing in the 55 localities of Cordoba, a province in Southern Spain. The populations studied varied in size from between 410 and 39,783 inhabitants. The mean population size was 6,072.67 (SD = 7,355). The participants answered the questionnaire in their homes. Participants (72.1%) were women and the total sample was spread across four age ranges: under 30 (29.92%), 31–50 (28.75%), 51–65 (19.91%), and over 66 (21.69%). Four collaborators were trained to administer the questionnaires.

Table 1. Evaluation questionnaire about self-regulating mechanisms of pro-environmental behaviour (Tabernero & Hernández, 2006): items to evaluate the level of self-efficacy to carry out ERB

Score the following statements relating to your waste separation habits in the home ...	Not at all	Not very	Average	Fairly	Very or completely
To what extent do you feel capable of separating ALL paper and cardboard and taking it to the right container?	1 2 3 4	5	6 7	8 9 10	
To what extent do you feel capable of separating ALL glass items and taking them to the right container?	1 2 3 4	5	6 7	8 9 10	
To what extent do you feel capable of separating ALL packaging (plastics, cans, and cartons) and taking them to the right container?	1 2 3 4	5	6 7	8 9 10	

Measures

Intrinsic Satisfaction

In order to ascertain *motives for past recycling behaviour,* the citizens were asked to identify the main reasons that motivated their behaviour in terms of separating waste in the home. They had to identify their motivations using the motivational continuum drawn up by Deci and Ryan (2000) using the seven response options included in Figure 1, namely: Because I have the opportunity ... accepting a rule, ... receiving a reward, ... avoiding penalisation or ... gaining social acceptance, ... contributing to something worthwhile, ... I enjoy doing it or ... contributing to the collective good.

Collective Efficacy for Recycling Behaviour

Self-efficacy refers to beliefs about one's capacity to develop the strategies and courses of action required to carry out different behaviours, in this case in relation to recycling (separating paper/cardboard, glass, and packaging). Collective efficacy can be evaluated as the mean of judgements about individual capacity, individual beliefs about collective capacity or collective belief about collective capacity (Bandura, 1997). This chapter considers collective efficacy as the mean of individual beliefs, in other words the extent to which people feel capable of doing something. Therefore, three specific items were drawn up (see Table 1) for each of these behaviours with a high level of reliability ($\alpha = .91$).

The responses followed a normal distribution pattern and citizens presented relatively high levels of self-efficacy ($M = 6.83$; $DT = 1.98$). In another study developed by Tabernero and Hernández (2006) with a sample of university students, nine items were used, similar to those proposed here but adapted to nine relevant environmental behaviours proposed by Osbaldiston and Sheldon (2003).

Observed Collective Recycling Behaviour

Finally, to gain an objective evaluation of the amount of waste recycled in each locality, data were provided by the local recycling company, in terms of kilograms of paper and cardboard recycled per inhabitant per year. The correlation between the two measures was high ($r = .43$, $p < .001$) and so a single observed recycling measure was created for each of the 55 localities evaluated. This collective behaviour measure was calculated by taking the total amount recycled in the locality in 2005, and dividing it by the number of households.

Results

To respond to the first aim of this study, the percentage of responses given for each of the environmental motives presented was analysed. The results show that the majority of pro-environmental behaviours are carried out due to intrinsic motivation and the desire to accomplish self-transcendent goals: "I value it," "I enjoy doing it," and "because it contributes to the collective good." Specifically, behaviours are based on the desire to contribute to the collective good (68% of participants declared they had engaged in ERB for this reason), having incorporated that behaviour into their system of values (27%), because others do it (7%), the mere fact of enjoying it (3%), having the obligation to do it (3%), the opportunity of obtaining a reward (2%), and to avoid criticism (1%).

A correlation analysis conducted between collective behaviour and each of the motivations revealed that communities that placed the highest value on ERB and enjoyed engaging in ERB presented a significant and positive correlation with the collective behaviour registered ($r - .25$, $p < .05$; $r = .28$, $p < .05$, respectively).

In relation to the second aim of the study regarding the link between population size and collective efficacy judgements, the correlation analysis did not reveal a significant relationship ($r = -.17$, $p = .07$), although the negative direction of the correlation does support the hypothesis that smaller populations present higher collective efficacy judgements than larger populations. By distributing the populations into 10 equal groups according to the number of inhabitants (1 = fewer than 948 inhabitants; 2 = up to 1,483; 3 = up to 1,809; 4 = up to 2,699; 5 = up to 3,576; 6 = up to 4,647; 7 = up to 5,660; 8 = up to 7,562; 9 = up to 18,355; and 10 = over 18,356 inhabitants), Figure 3 shows that smaller populations maintain higher judgements of collective efficacy than the rest.

As for the third aim of this study regarding the relationship between collective efficacy and collective behaviour, the results show that populations with a better judgement of collective capacity carry out a higher number of recycling actions ($r = .32$, $p < .01$).

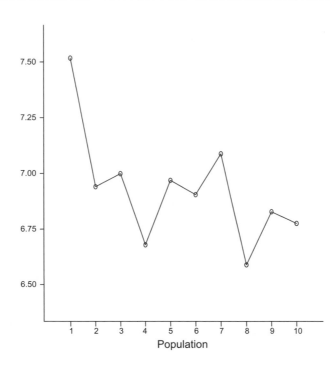

Figure 3. Relationship between population size according to the number of inhabitants and the perception of collective efficacy.

Discussion and Conclusion

The findings of this study support the relationship between collective efficacy and collective behaviour. Given that self-efficacy and collective efficacy are self-regulating mechanisms (motivators of behaviour) and, therefore, act as predictors of behaviour, the analysis performed supports the hypothesis that populations with a higher judgement of collective efficacy also recycle more. Furthermore, continuing with the aim of ascertaining the role of group efficacy in performance, when analysing the size of the population in relation to judgements of collective efficacy, it was found that smaller populations maintained higher judgements of collective efficacy. This result supports the thesis put forward by Kerr (1989) about the relationship between judgements of collective efficacy and group size. It would be interesting to analyse this relationship using the identity of the group or collective as a co-variable. According to Kerr and Kaufman-Gilliland (1997), identity has a decisive influence on performance in a group task. Following on from the work of Tabernero, Arenas, and Briones (2007), it also would be interesting to analyse the effect of previous experiences of cooperation on the community's judgement of collective efficacy.

Another significant finding of this chapter links the intrinsic and self-transcendent goals shared by the collective with CERB. Other authors (Eisler, Eisler, & Yoshida, 2003) have evaluated the effect of cultural differences on the perceived importance of protecting the environment. In their study, they demonstrate that certain cultures (Germany and Sweden) carry out a greater number of protective actions than others (Japan). These differences must be approached with caution since the sample used for the study was composed entirely of university students. Along the same lines, Corral-Verdugo and Frías (2006) indicate that most of the psychosocial models used to explain and predict ERB have not incorporated the importance of the cultural variable and this could explain their low predictive power.

In summary, the findings of this study highlight the importance of generating judgements of collective efficacy within the population and maintaining a high level of intrinsic satisfaction with environmental actions. Therefore, it would be useful to create environmental training programmes adapted to different contexts (work, home, and leisure) as well as environmental education programmes and publicity campaigns aimed at generating judgements of environmental self-efficacy within the population. Using four sources to generate judgements of self-efficacy (own experience, the model, persuasion, and psychophysiological states), environmental policies should aim to create confidence among citizens in their capacity to carry out specific environmental actions that help to protect the environment.

Acknowledgments

This chapter was based on two research projects supported by the Spanish Ministry of Science and Technology under Grants PSI2009-07423 and PSI2009-08896 in which Carmen Tabernero and Bernardo Hernandez are the main researchers, respectively.

References

Bandura, A. (1997). *Self-efficacy: The exercise of control*. New York: Freeman.
Bandura, A. (2002). Environmental sustainability by sociocognitive deceleration of population growth. In P. Schmuch & W. Schultz (Eds.), *The psychology of sustainable development* (pp. 209–238). Dordrecht, The Netherlands: Kluwer.
Corral-Verdugo, V., & Frías, M. (2006). Personal normative beliefs, antisocial behavior, and residential water conservation. *Environment and Behavior, 38*, 406–421.
Deci, E. L., & Ryan, R. M. (2000). The "what" and "why" of goal pursuits: Human needs and the self-determination behavior. *Psychological Inquiry, 11*, 227–268.
De Young, R. (2000). Expanding and evaluating motives for ennvironmentally responsible behavior. *Journal of Social Issues, 56*, 509–526.

Eisler, A. D., Eisler, H., & Yoshida, M. (2003). Perception of human ecology: Cross-cultural and gender comparisons. *Journal of Environmental Psychology, 23*, 89–101.

Geller, E. S. (2002). The challenge of increasing pro-environment behavior. In R. B. Bechtel & A. Churchman (Eds.), *Handbook of environmental psychology.* New York: Wiley.

Grouzet, F. M. E., Kasser, T., Ahuvia, A., Fernandez-Dols, J. M., Kim, Y., Lau, S., et al. (2005). The structure of goal contents across 15 cultures. *Journal of Personality and Social Psychology, 89*, 800–816.

Kasser, T., & Ryan, R. M. (1996). Further examining the American dream: Differential correlates of intrinsic and extrinsic goals. *Personality and Social Psychology Bulletin, 22*, 80–87.

Kerr, N. L. (1989). Illusions of efficacy: The effects of group size on perceived efficacy in social dilemmas. *Journal of Experimental Social Psychology, 25*, 287–313.

Kerr, N. L., & Kaufman-Gilliland, C. M. (1997). "... and besides, I probably couldn't have made a difference anyway": Justification of social dilemma defection via perceived self-inefficacy. *Journal of Experimental Social Psychology, 33*, 211–230.

Osbaldiston, R., & Sheldon, K. M. (2003). Promoting internalized motivation for environmentally responsible behavior. A prospective study of environmental goals. *Journal of Environmental Psychology, 23*, 349–357.

Schwartz, S. (1992). Universals in the content and structure of values: Theoretical advances and empirical tests in 20 countries. *Advances in Experimental Social Psychology, 25*, 1–65.

Shoda, Y., & Mischel, W. (2006). Applying meta-theory to achieve generalisability and precision in personality science. *Applied Psychology. An International Review, 55*, 439–452.

Tabernero, C., Arenas, A., & Briones, E. (2007). Previous experience and group efficacy on social dilemmas. *Psicologia, 11*, 83–105.

Tabernero, C., & Hernández, B. (2006). Environmental motivation: Self-regulation and environmental behaviour. *Bulletin of People-Environment Studies, 28*, 3–6.

The Ecological Concern in Consumer's Choices of Organic and Genetically Modified Food Products

Pierluigi Caddeo

Department of Economic and Social Research, University of Cagliari, Italy

Abstract

Different studies show that personal health and preservation of natural environment are strongly related to considerations about responsible food consumption behaviours. These considerations are often related to the difference between Organic (O) and Genetically Modified (GM) food products. The purpose of the present study is to explore consumer's evaluations towards food products composed of O and GM ingredients, and in particular to explore whether ecological motives underlying the food choice, such as the natural and healthy food content and the ethical concern, could play a role in consumer's evaluations of these food products. Fifty-three Italian students were asked to rate on a 7-point likert scale two pieces of cheese labelled as 95% O and 95% GM. Afterwards, participants' ecological motives for the food choices were assessed. Results show a more positive evaluation for O food products rather than for the GM ones in all evaluative dimensions. The health hazard related to the consumption was found to be affected by natural content motives for food choice, especially in consumers with high motivations. Instead, consumers with low natural content motives seem to be more confident in both these products.

Key words: consumer conducts, ecological concern, genetically modified food choices, health behaviours, organic food choices

People's well-being is one of the important factors in the multidimensional concept of quality of life (QoL). The World Health Organization Group (1998) defined QoL as a set of variables with regard to people's physical health, psychological conditions, social relationships, beliefs, and the relationship established with the salient characteristics of the environment in which people live. Starting from this perspective, personal well-being is considered to be related to a subjective evaluation of the personal condition ascribed in a specific social and environmental context. Thus, people's beliefs, evaluations, and attitudes toward both personal and environmental health could be considered as motives underlying specific choices and behaviours they direct to achieve and maintain health and well-being.

A particular kind of behaviour, such as making responsible food choices, seems to be strongly related to the considerations about consumption consequences on preservation of the natural environment and on personal health (Magnusson, Arvola, Koivisto Hursti, Åberg, & Sjöden, 2003; Wandel & Bugge, 1997).

Different studies provide evidence to the claim that people are more likely to believe that they will contribute to sustainability efforts by performing environmentally friendly purchasing behaviours (Ellen, Wiener, & Cobb-Walgren, 1991; Howard & Allen, 2006). Thus environmentally friendly behaviours are performed by people through their consumption patterns to sustain the environment and to protect the earth's natural resources (Mainieri, Barnett, Valdero, Unipan, & Oskamp, 1997).

With a pro-environmental sound definition of their lifestyle, people could define their consumption patterns, focusing attention on the difference between organic (O) and genetically modified (GM) food products. Previous research has shown that motivation for purchasing organic food products seems tied to motives such as the perceived benefit for one's health, and the related environmental and political considerations (Gaskell et al., 2000; Grankvist & Biel, 2001; Honkanen, Verplanken, & Olsen, 2006; Magnusson et al., 2003). In particular, environmental concern has been found to be a major determinant of buying organic food (e.g., Grunert, 1993; Van Dam, 1991).

A widely negative judgement, jointly associated with moral and ethical doubts, seems to be related to GM food products and to the perceived unknown long-term consequences for one's health and for the environment (Frewer & Shepherd, 1995; Magnusson & Koivisto Hursti, 2002; Magnusson et al., 2003). Nevertheless, recent studies demonstrated that when GM food products are assessed to provide tangible benefits for human health or to be "better for the environment," consumers are more likely to buy them (Frewer, Howards, & Shepherd, 1996; Townsend & Campbell, 2004).

Referring to food consumption, consumer's product judgements and decisions could be affected by the verbal labels used to describe specific product attributes (Johnson & Levin, 1985; Levin, Johnson, Russo, & Deldin, 1985). The psychological literature presents a few studies focusing on the role of verbal descriptions in positive versus negative ways upon O and GM food consumer conducts.

The effect of food attributes on consumer's judgements was assessed by Levin and Gaeth (1988) in a study in which people were asked to rate on several dimensions a piece of ground beef described as 75% lean or 25% fat. Results show a more favourable evaluation for the beef labelled 75% lean rather than for the 25% fat.

A strong link to the plausibility of an information framing effect toward O and GM food products may be found in Italian legislation about these types of products. In fact, food products must contain at least 95% of ingredients to acquire the biological certification. The legislation also defines a tolerance level for the accidental presence of GM organisms (lower than 0.9%), for a variety of GM organisms that have received one favourable scientific evaluation of related risks. In addition, if cows are fed with GM cereals, the cheeses produced with their milk would not be considered GM foods.

Given these considerations, the main aim of the present study is to explore consumer's evaluations toward foods composed of ingredients derived from O or GM organisms. More specifically, we want to assess empirically whether ecological motives underlying food choice that encompass natural and healthy food contents and the ethical and environmental concerns, can play a role in consumer's evaluations of food products labelled as organic or genetically modified.

In particular, on the basis of the literature reviewed so far, we hypothesize that:

H1: Consumer's evaluations will be more positive for products composed of organic ingredients rather than food composed of GM ingredients;
H2: Consumers with high ecological concerns will evaluate O food products more positively than people with low ecological motives.

Methods

Pre-experimental Phase

Two preliminary studies to provide the soundness of our procedures and to define experimental conditions for the main study were carried out. The first study, using the method of free association (Rozin, Kurzer, & Cohen, 2002), was conducted to identify evaluative dimensions for O and GM food products. A sample of 36 university students participated in the study. They were asked to write on a sheet of paper all the words that came to mind in response to the words "organic food" and genetically modified food. The terms were presented in random order. Findings of this study identified a set of the most representative adjectives as follows: (a) Good taste; (b) Healthy; (c) Bad; (d) Natural; (e) Tasty; (f) Dangerous; and (g) Genuine.

The second preliminary study was conducted to define the percentage of presence of O or GM ingredients that activated the high framing effect. Participants (75 University students) were asked to evaluate an Italian cheese on seven qualitative dimensions on the basis of the descriptive label. Participants were assigned randomly to one of the experimental conditions (95% – 75% – 50%). The descriptive label lists the typical characteristics of this product and it was maintained constant in all conditions. In the description, the different percentage of GM or organic milk contained in the cheese involved was underlined. Results show that the attribute framing manipulation leads participants to evaluate in more positive terms positive food products containing organic ingredients rather than food products containing GM ingredients. In particular, the presence of 95% of organic ingredients seems to be the most powerful in activating a framing effect.

Participants, Procedure, and Materials

A total of 53 undergraduates of the University of Cagliari (Italy) took part in this study. The sample consisted of 14 males and 39 females; mean age = 23 years (SD = 5 years). Participants were approached by trained interviewer and asked to participate in a University survey about people's food purchasing behaviours. They were assured about the anonymous nature of the survey. Data were collected during January 2007.

Participants were asked to imagine buying a piece of Italian cheese. Two food product labels representing two different Italian cheeses were presented. Presentation order was randomly assigned for each participant. The description, as in the second pilot study, lists the typical characteristics of this product. Cheeses were similar on all of their characteristics, except for the difference in the quality of the milk: (a) 95% from GM products and (b) 95% from organic products.

Participants were asked to rate the cheeses on seven semantic differential scales. The following bipolar evaluative adjectives were used: (a) Good taste-Bad taste; (b) Healthy-Unhealthy; (c) Good-Bad; (d) Natural-Artificial; (e) Tasty-Tasteless; (f) Safe-Dangerous; and (g) Genuine-Altered. A higher score indicates a more negative attribute evaluation than a lower score.[1] The right-left position of the adjectives was constant for both the conditions.

Afterwards, participants completed a questionnaire measuring motives underlying the selection of food selected from the *Food Choice Questionnaire* (Steptoe, Pollard, & Wardle, 1995). In particular, three subscales measuring three specific dimensions of the food choice were used: (a) *Natural Content*, composed of three items (i.e., contains no artificial ingredients); (b) *Health*, composed of six items (i.e., keeps me healthy); and (c) *Ethical Concern*, composed of three items. (i.e., Is it packaged in an environmentally friendly way?) Seven-step Likert scales were used for all the items.

Results

A mixed model of variance was used to test our hypotheses. Within-subjects measures were a 2 (Product: 95% O versus 95% GM) as a repeated factor on the 7 (evaluative dimensions: Good taste; Healthy; Good; Natural; Tasty; Safe; and Genuine) as dependent variables; whereas between-subjects factors were the ecological motives for food choice, respectively: Natural Content, Health, and Ethical Concern.[2]

---

[1]   In further analyses, data were reverse scored to associate high scores to positive evaluations.
[2]   Each factor was dichotomized (by a median split) in high and low motives for food choice.

A significant multivariate effect of the within subjects test was found for the product evaluations (Wilk's $\lambda = .56$, $F_{(7, 40)} = 4.38$, $p < .01$, $\eta^2 = .43$). In relation to H1, products containing organic ingredients received more positive evaluations than the GM ones. Independently from motives for food choice, since no statistically significant multivariate interactions between product evaluations and each one of the motives for food choice were found: (Natural Content: $F_{(2, 42)} = 1.15$; NS); (Health: $F_{(2, 42)} = 1.16$; NS); (Ethical Concern: $F_{(2, 42)} = 1.30$; NS). Also multivariate test of between-subjects effect was found to be not significant for each one of the factors: (Natural Content: $F_{(2, 42)} = 1.19$; NS); (Health: $F_{(2, 42)} = .94$; NS); and (Ethical Concern: $F_{(2, 42)} = .36$; NS).

The univariate contrast analyses show that product evaluations between O and GM products are significantly higher for O products than for GM in each of the seven evaluative dimensions. Results are summarized in Table 1.

Further, findings offer partial support to Hypothesis 2; in fact, only the natural content motive to food choice was found to affect consumers' evaluations. More specifically, consumers showing high motives for food choice related to the natural content seem to discriminate between O and GM food products only on evaluative dimensions regarding health and safety. Dimensions relevant to taste were not significant. Results of univariate test and estimated marginal means are summarized in Table 2.

Differences were found between consumers with low and high motives relative to the natural content of foods. Consumers with low motives seem to be more confident in GM products and, at the same time, they positively valued both products. Instead, people with high motives relative to natural content of foods seemed to express more criticism toward GM products rather than O products. In fact, they manifest lower evaluations toward GM products rather than those manifested by consumers with low motives. In particular, the degree of observed statistical power (η^2 index) revealed that the main effect relative to the differences in consumers with high and low motives regarding the evaluative dimensions is mainly in reference to the dimension of safety of the products as represented in Figure 1.

Table 1. Univariate test and estimated marginal means of product evaluations of O and GM food products

Product evaluations (N = 53)	95% O M (SD)	95% GM M (SD)	F	η^2
Good taste	5.31 (0.15)	4.83 (0.19)	4.10*	.082
Healthy	5.26 (0.15)	3.87 (0.24)	20.36**	.307
Good	5.30 (0.16)	4.59 (0.20)	8.02**	.148
Natural	5.66 (0.19)	3.53 (0.28)	30.01**	.395
Tasty	5.57 (0.16)	5.01 (0.17)	5.88*	.113
Safe	5.31 (0.18)	3.85 (0.24)	20.90**	.312
Genuine	5.57 (0.16)	3.49 (0.27)	31.17**	.404

$^*p < .05$, $^{**}p < .01$ (ratings from 1 to 7, with 1 = high negative evaluation and 7 = high positive evaluation).

Table 2. Univariate test and estimated marginal means of product evaluations of O and GM food products in high and low motives for food choice

Product evaluations (N = 53)	Natural content motives	95% O M (SD)	95% GM M (SD)	F	η^2
Good taste	Low	5.28 (0.22)	5.21 (0.29)	2.87	.059
	High	5.33 (0.20)	4.46 (0.25)		
Healthy	Low	5.19 (0.23)	4.51 (0.36)	5.11*	.100
	High	5.32 (0.20)	3.23 (0.31)		
Good	Low	5.13 (0.24)	4.97 (0.30)	4.91*	.097
	High	5.47 (0.21)	4.19 (0.26)		
Natural	Low	5.40 (0.29)	4.23 (0.42)	5.96*	.115
	High	5.91 (0.25)	2.83 (0.37)		
Tasty	Low	5.55 (0.24)	5.21 (0.26)	0.85	.018
	High	5.58 (0.21)	4.81 (0.23)		
Safe	Low	5.09 (0.27)	4.57 (0.36)	8.54**	.157
	High	5.53 (0.23)	3.14 (0.31)		
Genuine	Low	5.44 (0.24)	4.18 (0.41)	4.85*	.095
	High	5.70 (0.21)	2.79 (0.36)		

*$p < .05$, **$p < .01$ (ratings from 1 to 7, with 1 = high negative evaluation and 7 = high positive evaluation).

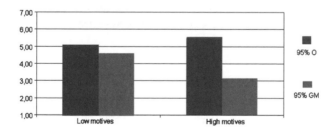

Figure 1. Estimated marginal means of evaluations on safety for O and GM food products as a function of motives underlying the food choice.

Discussion and Conclusions

This study, focusing on environmental concern as one of the main motives underlying people's consumption choices of organic and genetically modified food products, explored the role of health and environmental implications in motivating people to engage in sustainable consumption patterns.

Consistent with the literature, findings show that food products with O ingredients received more positive evaluations than the GM ones. A general negative evaluation towards food products composed of GM ingredients was discovered in each of the evaluative dimensions. Motives related to natural content of food products seem to affect specific evaluative dimensions of food. However, dimensions about perceived taste of the food do not discriminate between different kinds of these products, whereas safety and health hazard dimensions seem to cover evaluations of consumers with high or low natural content motives for food choices. The presence of organic or GM ingredients influenced consumers' evaluations of the perceived safety related to consumption consequences. It is particularly interesting that consumers with high motives related to natural content revealed high criticism towards GM food products. Consumers with low motives seem to be more confident about these kinds of products, and they positively valued both GM and O food products. Perhaps consumers with low motives could be less aware about differences between these products, or merely less interested in the possible consequences of the foods they consume.

These findings confirm that people aware of the environmental impact of their consumption choices are more likely to hold pro-environmental attitudes and to perform sustainable purchase conduct. Consequently, it is plausible to underline the need to sustain green consumption patterns by strengthening consumer's beliefs about environmental consequences of specific consumption choices (e.g., Mainieri et al., 1997).

Further replications and empirical evidence are needed to confirm these outcomes. In particular, future research must be addressed to explore, with more accuracy, the relationship between environmental antecedents and consequences of food choices and consumption conducts in terms of environmentally friendly behaviour (e.g., Bamberg, 2003; Fransson & Gärling, 1999; Thøgersen & Ölander, 2003). Moreover, food consumption patterns must be explored, taking into account consequences and implications for local versus global matters. Hence, a replication of the present study using other fundamental information for consumers (e.g., price labels) and observed measures of actual behaviours is probably needed.

In conclusion, the present findings may have practical implications that need to be focused. People who define their specific consumption lifestyle by pro-environmental motives are driven in their food choices by providing a sustainable effort. Nevertheless, these consumers had a few chances to find products with labels containing information that could affect their evaluations. In fact, on the one hand, food product labels do not always present information about some ingredient's origin because products composed of 95% of organic ingredients are considered totally organic. On the other hand, a food product composed in breeding that makes use of GM organics could be not sold as a GM food product.

Thus, public authorities must attend to the differences in individual motives and different levels of awareness on these issues to set up campaigns concerned with food-related policies and/or for environmental policy strategies. Moreover, consumers and pro-environmental associations must consider the need of even more complete information about food products to support and promote consumption lifestyles in a more environmental, sustainable, and health-care-related perspective.

References

Bamberg, S. (2003). How does environmental concern influence specific environmentally related behaviors? A new answer to an old question. *Journal of Environmental Psychology, 23*, 21–32.

Ellen, P. S., Wiener, J. L., & Cobb-Walgren, C. (1991). The role of perceived consumer effectiveness in motivating environmentally conscious behaviors. *Journal of Public Policy and Marketing, 10*, 102–117.

Fransson, N., & Gärling, T. (1999). Environmental concern: Conceptual definitions, measurement methods, and research findings. *Journal of Environmental Psychology, 19*, 369–382.

Frewer, L. J., Howards, C., & Shepherd, R. (1996). The influence of realistic product exposure towards genetic engineering of food. *Food Quality and Preference, 7*, 61–67.

Frewer, L. J., & Shepherd, R. (1995). Ethical concerns and risk perceptions associated with different applications of genetic engineering: Interrelationships with the perceived need for regulation of the technology. *Agriculture and Human Values, 12*(1), 48–57.

Gaskell, G., Allum, N., Bauer, M., Durant, J., Allansdottir, A., Bonfadelli, H., et al. (2000). Biotechnology and the European public. *Nature Biotechnology, 18*, 935–938.

Grankvist, G., & Biel, A. (2001). The importance of beliefs and purchase criteria in the choice of eco-labeled food products. *Journal of Environmental Psychology, 21*, 405–410.

Grunert, S. C. (1993). Green consumerism in Denmark: Some evidence from the OKO foods-project. *Der Markt, 32*(3), 140–151.

Honkanen, P., Verplanken, B., & Olsen, S. O. (2006). Ethical values and motives driving organic food choice. *Journal of Consumer Behaviour, 5*, 420–430.

Howard, P. H., & Allen, P. (2006). Beyond organic: Consumer interest in new labelling schemes in the central coast of California. *International Journal of Consumer Studies, 30*, 439–451.

Johnson, R. D., & Levin, I. P. (1985). More than meets the eye: The effect of missing information on purchase evaluations. *Journal of Consumer Research, 12*, 169–177.

Levin, I. P., & Gaeth, G. J. (1988). How consumers are affected by the framing of attribute information before and after consuming the product. *Journal of Consumer Research, 15*(3), 374–379.

Levin, I. P., Johnson, R. D., Russo, C. P., & Deldin, P. J. (1985). Framing effects in judgement tasks with varying amounts of information. *Organizational Behaviour and Human Decision Processes, 36*, 362–377.

Magnusson, M. K., Arvola, A., Koivisto Hursti, U.-A., Åberg, L., & Sjöden, P. O. (2003). Choice of organic foods is related to perceived consequences for human health and to environmentally friendly behaviour. *Appetite, 40*, 109–117.

Magnusson, M. K., & Koivisto Hursti, U.-A. (2002). Consumer attitudes towards genetically modified foods. *Appetite, 39*(1), 9–24.

Mainieri, T., Barnett, E. G., Valdero, T. R., Unipan, J. B., & Oskamp, S. (1997). Green buying: The influence of environmental concern on consumer behaviour. *Journal of Social Psychology, 137*, 189–204.

Rozin, P., Kurzer, N., & Cohen, A. B. (2002). Free associations to "food": The effects of gender, generation, and culture. *Journal of Research in Personality, 36*, 419–441.

Steptoe, A., Pollard, T. M., & Wardle, J. (1995). Development of a measure of the motives underlying the selection of food: The food choice questionnaire. *Appetite, 25*, 267–284.

Thøgersen, J., & Ölander, F. (2003). Spillover of environment-friendly consumer behavior. *Journal of Environmental Psychology, 23*, 225–236.

Townsend, E., & Campbell, S. (2004). Psychological determinants of willingness to taste and purchase genetically modified food. *Risk Analysis, 24*(5), 1385–1393.

Van Dam, Y. K. (1991). A conceptual model of environmentally conscious consumer behaviour. In *Proceedings of the European Marketing Academy's Conference – Marketing thought around the world* (Vol. 2, pp. 463–483). Dublin: Michael Smurfit Graduate School of Business.

Wandel, M., & Bugge, A. (1997). Environmental concern in consumer evaluation of food quality. *Food Quality and Preference, 8*, 19–26.

World Health Organization Group. (1998). *Group development of the World Health Organization WHOQOL*.

Diversity in Social Groups and Inclusive Urban Environments

Children in the Neighbourhood

Sense of Safety and Well-Being

Laura Migliorini[1] and Paola Cardinali[2]

[1]Department of Anthropological Sciences (DISA), University of Genova, Italy
[2]Department of Human Study (DISTUM), University of Genova, Italy

Abstract

A considerable body of research addresses the role of physical environment in child development. Children's experience of their environment is connected with their perception of safety and with the feelings of fear. Safety is an essential resource for everyday life that could influence the sense of well-being. The first purpose of this chapter is to analyse the feelings of safety and fear of crime that arise from living as a child in urban environments that differ in structural and social features; afterward to investigate children's self-esteem and well-being and their relationship with sense of security. 518 Italian students (average age 10 years) from primary schools of three different urban neighbourhoods participated in this study. The questionnaire was composed by demographic information, measures of urban sense of safety and self-esteem, and well-being scale that includes measures of outdoor and indoor activities. The children's personal sense of safety does not seem to be related to structural elements of neighbourhood. These data underline that more research is needed to analyse this construct in relation to neighbourhoods that are different in structural features. Furthermore, children who participate in more outdoor activities report higher levels of well-being and self-esteem.

Key words: childhood, neighbourhood features, outdoor activities, sense of safety, well-being

Stokols and Altman (1987), in their introduction of the first handbook of environmental psychology, defined environmental psychology as the study of behaviour and human well-being relative to the social-physical environment. Recently, environmental psychology focuses more on the relationship between inhabitants and place of residence. Identification of the pathways by which neighbourhoods affect well-being is critical to moving the field forward toward a more complete understanding of the complex relationships between residential environments and well-being (O'Campo, Salmon, & Burke, 2009).

This relationship assumes different features according to the particular ecological niche (Swenson & Prelow, 2005) and to the diversity of people's experiences, and it is increasingly important to understand its many forms, contradictions, and implications for environmental psychology. For these reasons, we consider it very relevant to focus our attention on multiple differences which not only characterise neighbourhood, but also the people who live in those neighbourhoods.

One of the main questions that arises from this study regards the relationship among differences in the sense of safety, people, and environment diversity. To study the interaction between the individual and the environment, the transactional and contextual approaches (Bonnes, Bonaiuto, & Lee, 2004) have focused on molar units of analysis, overcoming the tendency to look at very specific and fragmented aspects of the home environment. This approach recognizes the important role played by the affective and temporal dimensions of the environmental experience (Bonaiuto, Aiello, Perugini, Bonnes, & Ercolani, 1999). At first, this relationship was examined in relation to the quality of the physical characteristics of the residential environment, however, the current transactional perspective looks more at meaningful units, focusing on such aspects as the appraisal of residential satisfaction, attachment, or identification to place – variables that create stability and security and defend personal identity (Brown & Perkins, 1992; Uzzell, Pol, & Badenas, 2002). Within this theoretical framework, relevant contributions (Moser, 1995) have suggested that the feeling of insecurity is a multidimensional construct that is made up of three dimensions: Cognitive, emotional, and behavioural. One point that has excited researchers' curiosities ever since the very first studies on this subject is the lack of a direct relationship between objective insecurity (the risk of victimization) and subjective insecurity. Both subjective and objective dimensions of sense of safety can influence the sense of well-being, the possibility to enhance exploration of the environment, and to grow individual autonomy. Research on urban lack of safety has been carried out mostly on the adult and elderly populations; little has been written about this effect during childhood (Zani, 2003).

An increasingly popular approach to understanding the influence of the environment on development is through ecological models. Within these theories it is hypothesized that social systems are ecological influences which play a significant role in children's development. Adaptations of Bronfenbrenner's work to examine environmental influence on child development offer useful and important ways of conceptualizing and designing studies intended to improve community health. According to this theory, developmental transitions are viewed as a product of a developmental system that involves a person's biological predispositions and the environmental influences she/he experiences (Bronfenbrenner, 1986; Bronfenbrenner & Evans, 2000). Ecological theory and research indicate that neighbourhood and neighbours, at different levels, affect child development (Figure 1).

Leventhal and Brooks-Gunn (2000) reviewed the effects of residential neighbourhood on child and adolescent well-being. Specifically, studies point to structural characteristics such as poverty, mobility, and differences in social organization impacting levels of risk

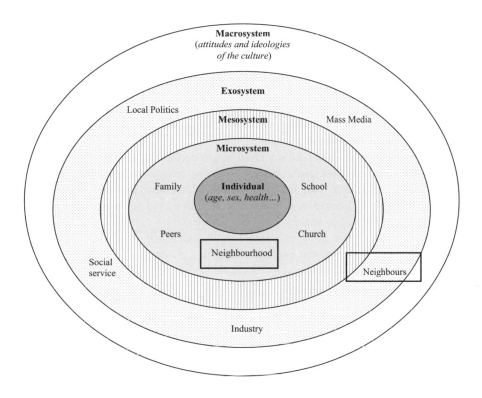

Figure 1. Ecological model, adapted from McLaren and Have (2005).

for children and youth. With an interest in the adaptive characteristics of neighbourhoods, other studies examine the availability of resources and positive opportunities such as education and employment as protective factors for children and youth. Access to resources for basic physical and social needs within one's own community is tied to a range of positive outcomes and creates a supportive residential community (Brower, 2005). Moreover, greater attention to neighbourhood research should be useful to help low-income urban families and children cope successfully with the challenges posed by their neighbourhoods (Roosa, Jenn-Yun Tein, & Cree, 2003).

Examinations of the neighbourhood as a context for development have met formidable challenges (Anthony & Nicotera, 2008). In particular, preliminary studies suggest that understanding how youth perceive and experience their neighbourhood is fundamental to understanding neighbourhood as an influential context. However, the specific processes and mechanisms of neighbourhood influences are not investigated very much nor well understood. The analysis of the complex relationship between structural neighbourhood variables, subjective experiences of those variables, and developmental outcomes is hindered by this lack of information.

Furthermore, neighbourhoods represent a relevant context for children, adults, and the elderly (Kahana, Lovegreen, Kahana, & Kahana, 2003), and researchers analyse which mechanisms are embedded in this relation (Sampson, 2001). In particular, Booth and Crouter (2001) study which elements "make a village" and what are the collective processes that contribute to making a neighbourhood environment healthy for children and adolescents. How are neighbourhood mechanisms measured? What are their structural sources of variation? Are neighbourhood mechanisms embedded in citywide processes that transcend local boundaries?

It is not very clear, however, how a child might define neighbourhood (as the street where she/he lives or as people who engage in the same activity in the neighbourhood) (Anthony & Nicotera, 2008; Min & Lee, 2006). Neighbourhood resources, both physical (such as availability of libraries and health care facilities), and socio-emotional (such as social support), contribute to healthy child development.

During childhood, the need to explore both one's self and one's environment becomes more significant and this expresses itself in a greater involvement in potentially risky situations. Some authors (Perkins, Meek, & Taylor, 1992; Perkins & Taylor, 1996) have shown that internal processes that produce levels of malaise characterized by anxiety and stress (e.g., living in an area that is not very safe) can limit people's movements, make changes in social relations, and increase conflicts between groups. The sense of insecurity is not necessarily connected to the existence of "objective" dangers but often varies according to subjective experiences or socio-demographic features such as age, sex, and social position. In a study by Farver, Ghosh, and Garcia (2000), preadolescents who considered their neighbourhood "unsafe" felt worried and powerless – independent of whether this danger was real or imagined. The subjective perception of a threat to one's own safety raises levels of anxiety, vulnerability, stress, and vigilance, thus undermining feelings of self-esteem and self-efficiency. The literature about this subject has shown how a strong sense of a common bond, the feeling of being integrated into a community, and attachment to a place can lower the sense of insecurity and protect people from the consequences of fear (Chipuer, 2001; Ross & Jang, 2000). Feelings of environmental insecurity and lack of trust in other people can have a strong impact on perceived quality of life and the condition of general well-being in urban contexts.

The relationship that children establish with their "ecological" life context is central and can influence their chances of optimal development, because it can represent a resource for development but also a danger to avoid. Worry about crime is associated in adolescence with lower levels of social and relational skills; such as, increased distrust and suspicion towards other people, lower self-esteem, lower school performance, and reduced activity in sports (Williams, Singh, & Singh, 1994).

This study is part of a wider project of research, by local governance, to analyse and study children living in three neighbourhoods in a peripheral area of Genoa to enhance well-being and adjustment by engaging in prevention programmes. The aim of this study is to analyse the feelings of safety/unsafety and fear of crime in children that arise from living in various urban environments that differ in structural and social features. Moreover, we have investigated children's self-esteem and well-being to examine the link between these variables and their sense of security.

Some key assumptions from the literature, form the basis of the study:

- The feeling of safety is expected to be stronger in the neighbourhood context than in the city as a whole.
- Sense of safety, fears of victimization, self-esteem, and well-being differ according to neighbourhood type.
- Sense of safety, fears of victimization, self-esteem, and well-being differ according to gender.
- There is a correlation among sense of safety, self-esteem, and well-being.

Method

Subjects

Participants are 518 preadolescents (mean age: 9.45 years), 50.4% males, living in three districts in the urban area of Genoa (Italy). We chose children at the end of primary school because during this period, youth experiment with greater autonomy and wider-reaching exploration of their environment, and with increasing exposure to potentially risky situations. This can be a source of higher levels of personal and social insecurity.

Procedures

The subjects were contacted at school and the data were collected by a self-report questionnaire. The students were informed that their answers would be confidential; participation was subject to parental consent.

Measures

The questionnaire was composed of the following instruments:

- *A socio-demographic information schedule:* A brief part of the questionnaire has been used to obtain information concerning subjects' age, sex, educational level, and ethnic identity.
- *Sense of safety in the neighbourhood* (1 item using a 10-point scale).
- *Sense of safety in the city* (1 item using a 10-point scale).
- *A scale of sense of safety in the residence neighbourhood* (12 items). The scale is composed of two factors: Structural features dimension and relational dimension (Migliorini, Zunino, & Piermari, 2004).

- *A fear of victimization measure* (1 item using a 10-point scale).
- *A well-being measure* (VSP-A, Simeoni, Sapin, Antoniotti, & Auquier, 2001). The scale – 34 items – investigates several dimensions of quality of life and includes measures of outdoor and indoor activities with peers.
- *The Rosenberg global self-esteem scales* (10-item version, Rosenberg, 1965). This scale provides a measure of self-esteem, defined as the emotional value perceived by an individual.

Results

As described above, the study surveys include a section about children's sense of safety in the neighbourhood and in the city, so it is possible to compare children's safety/unsafety in the two settings. Children think that their own neighbourhood is safer than the city as a whole ($t = 11.62**$). Nordström (2004) said that the environment of interest to and daily use by children depends on their age. Consistently, this result can be interpreted within the context of the literature about children in cities which shows that parents allowed their children greater autonomy in their own neighbourhoods (Prezza, Alparone, Cristallo, & Secchiano, 2005), favouring the development of a gradual sense of personal responsibility and a more positive relationship with the local district.

Moreover, females feel significantly less safe than their male peers ($M_{females} = 33.67$; $M_{males} = 35.71$). This confirms classic hypotheses about gender differences (Fisher & Sloan, 2003; Schafer, Huebner, & Bynum, 2006; Zani, Cicognani, & Albanesi, 2001) that point to women's greater insecurity in urban contexts, despite the fact that victimization indices are higher among males. Some authors (Stanko, 1995) have talked about the idea of danger socialization among women from infancy. Also the means for well-being ($t = -2.51*$) and self-esteem ($t = 2.72**$) were significantly different between males and females.

Regarding sense of safety construction, according to children, the relational dimension (e.g., *In my neighbourhood I feel secure when I meet persons that I recognize...*) is more relevant ($t = 6.14**$) than structural features of places (e.g., *When roads are not very illuminated I'm frightened*) (Figure 2) that are considered more important for adolescents and adults (Migliorini, Piermari, & Zunino, 2004).

Sense of safety seems to be characterized mainly by the possibility to stay in close relation with others, especially those with whom there is a close relationship. Environmental structural elements play a secondary role in the sense of safety, as compared to social relations. Also the absence of significant differences on the scale on the sense of safety among the three neighbourhoods suggests a minor role of the neighbourhood's structural features in the construction of a sense of safety in children. The item *"Being in places where I can do pleasant things gives me a sense of safety"* had the highest average, which supports the idea, according to the place theory (Canter, 1977), that activity is one of the main constitutive components of place. This experience emphasizes the active and conscious use of space as a means of recreation and to gain a sense of security. Moreover, there is evidence

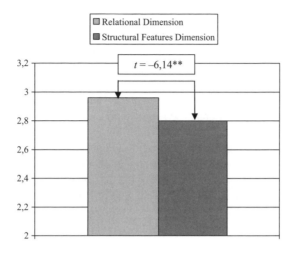

Figure 2. Relational and structural features of places.

that one's neighbourhood is the key setting for the time children spend outdoors (Klesges, Eck, Hanson, Haddock, & Klesges, 1990; Sallis, Prochanska, & Taylor, 2000). There is a significant difference ($F = 6.58**$) in children's outdoor activities among the three districts, but it is not clear if this diversity should be connected to variability in population or in neighbourhood's structural and/or environmental characteristics.

Children who live in neighbourhood 1, in which outdoor activities are more present (Figure 3), reported significantly higher levels of self-esteem ($F = 10.13**$) and less fear

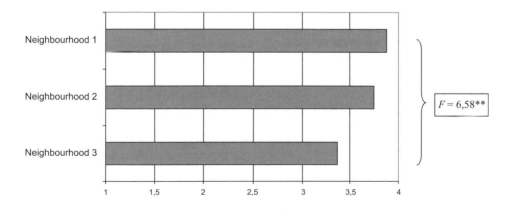

Figure 3. Outdoor children activities: Differences among neighbourhood.

of victimization than others, while there are no significant differences in the means regarding sense of safety among the three neighbourhoods.

In addition, individuals' socio-demographic characteristics may influence perceptions of their neighbourhoods. As previously shown, females and males tend to be socialized differently and use public spaces in different ways. Older children have been shown to use more extensive areas of the city than younger ones. The level of outdoor activities seems to have a positive affect on children's self-esteem and well-being. As shown in Figure 4, well-being increases when children report more outdoor activity. Also mean scores on self-esteem are statistically significant between low and high outdoor activity levels.

Table 1 shows the correlation matrix among the main variables when looking at the whole sample. This proves useful in verifying the assumption of this research about the relationships among sense of safety, self-esteem, and well-being. Sense of safety correlates stronger with fear of crime ($-.22^{**}$), which could indicate that safety is defined primarily as "absence of fear." On the contrary, the quality of relations seems to be the key element in a positive sense of security.

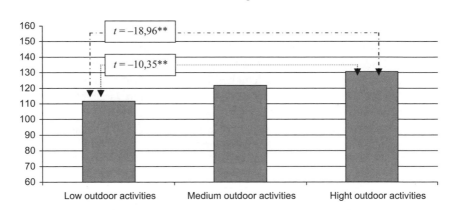

Figure 4. Outdoor activities with friends: Means in well-being.

Table 1. Correlation among variables

	Sense of safety	Fear of victimization	Well-being	Self-esteem	Outdoor activities
Sense of safety	1				
Fear of victimization	$-.22^{**}$	1			
Well-being	$.14^{**}$	$-.14^{**}$	1		
Self-esteem	$.07$	$-.11^{**}$	$.59^{**}$	1	
Outdoor activities	$.08^*$	$-.06$	$.38^{**}$	$.20^{**}$	1

Despite expectations, there is a strong correlation between well-being and self-esteem (.59**), but not as strong between well-being and sense of safety (.14**). According to the literature, children who participate in more outdoor activities have higher levels of well-being (.38**) and self-esteem (.20**).

Discussion and Conclusion

This chapter explores the sense of safety, well-being, and self-esteem in children. In conclusion, we might consider sense of safety as the most salient consequence of the child-environment relationship; however, many elements of this relation must be better explained. The first of these is that personal sense of safety does not seem to be related to structural elements of neighbourhood. This result underlines that more research is needed to analyse this concept in relation to various types of neighbourhoods in terms of structural features. We need to verify this outcome and to answer to the following questions: How are neighbourhood mechanisms measured? What are their structural sources of variation? (Booth & Cronter, 2001).

To discuss our results, we might hypothesize that the influence of neighbourhood on children well-being is probably indirect. One result, as previously stated, is that children who have more outdoor activities have higher levels of well-being and self-esteem. These data should be useful to planning interventions in order to promote the development of skills and interpersonal relationships that might affect the sense of safety in children. It would be particularly useful to develop the classification of criteria that take into account the relational and structural assessment of neighbourhoods according to the well-being of children. This should be accomplished within a molar perspective of intervention, which takes account of both objective and subjective elements. Perception of environmental quality has been measured in adult populations, but is understudied in children; future research might overcome this limitation improving the knowledge of psychological and psychosocial processes that underlie the feeling of safety in childhood. The neighbourhood level of analysis should be the most meaningful unit to study safety in the environment. It could be interesting to identify which kind of neighbourhood factors we must consider to study person-environment fit.

References

Anthony, E. K., & Nicotera, N. (in press). Youth perceptions of neighbourhood hassles and resources: A mixed method analysis. *Children and Youth Services. Review.* Available Online April 7 2008.

Bonaiuto, M., Aiello, A., Perugini, M., Bonnes, M., & Ercolani, A. P. (1999). Multidimensional perception of residential environment quality and neighbourhood attachment in the urban environment. *Journal of Environmental Psychology, 19*, 331–352.

Bonnes, M., Bonaiuto, M., & Lee, T. (2004). *Teorie in pratica per la psicologia ambientale*. Milano: Raffaello Cortina.

Booth, A., & Crouter, A. C. (2001). *Does it take a village? Community effects on children, adolescents, and families*. Mahwah, NJ: Erlbaum.

Bronfenbrenner, U. (1986). Ecology of the family as a context for human development: Research perspectives. *Developmental Psychology, 22*(6), 723–742.

Bronfenbrenner, U., & Evans, G. (2000). Developmental science in the 21st century: Emerging questions, theoretical models, research designs and empirical findings. *Social Development, 9*, 115–125.

Brower, S. (2005). Community-generating neighbourhoods. In B. Martens & A. Keul (Eds.), *Designing social innovation, planning, building, evaluating* (pp. 273–281). Washington: Hogrefe & Huber.

Brown, B. B., & Perkins, D. D. (1992). Disruptions in place attachment. In I. Altman & S. Low (Eds.), *Human behaviour and environment: Advances in theory and research. Volume 12: Place attachment* (pp. 279–305). New York: Plenum Press.

Canter, D. (1977). *The psychology of place*. London: Architectural Press.

Chipuer, H. (2001). Dyadic attachments and community connectedness: Links with youth's loneliness experiences. *Journal of Community Psychology, 29*, 429–446.

Farver, J. A. M., Ghosh, C., & Garcia, C. (2000). Children's perception of the neighbourhoods. *Journal of Applied Developmental Psychology, 21*, 139–163.

Fisher, B. S., & Sloan, J. J. (2003). Unraveling the fear of victimization among college women: Is the "shadow of sexual assault hypothesis" supported? *Justice Quarterly, 20*, 633–659.

Kahana, E., Lovegreen, L., Kahana, B., & Kahana, M. (2003). Person, environment, and person-environment fit as influences on residential satisfaction of elders. *Environment and Behavior, 35*(3), 434–453.

Klesges, R., Eck, L., Hanson, C., Haddock, C., & Klesges, L. (1990). Effects of obesity, social interactions, and physical environment on physical activity in preschoolers. *Health Psychology, 9*(4), 435–449.

Leventhal, T., & Brooks-Gunn, J. (2000). The neighbourhoods they live in: The effects of neighbourhood residence upon child and adolescent outcomes. *Psychological Bulletin, 126*, 309–337.

McLaren, L., & Have, P. (2005). Ecological perspective in health research. *Journal of Epidemiology and Community Health, 59*, 6–14.

Migliorini, L., Zunino, A. & Piermari, A. (2004). *Sense of safety and perception of life environment: The preadolescent and their parent perception*. Paper presented at 18 Conference of the International Association for People Environment Studies, 7–10 July 2004, IAPS, Wien.

Min, B., & Lee, J. (2006). Children's neighbourhood place as a psychological and behavioural domain. *Journal of Environmental Psychology, 26*, 51–71.

Moser, G. (1995). *Gli stress urbani*. Milano: Edizioni universitarie di Lettere, Economia e Diritto.

Nordström, M. (2004). *How is environment reflected in children's notions of child-friendly environments? Comparing the notions of children living in different environments*. Paper presented at 18 Conference of the International Association for People Environment Studies, 7–10 July 2004, IAPS, Wien.

O'Campo, P., Salmon, C., & Burke, J. (2009). Neighbourhoods and mental well-being: What are the pathways? *Health & Place, 15*, 56–68.

Perkins, D. D., Meek, J. W., & Taylor, R. B. (1992). The physical environment of street blocks and resident perception of crime and disorder: Implication for theory and measurement. *Journal of Environmental Psychology, 12*, 21–34.

Perkins, D. D., & Taylor, R. B. (1996). Ecological assessment of community disorder: Their relationship to fear of crime and theoretical implication. *American Journal of Community Psychology, 24*, 63–107.

Prezza, M., Alparone, F. R., Cristallo, C., & Secchiano, L. (2005). Parental perception of social risk and of positive potentiality of outdoor autonomy for children: The development of two instruments. *Journal of Environmental Psychology, 25*(4), 437–453.

Roosa, M. W., Jenn-Yun Tein, S. J., & Cree, W. (2003). Prevention science and neighborhood influences on low-income children's development: Theoretical and methodological issues. *American Journal of Community Psychology, 31*, 55–72.

Rosenberg, M. (1965). *Society and the adolescent self-image*. Princeton, NJ: Princeton University Press.

Ross, C. E., & Jang, S. J. (2000). Neighborhood disorder, fear, and mistrust: The buffering role of social ties with neighbors. *American Journal of Community Psychology, 28*, 401–420.

Sallis, J. F., Prochaska, J. J., & Taylor, W. C. (2000). A review of correlates of physical activity of children and adolescents. *Medicine & Science in Sports & Exercise, 32*(5), 963–975.

Sampson, R. J. (2001). How do communities undergird or undermine human development? Relevant contexts and social mechanisms. In A. Booth & A. C. Crouter (Eds.), *Does it take a village? Community effects on children, adolescents, and families* (pp. 3–30). Mahwah, NJ: Erlbaum.

Schafer, J. A., Huebner, B., & Bynum, T. S. (2006). Fear of crime and criminal victimization: Gender-based contrasts. *Journal of Criminal Justice, 34*, 285–301.

Simeoni, M. C., Sapin, C., Antoniotti, S., & Auquier, P. (2001). Health-related quality of life reported by French adolescents: A predictive approach of health status?. *Journal of Adolescent Health, 28*(4), 288–294.

Stanko, E. (1995). Women, crime and fear. *Annals of the American Academy of Political and Social Science, 539*, 47–58.

Stokols, D., & Altman, I. (1987). *Handbook of environmental psychology* (Vol. 1). New York: Wiley.

Swenson, R. R., & Prelow, H. M. (2005). Ethnic identity, self-esteem, and perceived efficacy as mediators of the relation of supportive parenting to psychosocial outcomes among urban adolescents. *Journal of Adolescence, 28*, 465–477.

Uzzell, D., Pol, E., & Badenas, D. (2002). Place identification, social cohesion, and environmental sustainability. *Environment and Behavior, 34*(1), 26–53.

Williams, J. S., Singh, K. B., & Singh, B. B. (1994). Urban youth, fear of crime and defensive actions. *Adolescence, 29*(114), 323–330.

Zani, B. (a cura di). (2003). *Sentirsi in/sicuri in città*. Bologna: Il Mulino.

Zani, B., Cicognani, E., & Albanesi, C. (2001). Adolescents' sense of community and feeling of unsafety in the urban environment. *Journal of Community and Applied Social Psychology, 11*, 475–489.

Fencing in the Bay? Place Attachment, Social Representations of Energy Technologies, and the Protection of Restorative Environments

Patrick Devine-Wright

University of Exeter, UK

Abstract

Although numerous UK and European opinion polls have indicated public support for more renewable energy, actual developments have often met with local opposition, typically described as "NIMBYism" (not in my back yard). Although the NIMBY concept has been used both to describe and explain local opposition, the pejorative nature of the concept has led some researchers to recommend that the concept be abandoned. An alternative explanation has been proposed, where so-called "NIMBY" responses are reconceived as place-protective actions, founded upon processes of place attachment and place identity. This chapter empirically explores this alternative perspective, drawing on mixed method data from a case study of a proposed offshore wind farm in North Wales, UK. Results indicated that place attachment negatively correlated with support for the wind farm. Analysis of place-related meanings and of perceived project impacts suggested that the project threatened place-related identities and attachments since it was objectified to 'fence in the bay', thereby closing off the horizon, damaging the distinctiveness and historical continuity of the place, as well as its ability to provide a restorative environment for visitors. The implications of the findings for theory and practice are explored.

Key words: NIMBY, place attachment, social representations, renewable energy

The term "NIMBY" (not in my back yard) refers to public opposition to unwanted local developments, ranging from landfill waste dumps to wind farms (Burningham, Barnett, & Thrush, 2007). Although numerous UK and European opinion polls have indicated public support for more renewable energy, actual developments have often met with local opposition, which has typically been described as "NIMBYism," leading to delayed or even abandoned projects (Toke, 2005). NIMBY has been used both to describe and explain local opposition:

> In plain language . . . [NIMBYs are] residents who want to protect their turf. More formally, NIMBY refers to the protectionist attitudes of and oppositional tactics adopted by community groups facing an unwelcome development in their neighbourhood . . . residents usually concede that these 'noxious' facilities are necessary, but not near their homes, hence the term 'not in my back yard' (Dear, 1992, p. 288).

However, the pejorative nature of the concept has led some researchers to recommend that the concept be abandoned (e.g., Devine-Wright, 2005; Wolsink, 2006).

An alternative explanation has been proposed (Devine-Wright, forthcoming), where so-called "NIMBY" responses are reconceived as place-protective actions, founded upon processes of place attachment and place identity. Place attachment is a positive emotional connection with familiar locations such as the home or neighbourhood (Manzo, 2005), correlating with length of dwelling (Brown & Perkins, 1992), featuring social and physical sub-dimensions (Hidalgo & Hernandez, 2001) and leading to action, both at individual and collective levels (Manzo & Perkins, 2006).

The impact on individuals and groups of change to places has sometimes been labelled as "disruption" to place attachment (Brown & Perkins, 1992) or "threat" to place identity (Bonaiuto, Breakwell, & Cano, 1996). In both cases, change can result in emotional responses such as grief and loss (Fried, 2000) and lead to specific forms of action. For example, Stedman (2002) showed how opposition to new housing proposals in a lakeside area of Wisconsin was contingent upon strong place attachments and the adoption of symbolic meanings. He concluded "we are willing to fight for places that are central to our identities . . . this is especially true when important symbolic meanings are threatened by prospective change" (p. 577). However, Stedman recognised that "the source of cognition is a relative mystery using this framework and data. More research is needed on the source of symbolic meanings" (Stedman, 2002, p. 577).

Social representations theory (Moscovici, 2000) is a useful means to explore such symbolic meanings. It addresses commonsense understandings of the world and how these evolve, rendered by processes of anchoring (the connecting of new ideas to familiar knowledge) and objectification (the making concrete of abstract ideas) that occur across multiple levels, connecting the cognitive system with the social meta-system. Although the theory has been applied to the study of environmental concern (Castro, 2006), it has yet to be fruitfully applied to the study of prospective change to places, despite the fact that it offers a useful approach to understand how change becomes identified, interpreted, and evaluated by local residents, and may be perceived to disrupt or threaten identity processes.

This chapter describes an empirical study of public responses to a proposed offshore wind farm in the UK. Although many experts view offshore wind as the most likely vehicle for meeting national energy policy targets, often assuming that offshore wind farms will prove less controversial than those onshore, to date there is a dearth of empirical research on public responses. Furthermore, across different renewable energy sources, few empirical studies have addressed links between place attachment and public responses. One exception is Vork-inn and Riese's study of a proposed hydropower project in Norway (2001), with findings indicating that place attachment significantly explained attitudes to the development, with residents who were more attached to the impacted area expressing more negative attitudes to the project. However, the study overlooked how local people interpreted the project, whether respondents felt emotionally threatened by change, and to what extent negative attitudes may lead to active opposition. Accordingly, this study aimed to address these gaps, conceiving so-called "NIMBY" opposition as arising from specific ways of representing energy technologies that disrupt place attachments and threaten place identities.

Methodology

Context: Place and Project

The study was conducted in Llandudno, a seaside town in North Wales situated opposite the proposed site of the offshore wind farm (see Figure 1). Llandudno was founded in the 19th century as a respite for urban dwellers from the industrial cities of Manchester and Liverpool. Today, it remains an important holiday resort, receiving 20% of Welsh national tourist income (Haggett, 2008). In 2001, the town had a population of 20,090, and a substantial minority (26%) of residents over 65 years of age, indicating its importance as a retirement location. The project is an offshore wind farm called "Gwynt y Mor" that, if approved, will install about 250 turbines, each over 100 m tall, approximately 9 miles out to sea. There are several other wind farms in the area: North Hoyle and Burbo Bank, as well as Rhyl Flats (in construction). Some local residents have set up an opposition group

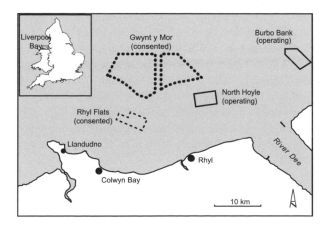

Figure 1. The site of the Gwynt y Mor offshore wind farm.

called "Save Our Scenery," arguing that the wind farm will damage tourism, for example by "fencing in" the bay. Whether local residents adopted ways of thinking propagated by the opposition group or the developer was investigated in the survey.

Procedure and Sample

Two hundred and fifty questionnaires were distributed to residents using a "drop and collect" procedure, involving repeat visits to each household to personally drop off and later collect a completed survey. Two hundred and nineteen completed questionnaires were returned, with a response rate of 87.6%. Respondents' average age was 61.11 (SD = 15.44), 54% were male and the average length of local residence was 21.45 years (SD = 17.40). Respondents (55.8%) were retired, 31.6% worked full-time, and 12.6% part-time. Most respondents (91.7%) owned their house, 21.3% reported completing O levels, 11.2% A levels, and 36% held at least one University degree. The sample is representative of the local population in consisting of predominantly older individuals, although the proportion of those working full- and part-time is slightly lower than in Llandudno more generally.

Measures

The survey began with a section on place, capturing representations of Llandudno, using a free association task, and levels of attachment, using a standardised 8-item scale (Hidalgo & Hernandez, 2001) that had a high level of reliability (alpha = .94), and with a five-point response format from 1 (weak attachment) to 5 (strong attachment). Following this, emotional response to the project was measured using 11 specific forms of affect (e.g., happy, proud, and threatened), with responses scored between 1 (not at all) and 5 (extremely). Attitude to the project was measured using two items (e.g., *I support the Gwynt y Mor offshore wind farm*), which correlated highly (r = .74, n = 201, p < .01), with scores between 1 (weak support) and 5 (strong support). Representations of the project were measured using 9 items drawn from the developer and opposition group's communication, mixing positive and negative outcomes from local (e.g., industrialise the area, "fence in" the bay, provide jobs) to national (help meet national energy policy targets) and beyond (help tackle climate change), with responses between 1 (strongly disagree) and 5 (strongly agree). Behaviour was measured using 11 items, capturing the frequency of undertaking certain actions (e.g., writing a letter to the paper in support/opposition, signing a petition against/in favour). The items were clustered into composite measures of "supportive" and "oppositional" behaviour where a high score means a greater frequency of undertaking such action.

Results

The Results section is in three parts. First, place attachment and place-related meanings are analysed. In the second, different aspects of the project are explored: perceived impacts, affect, support, and behavioural responses. Finally, links between place attachment and representations of the project are investigated.

Representations of and Attachment With Place

Thematic analysis was used to analyse data from the free association task, identifying manifest and latent themes (Joffe & Yardley, 2004). The analysis was conducted using a coding template that contained 54 codes against which the first three words or phrases written by each respondent were analysed. Inter-rater reliability analysis was conducted raising the level of agreement from 97% to 99%. For the first association, the most frequently mentioned thematic categories were aesthetic beauty (21%), pleasant living (13%), holiday resort (12%), coastal features (11%), Victorian (7%), unique place (5%), retirement location (4%), home (4%), friendly (3%), and clean (3%), with 17% listing diverse responses categorised as "other." Further analysis indicated that aesthetic beauty was the top-ranked category in all three associations with the place, with coastal features ranking 4th, 2nd, and 2nd, respectively. Details of the kinds of thematic references for "aesthetic beauty" include words or phrases such as "beautiful view of the bay," "picturesque," and "stunning location"; while "coastal features" included references to the "seaside," "bay," "promenade," and "horizon." The results suggest that Llandudno is predominantly represented in terms of visual aesthetics, emphasising the place's scenic beauty linked to its coastal situation and environmental features. Mean levels of attachment to Llandudno were generally high (4.40, $SD = 0.74$).

Project-Related Attitudes, Perceived Impacts, Affect, and Behavioural Responses

Mean levels of project support were just below the mid-point of the scale (2.79, $SD = 1.51$) reflecting a "neutral" position as opposed to a strongly positive or negative attitude; however, the average masks considerable levels of opposition, revealed in Figure 2 illustrating responses for the item "I support the Gwynt y Mor offshore wind farm."

The project was represented mainly in terms of local and negative impacts. "Creating an eyesore" was the most highly rated perceived impact (see Table 1 for descriptive data). This was followed by other negative local impacts such as "fencing in the bay," "industrialising the area," and "damaging tourism." Positive or distant impacts were less agreed with, for example "providing jobs." Despite the size of the project, respondents did not agree that it would "help to tackle climate change" (mean 2.97). Descriptive data for emotional responses indicated generally higher levels of negative affect (e.g., sceptical, threatened, angry, and frustrated) in comparison to positive affect (e.g., excited, proud, happy, and hopeful), averaging "a little" (score of 2) or "somewhat" (score of 3) rather than "not at all" (score of 1) (see Table 1).

In terms of behavioural engagement, frequency analysis suggested that levels of engagement were predominantly low. The most frequently cited response was to sign a petition against the project (40.2%); 22% of respondents reported attending a public

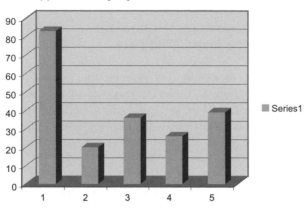

Figure 2. Levels of support for the offshore wind farm.

meeting or exhibition, 26.9% reported joining a group in support of the project, while 21.5% reported joining an opposition group.

Linking Place Attachment and Project Variables

Links between place attachment and project-related measures were analysed using two methods. Firstly, bivariate correlations were performed (see Table 2), indicating a consistent trend. The more strongly individuals felt attached to the place, the more they perceived local impacts to be negative, felt negative emotional responses suggesting a sense of threat, adopted a negative attitude to the project, and engaged in oppositional behaviour.

To explore links between place attachment and objectification, two multiple regressions were conducted (correlations between the variables are summarised in Table 3).

Firstly, place attachment and sociodemographics (age and gender) were regressed onto the item "fence in the bay." Using a stepwise procedure, only the place attachment scale proved significant, $F = 3.328$; $p < .021$, $r^2 = 5.1\%$. The beta weight was $+.187$ ($t = 2.606, p < .01$), indicating that the more one felt attached to the place, the more likely one was to agree that the wind farm would "fence in the bay." To investigate the importance of objectification for shaping attitudes to the project, a second regression was conducted, with project attitude as the dependent variable and the item "fence in the bay" as the independent variable. The regression was significant, $F = 240.991$, $p < .000$, $r^2 = 55\%$. The beta weight for "fence in the bay" was $-.743$ ($t = -15.524, p < .000$), suggesting that adopting the belief that the project would fence in the bay strongly shaped levels of opposition to the project.

Table 1. Descriptive data for levels of project support, impacts, and affective responses

	Mean	SD
Project support	2.79	1.51
Perceived impacts		
Create an eyesore	3.82	1.42
Fence in the bay	3.53	1.50
Industrialise the area	3.43	1.37
Damage tourism	3.41	1.50
Reduce property values	3.22	1.43
Help meet national policy targets	3.05	1.34
Tackle climate change	2.97	1.34
Have a positive impact upon wildlife	2.59	1.39
Provide jobs	2.46	1.20
Emotional responses		
Sceptical	3.02	1.47
Curious	2.76	1.29
Threatened	2.46	1.58
Angry	2.40	1.58
Frustrated	2.37	1.60
Hopeful	2.33	1.36
Shocked	2.11	1.42
Indifferent	1.88	1.06
Happy	1.73	1.19
Proud	1.52	0.94
Excited	1.48	0.92

Discussion

This study aimed to take forward understandings of the psychological processes underlying so-called "NIMBY" responses to proposed renewable energy technology projects. An approach was proposed (see Devine-Wright, forthcoming) drawing upon disruption to place attachment (Brown & Perkins, 1992) as a means of accounting for attitudinal and behavioural responses, and using social representations theory (Moscovici, 2000) to interpret place and project-related meanings. Within social representations, the dialogical approach (Marková, 2003) emphasises the significance of contradiction, particularly the prevalence of oppositional dyads or themata. In this case, a themata contrasting "natural" with "industrial" was suggested by the free associations with the place and with the Likert items capturing perceived impacts of the project. The results indicated predominantly visual associations with Llandudno, a place characterised in terms of its scenic beauty

Table 2. Bivariate correlations between place attachment, affect, specific project impacts, project support, and behavioural engagement

	Place attachment	
	Pearson r	p
Project support	−.16	.03
Emotional responses		
Angry	.19	.01
Threatened	.17	.02
Sceptical	.14	.05
Happy	−.15	.05
Excited	−.14	.07
Perceived impacts		
Create an eyesore	.20	.00
Will "fence in" the bay	.20	.00
Will "industrialise" the area	.20	.00
Behavioural engagement		
Supportive behaviour	−.03	n.s.
Opposition behaviour	.22	.00

Table 3. Bivariate correlations between place attachment, sociodemographics, fence in the bay, and project support

	Place attachment	Age	Gender	Fence in the bay	Project support
Place attachment	1	.121	.065	.200**	−.160*
Age		1	.073	.107	−.246**
Gender			1	−.021	.055
Fence in the bay				1	−.743**
Project support					1

*$p < .01$ (two-tailed), **$p < .01$ (two-tailed).

and coastal features. These contrasted with how the energy project was interpreted as an "eyesore" that threatened to "industrialise" the place, with consequent damage to the tourism industry upon which local livelihoods depended.

In terms of objectification, the impact that the project would have upon the place was made concrete by constructing the turbines as a "fence" that would alter the horizon, replacing it with an array of vertical turbines. In his prize-winning novel, the novelist John Banville (2005) has drawn attention to the "horizontal" nature of seaside views: *"at the seaside all is narrow horizontals, the world reduced to a few long straight lines pressed between earth and sky"* (Banville, 2005). The local opposition group have argued that this horizontal vista is threatened by the proposed wind farm, suggesting that Llandudno, as a place, does not cease at the water's edge but includes the view out to sea as much as its Victorian facades on the promenade.

Attention Restoration Theory (Kaplan & Kaplan, 1989) aims to account for the health benefits of natural environments, understanding restorative experience as alleviating cognitive fatigue and enabling reflection, with four basic principles: coherence, being away, fascination, and extent. It is a valid assumption that Llandudno's success as a holiday resort stems from its ability to provide all four aspects of a restorative experience: Enabling holidaymakers *to be away from* daily concerns, in an environment that is *coherent* due to the symmetry of the headlands and the conservation of Victorian facades along the promenade, offering the *fascination* of sea views and the *extent* of an unbroken horizon. By objectifying the wind farm as a "fence," the project is constructed in such a way as to reduce the extent of its sea views, potentially damaging the place's potential to provide a restorative experience, with economic consequences for the tourism industry.

That objectifying the wind farm in this way linked to place attachment and place identity was indicated by the correlational and regression analyses. The more an individual felt attached to Llandudno, the more they perceived the wind farm to "fence in the bay." Since high levels of attachment correlated with negative emotions, notably a sense of threat, this suggests that the wind farm proposal has disrupted place attachments and threatened place identities. By altering the horizon, the project may be perceived to threaten specific identity principles (Twigger-Ross & Uzzell, 1996), reducing Llandudno's *distinctiveness* as a unique seaside resort and creating *discontinuity* in a physical form that has been conserved since the Victorian era. The positive correlation between attachment and oppositional behaviour supports Stedman's (2002) conclusion that threats to place identities can lead to place-protective actions.

In conclusion, the findings suggest a promising alternative to the "NIMBY" explanation, drawing upon place attachment, place identity, and social representations theory to deepen our understanding of public responses to proposed renewable energy projects. However, caution is required before generalising from the findings since the study has a number of limitations, being based upon a sample not entirely representative of the town's population and a research design unable to demonstrate causal relations among variables. Notwithstanding these, the results suggest a number of implications for policy and practice, for example challenging presumptions that offshore wind farms will be uncontroversial and raising the importance of engagement processes that involve different actors and make explicit "commonsense" beliefs in order to promote conflict resolution.

Acknowledgments

The author thanks his colleagues Yuko Howes and Hannah Devine-Wright; project team, survey distributors, and all participants; and the funding agency: Research Councils' Energy Programme/Economic and Social Research Council (Grant Ref: RES-125-25).

References

Banville, J. (2005). *The sea*. London: Picador.

Bonaiuto, M., Breakwell, G. M., & Cano, I. (1996). Identity processes and environmental threat: The effects of nationalism and local identity upon perception of beach pollution. *Journal of Community and Applied Social Psychology, 6*, 157–175.

Brown, B., & Perkins, D. D. (1992). Disruptions to place attachment. In I. Altman & S. Low (Eds.), *Place attachment* (pp. 279–304). New York: Plenum.

Burningham, K., Barnett, J., & Thrush, D. (2007). *The limitations of the NIMBY concept for understanding public engagement with renewable energy technologies: A literature review.* Manchester: Manchester Architecture Research Centre, University of Manchester.

Castro, P. (2006). Applying social psychology to the study of environmental concern and environmental worldviews: Contributions from the social representations approach. *Journal of Community and Applied Social Psychology, 16*, 247–266.

Dear, M. (1992). Understanding and overcoming the NIMBY syndrome. *Journal of the American Planning Association, 58*, 288–300.

Devine-Wright, P. (2005). Beyond NIMBYism: Towards an integrated framework for understanding public perceptions of wind energy. *Wind Energy, 8*, 125–139.

Devine-Wright, P. (2009). Rethinking NIMBYism: The role of place attachment and place identity in explaining place-protective action. *Journal of Community and Applied Social Psychology, 19*, 426–441.

Fried, M. (2000). Continuities and discontinuities of place. *Journal of Environmental Psychology, 20*, 193–205.

Haggett, C. (2008). Over the sea and far away? A consideration of the planning, politics and public perception of offshore wind farms. *Journal of Environmental Policy & Planning, 10*, 289–306.

Hidalgo, M. C., & Hernandez, B. (2001). Place attachment: Conceptual and empirical questions. *Journal of Environmental Psychology, 21*, 273–281.

Joffe, H., & Yardley, L. (2004). Content and thematic analysis. In D. F. Marks & L. Yardley (Eds.), *Research methods for clinical health psychology* (pp. 56–68). London: Sage.

Kaplan, R., & Kaplan, S. (1989). *The experience of nature: A psychological perspective*. New York: Cambridge University Press.

Manzo, L. (2005). For better or for worse: Exploring multiple dimensions of place meaning. *Journal of Environmental Psychology, 25*, 67–86.

Manzo, L., & Perkins, D. (2006). Finding common ground: The importance of place attachment to community participation in planning. *Journal of Planning Literature, 20*, 335–350.

Marková, I. (2003). *Dialogicality and social representations: The dynamics of mind.* Cambridge: Cambridge University Press.

Moscovici, S. (2000). *Social representations: Explorations in social psychology.* London: Polity Press.

Stedman, R. (2002). Toward a social psychology of place: Predicting behaviour from place-based cognitions, attitude, and identity. *Environment and Behaviour, 34*, 561–581.

Toke, D. (2005). Explaining wind power planning outcomes: Some findings from a study in England and Wales. *Energy Policy, 33*, 1527–1539.

Twigger-Ross, C. L., & Uzzell, D. (1996). Place and identity processes. *Journal of Environmental Psychology, 16*, 205–220.

Vorkinn, M., & Riese, H. (2001). Environmental concern in a local context: The significance of place attachment. *Environment and Behaviour, 33*, 249–263.

Wolsink, M. (2006). Invalid theory impedes our understanding: A critique on the persistence of the language of NIMBY. *Transactions of the Institute of British Geographers, NS31*, 85–91.

From Divided Space to Shared Space

How Might Environmental Psychology Help Us to Understand and Overcome the Tenacity of Racial Segregation?

John Dixon,[1] Kevin Durrheim,[2] and Colin Tredoux[3]

[1]Department of Psychology, Lancaster University, UK
[2]School of Psychology, University of KwaZulu-Natal, South Africa
[3]Department of Psychology, University of Cape Town, South Africa

Abstract

Segregation is a notoriously obdurate system for organising social life: once established, it is often difficult to eradicate. In this chapter, drawing on research conducted in post-apartheid South Africa, we argue that this feature of segregation has an environmental psychological dimension, being grounded in processes of place identification, territorial boundary construction, and socio-spatial exclusion. As such, if the ideal of integration is to be realised, we need to know how to create material environments in which person-place relationships sustain rather than destabilise contact and solidarity between members of historically divided communities. We argue that this is a problem that should engage environmental psychologists.

Key words: desegregation, environmental psychology, place identity, segregation

If the ideal city promotes diversity, interaction among its citizens, and social justice, then the apartheid city, which characterised South African society during the latter half of the 20th century, stands as the antithesis of this ideal (see Figure 1). The design of the apartheid city entrenched the ideological belief that racial diversity and contact were problems to be managed rather than opportunities to be encouraged. It also entrenched forms of inequality that belied official protests to the contrary. While other groups languished in

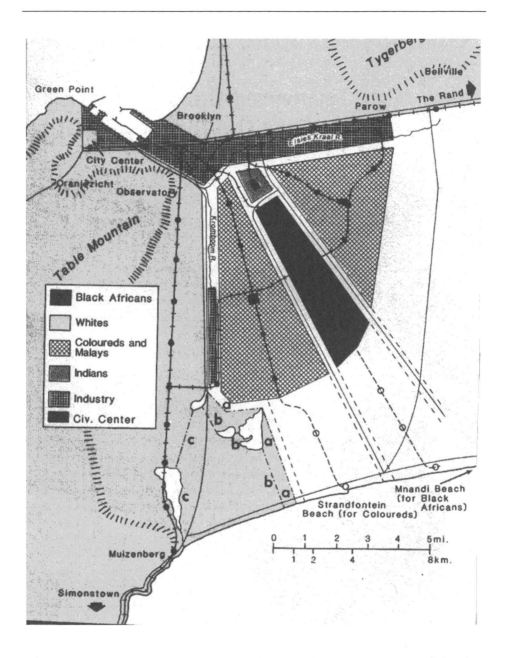

Figure 1. A representation of the apartheid ideal as applied to Greater Cape Town (taken from Western, 1996).

impoverished environments, most white South Africans retreated to the comparative luxury of their designated "group area," sequestered by the buffer zones, territorial barriers, and legal restrictions of the apartheid system. The authors were among the privileged few who lived in the "white" suburbs of Cape Town. All three of us were educated in all white schools and afterwards attended together the University of Cape Town (then predominantly white, though perhaps reluctantly so). We enjoyed "whites only" leisure spaces such as Muizenberg Beach (Figure 1) and, for much of our lives, had little opportunity to form friendships with members of other "race" groups.

The problem with (racial) segregation is that it amplifies group divisions and prejudices, creates environments comprised of relatively homogeneous enclaves, and all this at the cost of considerable social injustice (Massey & Denton, 1993). The solution, however, is rarely simple. Once established, the grip of segregation is notoriously difficult to prise apart. It is adaptable to changing circumstances, mutating constantly into new forms that are legitimated in new ways. This brief chapter argues that the tenacity of segregation has an environmental psychological dimension and that, by implication, environmental psychologists have an important role in transforming the kind of spatial formation represented *in extremis* in Figure 1. We develop this argument by drawing examples from a program of research on the dynamics of desegregation and re-segregation in post-apartheid South Africa, which is exploring changing relations in residential, educational, and leisure spaces in this country. To begin with, we sketch the context in which this work has been located.

The Tenacity of Segregation in Post-Apartheid Society

The human geography of post-apartheid society offers a stark testament to the tenacity of segregation. We do not dispute, of course, that much progress has been made. Since the official demise of the apartheid regime and the election of South Africa's first democratic government in 1994, there have been many profound changes. The legal basis of the old system of racial segregation has been abolished, with legislation such as the Group Areas Act of 1950 and the Prohibition of Mixed Marriages Act of 1949 being struck from the statutes. In their place, the ANC government has implemented a constitution that enshrines the ideal of racial equality and that, at least in principle, affords all citizens new freedoms of association, movement, and residential choice. It has implemented, too, a range of policies designed to encourage the desegregation of institutions of housing, education, and employment.

The geographic consequences of this (still unfolding) process have been mapped by a number of researchers, whose work provides a richer and more nuanced picture than can be achieved in this chapter. Saff (1998) and Beal, Crankshaw, and Parnell (2002), for example, have explored the dynamics of transformation in cities, while Lemon and

Clifford (2005) and Oldfield (2004) have explored transformation at more local scales. The point we wish to make here is a simplification but one that has heuristic value. Almost 15 years after the official end of apartheid, the apartheid city is alive and well. Racial segregation continues to exercise a powerful impact on South African society and to determine to a large extent the everyday patterning of contact and isolation.

Christopher's (2005) analysis of national patterns of residential distribution, for example, reveals a society marked by continuing and substantial levels of racial segregation. To be sure, the residential contours of many South African cities have changed and population distributions have altered, sometimes dramatically. However, in many locations practices of segregation have adapted accordingly, resulting in new forms of isolation, avoidance, and exclusion. The proliferation of gated communities, for instance, arguably represents the defensive architecture of the "new segregation" in South Africa. Although justified in non-racial terms (crime prevention and personal safety), these territorial formations communicate a powerful message about the continuing salience of racial boundaries in the "new" South Africa (e.g., Hook & Vrdoljak, 2002). Who is being fenced in and who fenced out?

Segregation also persists at more intimate scales of analysis, that is, beneath the global contours of the apartheid city and within its "nooks and crannies." In a series of studies designed to explore the so-called "micro-ecology" of contact and segregation, we have shown how racial isolation all too frequently characterises intimate relations within material environments that are ostensibly "integrated." If one looks closely, for example, at the spatial patterning of relations in university residences, tutorials, lecture theatres, and dining halls; in school classrooms and playgrounds; in public seating areas and spaces of leisure; in the night-time economy of bars and clubs; then one finds stable, routine patterns of racial isolation, enacted as people go about the mundane business of their everyday lives (see Dixon, Tredoux, Durrheim, Finchilescu, & Clack, 2008). What do such patterns tell us about the nature of "race relations" in this country? What do they tell us about the meaning and salience of "race" itself?

The project of explaining (the tenacity of) racial segregation is complex one that has preoccupied researchers in fields as diverse as geography, urban sociology, architecture, and demography. Indeed, segregation classically exemplifies the problem of causal "over-determination; in any given context, it may result from multiple sufficient causes that operate through multiple causal pathways." The explanation of segregation is further complicated by the fact that different forms of segregation require different theoretical accounts, for example, the processes that lead children to isolate themselves in the school playground of cafeteria (e.g., Schofield, 1986) are not the same as the processes that produce racially polarised neighbourhoods (e.g., Massey & Denton, 1993).

The premise of our research programme is that many forms of segregation have a psychological dimension and that a psychological level of explanation is necessary if we want to understand why people act in ways that establish, reproduce, defend, modify, or reject racial boundaries. This premise finds support in the wider literature on segregation, which has increasingly focused on the psychological factors that foster "preferential segregation,"

J. Dixon et al.
From Divided Space to Shared Space

241

including racial prejudice and perceived group threat (e.g., see Dawkins, 2004). Interestingly, this literature has also begun to consider processes directly related to the perception and evaluation of place. It has explored, for example, the role of cultural differences in housing "tastes" and (race stereotypic) projections about the future of given neighbourhoods in maintaining systems of residential segregation (e.g., Ellen, 2000).

In the next section, we suggest that environmental psychological processes may also help to explain how and why members of historically advantaged groups resist desegregation, focusing on the problem of understanding white opposition to socio-spatial change in post-apartheid South Africa.

Desegregation and the "Transgression" of Person-Place Relations

Whatever other changes it entails, the process of racial desegregation always entails a reorganisation of society's spaces and places. By definition, this process breaks down established geographic boundaries and creates new relations of proximity, co-presence, and inclusion. It is not surprising, then, that participants' accounts of their "lived experiences" of desegregation often highlight changes in place meanings. Nor is it surprising that resistance to desegregation is frequently grounded in the desire to preserve or reinstate particular types of person-place relations (see Dixon & Durrheim, 2004).

Our interest in the environmental psychological implications of desegregation initially arose during a case study of residential change in South Africa's "transitional" phase (roughly 1989–1994). Under apartheid, the coastal village of Hout Bay, located on the South West of the Cape Peninsula, was legally classified as a "white area." In April of 2001, however, a community of around 2,000 mostly black "Squatters" were given historical rights of legal residence in the village and the community of Imizamo Yethu was founded. Imizamo Yethu means "through our collective efforts" and the name hints at the protracted struggle that preceded (and indeed succeeded) the community's establishment. The nature and consequences of this "struggle" for inclusion in a formerly segregated enclave has been elaborated elsewhere (e.g., Dixon, Reicher, & Foster, 1997). Here we wish simply to outline a few key themes.

From the outset, local resistance to the new settlement of Imizamo Yethu was based around the idea that it was somehow "out-of-place" in Hout Bay, that it "transgressed" the character and identity of place (see Sibley, 1995). In a concerted campaign of letters to local newspapers, for example, representatives of the established "white" community argued that the settlement was not in keeping with the "village character" of Hout Bay, that its location in a disused forestry station constituted a threat to the fragile local ecosystem, and, above all, that its visual prominence marred the "scenic beauty" for which Hout Bay is famous. Located on a hillside visible from the main entry road to Hout Bay (Figure 2), Imizamo Yethu was frequently described in terms of metaphors of visual misplacement, for example, as an "eyesore," a "scar," and a "blot on the landscape."

Figure 2. Imizamo Yethu, Hout Bay. *Note*: We have also noted the locations of two neighbouring estates of "Penzance" and Hughenden.

Extract 1
The beauty of Hout Bay should have been preserved for all the people in the Cape; it is a famous tourist attraction. The present Squatter Camp is enough of an eyesore, being the first thing one sees when one drives along Victoria road. It certainly shouldn't be enlarged (Letter to the Editor, The Argus, October 1992).

Extract 2
Hout Bay just isn't the same. I mean even in our village nobody's bothered me. But it's just what they've done to our valley that bugs the hell out of me. And that it's no longer a pretty place. That it's now got this eyesore. Also they lied about – they said they were going to sustain the trees, that it wouldn't be such a blot. They haven't. You can see them very clearly from the road site . . . (Interview with a local resident).

Extract 3
As one of the oldest residents of this valley, I hang my head in shame over what is being done at present to destroy this last peaceful rural area located within the Cape Peninsula (Letter to the Editor, The Argus, February 1993).

Each of these extracts proclaims an event of place transgression: they are designed to expose the new settlement as a foreign and adulterating presence. Yet they also imply that something else has occurred: a cherished relationship between people and place has been ruptured or "dislocated" (Dixon & Durrheim, 2004). In Extracts 1 and 2, the disruption of residents' sensuous and aesthetic contemplation (and appropriation) of place is emphasised. Extract 2 additionally emphasises the degradation of the *local community* of insiders ("our valley," "our village") by a community of outsiders. One might say that the speaker's sense of "social insideness" (Rowles, 1983), her sense of "us" in "our" place, has been disturbed. A comparable theme arises in Extract 3, where "one of oldest residents of this valley" laments the destruction of his rural home, hinting at a disruption of so-called "place-referent continuity" (Twigger-Ross & Uzzell, 1996). In each extract, then, desegregation is constructed as a threat to what environmental psychologists have called place identity (Proshansky, Fabian, & Kaminoff, 1983).

Our reading of such accounts has drawn heavily on work in discursive and critical psychology (e.g., Potter & Wetherell, 1987), a research tradition that is beginning to influence environmental psychology (e.g., Aiello & Bonaiuto, 2003). It is vital, in our view, not to treat self-reports of the "dislocation" of place identity only as reflecting the disruption of some kind of authentic or natural environmental bond. To do so is to neglect a deeper politics of person-place relations that operates to conserve and reproduce systems of "racial" segregation. Clearly, such accounts are both rhetorically designed (e.g., organised to warrant the exclusion of "squatters" from Hout Bay) and ideologically loaded (e.g., reproducing political assumptions about who can claim to belong in the village and whose place values and meanings *should* be inscribed there). In this regard, it is instructive to consider how the establishment Imizamo Yethu has transformed the material environment of Hout Bay, simultaneously undermining and reproducing a landscape of racial division.

Material Landscapes of Inclusion and Exclusion

As it presently stands, the settlement's design and layout represents a kind of compromise formation, the result of a turbulent struggle between interest groups in the village. On the one hand, the mere existence of Imizamo Yethu is a significant political advance, part of a broader "deracialization of space" (Saff, 1998). Up until the 1980s, the state's response to squatting mainly consisted of forced removal, a tactic that was vigorously enforced in Hout Bay. Alternatively, squatters were encouraged to settle on the urban fringes in areas distanced from white suburbs, a policy sanitised by the label "orderly urbanization." Compared to these practices, the establishment of Imizamo Yethu within the municipal boundaries of Hout Bay was a progressive moment. It accorded the town's "squatters" the rights of residence, entitling them to municipal services, amenities, and land ownership.

On the other hand, the design of Imizamo Yethu has continued to underscore the "foreign" status of the settlement and its residents in various ways. First of all, buffer zones have been implanted on both sides of the new settlement. These zones are around two hectares in extent and vary between 60 and 100 m in width. As their name implies, the buffers were designed to minimise the possibility of interaction between communities. Second, a series of wire fences reinforce the buffer zones and delimit the perimeter of the settlement, some of which are built from "razor wire" and recall the militaristic barriers of the old regime. Third, "visual screens" of trees have been left in the buffer zones on both interface regions, to some extent obscuring Imizamo Yethu from view from the neighbouring estate of Penzance and Hughendon. A final kind of boundary is defined by an absence rather than a presence. There are no connecting roads running from

Imizamo Yethu to neighbouring areas, this possibility having been strenuously rejected by local ratepayers' associations.

In sum, in several respects, the architecture of the new settlement recapitulates the architecture of apartheid. It is designed to minimise the social impact of the township's inhabitants on the surrounding (white) communities and to emphasise the separation of Imizamo Yethu from the rest of Hout Bay. Contemplating this emergent racial ecology, which has resulted from a broader historical, material, and symbolic struggle over space in Hout Bay, one is reminded of Goldberg's (1993, p. 46) observation that: ". . . threatening to transgress or pollute the spatial order necessitates its reinvention, first by conceptualising the order anew and then by reproducing spatial confinement and separation in these modernized terms."

How Do We Create Landscapes of Inclusion and Solidarity?

If environmental psychological processes help us to understand the tenacity of systems of racial and ethnic segregation, then they are also part of the solution. At a fundamental level, we clearly need to avoid creating the kinds of "strongly classified spaces" (Sibley, 1995) represented in Figure 1. We need instead to build environments in which "us" and "them" become "we," or at least where the overwhelming salience of racial classification is attenuated. In other words, we need to create environments where the sharp distinctions between (racial) insiders and outsiders are blurred.

Reflexivity About Urban Design Practice

In societies where place and identity are so strongly interlinked and where the demarcation of racial boundaries is so much a part of everyday life, this is no easy matter. Indeed, our research shows that the strong classification of social space is sometimes perpetuated inadvertently by the tacit assumptions and behaviours of ordinary people, whose patterns of movement, assembly, and avoidance work to reproduce (racially) divided spaces (e.g., Dixon et al., 2008). Similarly, it is perpetuated by the working practices of urban designers (not to mention real estate agents, architects, mortgage lenders, and other institutional gatekeepers). We have mentioned already the insidious spread of security complexes in the post-apartheid era, which convey subtle (and not so subtle) information about who belongs in given space and about the nature of the relationship between different communities in South Africa.

Lemanski's (2006) case study of an ostensibly "progressive" mixed housing development near Cape Town provides an equally instructive example, for it demonstrates how strongly classified spaces may re-emerge even when designers have noble intentions. Westlake Village has been (and is) marketed as a shining example of a development that successfully integrates different communities and uplifts historically disadvantaged South

J. Dixon et al.
From Divided Space to Shared Space

245

Africans; and, in some respects, this is true. In other respects, however, as Lemanski's work evinces, the village's layout and spatial relationship to the neighbouring (mainly white) suburb of Silvertree has quietly reiterated in practice the very forms of (racialised) division and hierarchy that the development was intended in principle to overcome . . . In its use of visual buffers and territorial barriers, this new "progressive" settlement ironically echoes the very design features that characterised the long era of *de jure* segregation in South Africa, and crucially from an environmental psychological perspective, is experienced as such by Westlake residents themselves.

Taking Advantage of, and Defending, "Open Minded Spaces"

Integrated social spaces do not emerge overnight: they entail complex, historically evolving, often conflict ridden, sets of place meanings, values, and practices. When they do emerge, such spaces are thus a valuable source of information about the kinds of environmental psychological processes that may nurture stable, integrated communities. As important, they instantiate forms of human geography that, in their own right, must be defended against the resurgence of jingoistic, exclusive, or reactionary forms of localism. To conclude the chapter, we shall briefly illustrate this theme by drawing on an ongoing case study of changing relations in the Long Street in Cape Town (e.g., see Tredoux & Dixon, 2009).

During the apartheid era, Long Street acquired a reputation as the street that apartheid could not tame, a "grey area" where conventional norms broke down and where residents and visitors engaged in various bohemian, artistic, and countercultural activities (including activities of racial mixing). Whatever the accuracy of this version of place history, the street's reputation has grown in the post-apartheid era. It is not an exaggeration to claim that it has become a kind of metonym for the new South Africa (see Extract 4 below). In particular, its vibrant nightlife is often held up as an example of what a diverse and integrated public domain might ultimately look like in this society.

Interestingly, if one observes the nature of racial interaction in Long Street's nightlife one actually finds evidence of segregation (Tredoux & Dixon, 2009). Our observational work there, for example, has tracked racial distributions across venues over time, mapped the ecology of seating arrangements within particular establishments, and noted micro-interactional patterns (who drinks with whom, who dances with whom, and so on). We have found that contact between members of different race groups remains relatively limited. Even so, in interviews with patrons, the street's status as a space of racial integration and diversity is repeatedly emphasised. Their accounts suggest that this status derives as much from (a certain version of) the street's identity and from the kinds of person-place connections it establishes, as from the nature of actual interactions between those who enjoy its network of bars, eateries, clubs, and cafés.

Extract 4
I mean really, it's like South Africa on its own. It's an interracial country. It's like a mix. Places, there are some places more coloureds hang out. But there's places that

basically mix black people's places with white people's places. Like places like Jo'burg, Marvel, and here. I mean you find mostly white people, but sometimes you find black people coming in here (Black patron on Long Street).

Extract 5
It's a lot more black people mingling with the white people. The major change is whites and blacks dancing next to each other, drinking next to each other. It's no problems. But atmosphere, I can tell you now at the moment is very cosmopolitan, it's it colourful (White patron of Long Street).

These extracts illustrate the potential role of place meanings in facilitating and under-pinning processes of racial integration. In both interview accounts, Long Street is clearly depicted not only as a place *of* racial diversity, but also, in some deeper sense, as a place *for* social diversity and integration. Its hybrid mix of different kinds of spaces ("black" and "white"), its "cosmopolitan" and "colourful" atmosphere, and the visible diversity of its patrons – all of these place characteristics allow the street to become emblematic of the "new" South Africa ("an interracial country," no less). Far from representing a boundary threat, the sharing of social spaces by different groups is here conceived as part of the *normative* meaning and function of activity on the street. Indeed, to employ Gustafson's (2001) taxonomy, one might say that the identity of place is defined precisely by the complex interactions between self, other, and local environment. To curb visible diversity there would be to impoverish the very nature of place itself.

In closing the chapter, however, we feel obliged to warn that such shared spaces of encounter are fragile and often transitory. In Long Street, for example, unfolding processes of urban renewal and gentrification are currently eroding the very features of place that have made the street such an attractive proposition for developers in the post-apartheid era (i.e., its "colourful" and "cosmopolitan" atmosphere). As a cautionary illustration, consider Extract 6 below in which a (black African) patron reflects upon the changing "servicescape" (Rosenbaum & Montoya, 2006) of the street and what it communicates about who belongs and who does not belong there.

Extract 6
I1: There are places you get in and looks like a place only belongs to one race of people [. . .] Let me give you an example of some places. Like Miau Miau, that place down there is a white place. There is of course black waiters working there, but there is no black barmen. So what happens is: One, the music people who like black music they want to feel like just jumping music, dance hall music so they can bounce. [. . .] Two, if the managers and staff are white, they just want rich people. It's not okay it's not at all. Cause me myself I am black, I am African and I am in Africa, so I don't want to be like . . . so if I go to Miau Miau and they say no let's see only the guest list or are you on the guest list? (Two black patrons of Long Street).

J. Dixon et al.
From Divided Space to Shared Space

247

Conclusions

Segregation is an obdurate system for ordering social life: Once established, it has the capacity to survive long periods of upheaval. At least in part, this force of inertia reflects deep-seated processes of institutionalisation. In South Africa, it took an enormous invest-ment of economic, legal, and political resources (and considerable violence) to entrench a system where the entire infrastructure of the city maintained the division of racialised com-munities: It may take an equal investment to dismantle this landscape of division. Clearly, too, even after its institutional foundations have been removed, segregation in South Africa – as in many other societies – is perpetuated by economic disparities between groups.

In this chapter, we have suggested that the tenacity of segregation also has an environ-mental psychological dimension. Above all else, segregation is a socio-spatial order that regulates who belongs where, maintaining the integrity of certain versions of (racial) iden-tity. Because desegregation undermines this way of ordering human relations and the forms of located subjectivity that it upholds, it is often conceived as a "boundary-trans-gressive" process. It is not surprising, then, that a common response to desegregation is re-segregation, as communities seek to re-establish symbolic and material landscapes of division.

If we are committed to the project of creating (racially) integrated societies, then we also need to be committed to the project of creating places in which the ideal of integration can be concretely realised. What are the defining features of these kinds of places? What kinds of person-place relationships might flourish there? How can we ensure their stabil-ity? These are environmental psychological questions in the fullest sense of the phrase.

References

Aiello, A., & Bonaiuto, M. (2003). Rhetorical approach and discursive psychology: The study of environmental discourse. In M. Bonnes, T. Lee, & M. Bonaiuto (Eds.), *Psychological theories for environmental issues*. Aldershot, England: Ashgate.

Beal, J., Crankshaw, O., & Parnell, S. (2002). *Uniting a divided city: Governance and social exclusion in Johannesburg*. London: Earthscan.

Christopher, A. J. (2005). The slow pace of desegregation in South African cities, 1996–2001. *Urban Studies, 42*, 2303–2320.

Dawkins, C. J. (2004). Recent evidence on the continuing causes of black-white residential segregation. *Journal of Urban Affairs, 26*, 379.

Dixon, J. A., & Durrheim, K. (2004). Dislocating identity: Desegregation and the transformation of place. *Journal of Environmental Psychology, 24*, 455–473.

Dixon, J. A., Reicher, S., & Foster, D. (1997). Ideology, geography and racial exclusion: The squatter camp as 'blot on the landscape'. *Text, 17*, 317–348.

Dixon, J. A., Tredoux, C., Durrheim, K., Finchilescu, G., & Clack, B. (2008). "The inner citadels of the color line": Mapping the micro-ecology of segregation in everyday life spaces. *Personality and Social Psychology Compass, 2*, 1–23.

Ellen, I. G. (2000). Race-based neighbourhood projection: A proposed framework for understanding new data on racial integration. *Urban Studies, 37*, 1513–1533.

Goldberg, D. T. (1993). Polluting the body politic: Racist discourse and urban location. In M. Cross & M. Ketih (Eds.), *Racism, the city and the state* (pp. 45–60). London, UK: Routledge.

Gustafson, P. (2001). Meanings of place: Everyday experience and scientific conceptualizations. *Journal of Environmental Psychology, 21*, 5–16.

Hook, D., & Vrdoljak, M. (2002). Gated communities, heterotopia and a 'rights' of privilege: A heterotopology of the South African security-park. *Geoforum, 33*, 195–219.

Lemanski, C. (2006). Spaces of exclusivity or connection. Linkages between a gated community and its poorer neighbour in a Cape Town Master Plan Development. *Urban Studies, 43*, 397–420.

Lemon, A., & Clifford, D. (2005). Post-apartheid transition in a small South African town: Interracial property transfer in Margate, KwaZulu-Natal. *Urban Studies, 42*, 7–30.

Massey, D. S., & Denton, N. A. (1993). *American apartheid: Segregation and the making of the underclass.* Cambridge: Harvard University Press.

Oldfield, S. (2004). Urban networks, community organizing and race: An analysis of racial integration in a South African neighbourhood. *Geoforum, 35*, 189–201.

Potter, J., & Wetherell, M. (1987). *Discourse and social psychology.* London: Sage.

Proshansky, H. M., Fabian, A. K., & Kaminoff, R. (1983). Place identity: Physical world socialization of the self. *Journal of Environmental Psychology, 3*, 57–83.

Rosenbaum, M. S., & Montoya, D. Y. (2006). Am I welcome here? Exploring how ethnic consumers assess their place identity. *Journal of Business Research, 60*, 206–214.

Rowles, G. D. (1983). Place and personal identity in old age: Evidence from Appalachia. *Journal of Environmental Psychology, 3*, 299–313.

Saff, G. (1998). *Changing Cape Town.* New York: University of America Press.

Schofield, J. W. (1986). Black-white contact in desegregated schools. In M. Hewstone & R. Brown (Eds.), *Contact and conflict in intergroup encounters* (pp. 79–92). Oxford: Basil Blackwell.

Sibley, D. (1995). *Geographies of exclusion: Society and difference in the west.* London: Routledge.

Tredoux, C., & Dixon, J. A. (2009). Mapping the multiple contexts of racial isolation: Some reflections on the concept of scale in segregation research. *Urban Studies, 46*, 761–777.

Twigger-Ross, C., & Uzzell, D. (1996). Place and identity processes. *Journal of Environmental Psychology, 16*, 205–220.

Western, J. (1996). *Outcast Cape Town.* California: University of California Press.

Authors

Nancy H. Blossom
Interdisciplinary Design Institute
Washington State University
PO Box 1495
Spokane, WA 99210-1495
USA
blossom@wsu.edu

Marino Bonaiuto
Sapienza University of Rome
Department of Social and Developmental
Psychology
Via dei Marsi 78
00185 Rome
Italy
marino.bonaiuto@uniroma1.it

Paolo Bonaiuto
Department of Psychology
Sapienza University of Rome
Via Caio Mario, 8
00192 Rome
Italy
paolo.bonaiuto@uniroma1.it

Mirilia Bonnes
Sapienza University of Rome
Department of Social and
Developmental Psychology
Via dei Marsi 78
00185 Rome
Italy
mirilia.bonnes@uniromal.it

Pierluigi Caddeo
DRES – Department of Economic and
Social Research
University of Cagliari
V.le S. Ignazio-da-Laconi 78
09123 Cagliari
Italy
pierluigi.caddeo@uniroma1.it

Paola Cardinali
Department of Human Study (DISTUM)
University of Genova
C.so A. Podestà 2
16121 Genova
Italy
paola.cardinali@unige.it

Ruth Conroy Dalton
Bartlett School of Graduate Studies
University College London
1-19 Torrington Place
London, WC1E 6BT
UK
r.conroy-dalton@ucl.ac.uk

Antônio Tarcísio da Luz Reis
School of Architecture/PROPUR
Federal University of Rio Grande do Sul
Praça Carlos Simão Arnt 21, apto. 202
Bela Vista
Porto Alegre, RS
CEP 90450-110
Brazil
tarcisio@orion.ufrgs.br

Patrick Devine-Wright
College of Life and
Environmental Sciences
University of Exeter
Amory Building, Rennes Drive
Exeter, EX4 4RJ
UK
P.G.Devine-Wright@exeter.ac.uk

Keith Diaz Moore
School of Architecture and
Urban Planning
The University of Kansas
1465 Jayhawk Blvd., Marvin 205

Lawrence, KS 66045-7614
USA
diazmoore@ku.edu

John Dixon
Department of Psychology
Lancaster University
Lancaster, LA1 4YF
UK
j.a.dixon1@lancaster.ac.uk

Susan Drucker
Hofstra University
Department of Journalism,
Media Studies and Public Relations
Dempster Hall
Hempstead, NY 11549
USA
sphsjd@hofstra.edu

Ferdinando Fornara
Department of Psychology
University of Cagliari
Via Is Mirrionis, 1
09123 Cagliari
Italy
ffornara@unica.it

Claudia García-Landa
School of Psychology
National Autonomous University of
Mexico
Sur 73 No. 210 PH3
Col. Sinatel, México DF
CP 09460
México
cgarlan1@yahoo.com.mx

Bernardo Hernández
Department of Social Psychology
University of La Laguna
Campus de Guajara
38071 La Laguna
Tenerife

Spain
bhdezr@ull.es

Christoph Hoelscher
Center for Cognitive Science
University of Freiburg
Germany
hoelsch@cognition.uni-freiburg.de

Maritza Landázuri
Facultad de Estudios Superiores Iztacala
UNAM
Av. de los Barrios 1
Los Reyes Iztacala, Tlalnepantla
CP 54090
México
alandazu@yahoo.com

Roderick J. Lawrence
Human Ecology and Environmental
Sciences
Faculty of Social and Economic Sciences
University of Geneva
7 route de Drize
1227 Carouge (GE)
Switzerland
Roderick.lawrence@unige.ch

Terence R. Lee
School of Psychology
University of St. Andrews
St Andrews, KY16 9JP
UK
trl@st-andrews.ac.uk

Serafín J. Mercado
Facultad de Psicología
UNAM
Cubículo 5
2° piso del Edificio "D"
Av. Universidad 3004
Col. Copilco Universidad
México DF 04510
México
serafin.mercado@gmail.com

Laura Migliorini
Department of Anthropological Sciences
(DISA)
University of Genova
C.so A. Podestà 2
16121 Genova
Italy
migliori@nous.unige.it

María Montero
School of Psychology
National Autonomous University of
Mexico
Sur 73 No. 210 PH3
Col. Sinatel
México DF CP 09460
México

Anna Maria Nenci
Università LUMSA, Roma
Facoltà di Scienze della Formazione
Piazza delle Vaschette 101
001935 Rome
Italy
nenci@lumsa.it

Sarah R. Payne
Manchester Architecture Research Centre
School of Environment and Development
The University of Manchester
Humanities Bridgeford Street
Manchester, M13 9PL
UK
SarahRPayne@yahoo.co.uk

Adriana Portella
School of Architecture and Planning,
Federal University of Pelotas
Bartlett School of Planning,
University College London
Joint Centre for Urban Design,
Oxford Brookes University
Rua Andrade Neves, n.3021, apto 202
Pelotas/Rio Grande do Sul

CEP 96020-080
Brazil
adrianaportella@yahoo.com.br

Ombretta Romice
Department of Architecture
University of Strathclyde
131 Rottenrow
Glasgow, G4 0NG
UK
ombretta.r.romice@strath.ac.uk

Paula Silva Gambim
School of Architecture/PROPUR
Federal University of Rio Grande do Sul
Rua Vicente Pallotti 284
Bairro Passo D'Areia
Porto Alegre, RS
CEP 91030-120
Brazil
pgambim@terra.com.br

Carmen Tabernero
Department of Psychology
University of Córdoba
Avenida San Alberto Magno s/n
14004-Córdoba
Spain
carmen.tabernero@uco.es

Alejandra Terán
Facultad de Estudios Superiores Iztacala
UNAM
Av. de los Barrios número 1
Los Reyes Iztacala, Tlalnepantla
CP 50490
México
aleteran@yahoo.com

Renato Troffa
DRES – Department of Economic and
Social Research
University of Cagliari
V.le S. Ignazio-da-Laconi 78
09123 Cagliari

Italy
renato.troffa@uniroma1.it

John Zacharias
Department of Geography,
Planning and Environment

Concordia University
1455 de Maisonneuve Blvd W
Montréal, QC H3G 1M8
Canada
zachar@alcor.concordia.ca

Index